Anna Hampton's book on risk is one of the weightiest books I have ~ the subject. It is not a textbook, it is not a book on spiritual formation, it is not a theology of suffering, and it is not a guidebook for leaders in times of risk and danger—yet it is all of these and much, much more. This powerful and profound book has many provocative questions, lists of key points, intriguing quotations from thinkers, and personal stories.

Some of the concepts that impacted me were the references to risk in the New Testament; warfare preparation; "custodians of the alabaster vase" (stewardship); Paul's four ways of mitigating or managing risk; "the key idea in discernment is to know what we see rather than see what we know"; seven areas to keep in mind with regard to our own or others' spiritual maturity; depth theology; the message of the wilderness; developing endurance strategies; shepherding and leading in a time of risk.

Each chapter ends with a summary and a robust bibliography. This book is a classic for cross-cultural ministry workers in places of risk and danger. It should be required reading. The author has been there. The book is field-tested. I can't recommend it highly enough.

DR. LAURA MAE GARDNER
Former International Vice President for Personnel for Wycliffe Bible
Translators and SIL International
Author of *Healthy, Resilient and Effective in Cross-cultural Ministry*

Responding to God's call means facing decisions about stepping out of the boat when the wind is blowing and the seas are the roughest. Peter's first step onto the water was only possible because he knew with certainty that Jesus was reaching out for him. This outstanding book draws from years living with risk and danger while ministering in Afghanistan and Central Asia. I found the personal stories of difficult and risky choices to be compelling; they gave life to the theory and its practice. This book is a must read for those who are facing decisions about following Jesus into dangerous situations.

CHARLES SCHAEFER, PhD
Coauthor of *Trauma and Resilience: Effectively Supporting Those Who Serve God*

With friends, families, churches, and organizations confused by the fact that Christian workers knowingly step into situations that are dangerous and even life-threatening, I wonder why it has taken so long for us to engage with the content covered in Anna Hampton's book. This book will prove invaluable for those planning to serve God in dangerous settings and those who need faith to stand with them.

MARTIN CAMPBELL
Principal, EastWest College of Intercultural Studies, New Zealand

Facing Danger: A Guide through Risk is a compelling read for any worker living in a high-risk area. When I moved overseas nearly ten years ago, I did not have a theology of risk, and I wish I had this book in training. Anna Hampton is a veteran worker in hostile areas, and she helps bring clarity to a theology of risk based on decades of ministry experience, research, and a life led by the Spirit. After reading this book I have more confidence for facing crisis situations and a better understanding of how God's call and risk work together.

LESLIE TAYLOR
Worker in a Muslim Country

Many books either focus on trusting God in the midst of risk or contingency planning to mitigate that risk; this book walks the no-man's-land between those two extremes, the place where so many of us on the field actually live.

Pastor to the International Christian Community, Kabul, Afghanistan

Someone has said that all the easy places have already been reached with the gospel. It is now the riskier and difficult places on the rough edges of our world that yet need the good news of Jesus Christ. *Facing Danger* delivers more than what we would expect from an armchair theologian or missiologist. It is born out of the author's diligent research set in the complicated context of a decade living and working in war-ravaged Afghanistan. *Facing Danger* will be read by responsible leaders before placing workers in high-risk areas. It should find its way to the required reading lists of cross-cultural Christian courses. This is perhaps the most authoritative book in this field.

RONALD BROWN, DMIN
Former International Worker, Africa, Senior Associate, Mobile Member Care Team
Missions Coach, Christian and Missionary Alliance in Canada

Having lived with our family for many years in high-risk countries and spiritually dark places, facing danger and threats on numerous occasions, I am thankful to Anna Hampton for writing this book. She challenges readers on various levels to be spiritually sensitive and discerning, to follow God's call, and to count the cost. Anna shares deep theological insights from the Old and New Testaments, reflecting on the cosmic battle we are in, and thus making workers aware that reaching tough places with the truth of Christ needs more than an adventurous spirit. Her section on rearing children in risk environments is insightful and helpful.

Anyone going to or already working in high-risk countries should read this book and honestly assess their motivation, their personal relationship with the Lord, and their biblical understanding of risk.

A. G.

Psychologist, Member Care Partners Germany

This book would have been most helpful in my preparation for cross-cultural work! Years ago, while serving in a country next to Afghanistan, our family was attacked by a frenzied mob. We lived through it (by God's grace) and after that saw more fruit. Eventually we left the field, but what I have learned over the last twenty years of equipping workers for ministry in Muslim contexts is that *Facing Danger* is more needed today than ever before.

This text draws from both Testaments to show that risk taking is biblical. For example, it points out that the church in Jerusalem chose men like Barnabas and Paul because they had "risked their lives" for the sake of the gospel (Acts 15:25–26). A number of passages are exegeted to demonstrate that there is a difference between taking risks and suffering—something that is easily missed in our study of Scripture.

Finally, Anna Hampton interjects a number of personal experiences that add credibility and make for interesting reading. I highly recommend this book as a training manual for cross-cultural workers in areas of high risk.

WARREN LARSON, PhD

Professor Emeritus, Muslim Studies at CIU and Senior Fellow, Zwemer Center

In all of my years of studying this subject, there has never been a book written by an individual who has been able to blend so well the excellence of biblical theology interspersed with relevant testimony and practical application. In *Facing Danger: A Guide through Risk*, academic rigour has not dumbed down emotions nor has the importance of the emotions compromised robust and sound research. Practice informs theology, as it should, but theology is not manipulated by the drama of real-life stories that are woven into each page. This is a rare and unique contribution to not only the study and practice of risk but also to the whole global church.

Facing Danger has everything to say to a cross-cultural worker in Pakistan, a pastor in Iraq, or a student leader in a megacity anywhere in the world. Anna's realism and experiences write as a person still humble to learn herself but has so much to teach us, the readers. Download it, buy it, give it away, and keep it. There will be nothing else like it.

EMMA DIPPER
Associate Lecturer, All Nations Christian College, UK

There are few people alive today whom I respect more highly than Anna and Neal Hampton. For years I have watched them wrestle in the chaos while grounding themselves and their team in a scripturally rooted, authentic, lived experience of God. In *Facing Danger*, Anna Hampton develops a much-needed God-centered understanding of risk that is forged out of her "doing theology" and learning to "walk in the Spirit" in the context of Afghanistan. She takes the conversation deeper, avoiding the common moralizing approach to Scripture seen in many books on risk and suffering. Anna writes with the kind of substance, practicality, self-awareness, and insight that develops by coming to know God anew from within the experience of prolonged risk. *Facing Danger* should be required reading for ministry leaders who send staff to high-risk areas, as well as for individuals who live and work in those locations.

DAVID BOCHMAN, PHD
Organizational Development, Paraclete Mission Group

While the audience for *Facing Danger* is cross-cultural Christian workers living in high-risk nations, I would encourage anyone and everyone to read this book, whether or not you belong to the group of cross-cultural workers. In these fast-changing times, with more and more incidents deeply impacting societies all over our world, it is helpful for all of us to understand the issues of risk, not just those of us living in an international culture.

Anna and Neal's own experience in high-risk nations makes this book honest, realistic, and gives the reader a helpful tool. She helps you face your own situation, thought patterns, and personality, gracefully inviting you to connect with your Creator and Father when facing and managing risk. God's promise that he will always be with you stands firm.

LENY BREUR
Dutch Coworker and Friend in Afghanistan

There can be a tendency in the evangelical world to overspiritualize or be dismissive of risk and its deep and lasting impact. Anna provides a path down the middle of those two extremes with this profoundly insightful and helpful resource. This book is not written from either a theoretical posture or a "low-risk" location; she writes from life experience in some of the most volatile locations in the world, having lost numerous close friends and yet willing, along with her family, to live and work amidst these realities. This will be a book I will utilize for my own as well as organizational discernment as we have staff moving in and out of high-risk regions of the world.

SCOTT E. SHAUM
Director of Staff Development, Barnabas International

I have been involved in Anna Hampton's life since she was a teenager, shared leadership with her on cross-cultural trips around the world, observed her and Neal firsthand in Afghanistan, and count them as friends. Anna has experienced the terror, gone through the process of healing, and studied the subject of risk in-depth. She brings personal experience and well-researched and practical insights to this much-needed area. Although it is written for cross-cultural work, I have found it also has application for everyone, regardless of where they live or what they do. What could have driven Anna and Neal out of cross-cultural work instead has resulted in a unique and much-needed ministry for those who are thinking about or are in cross-culture ministries.

REV. LOUIS INKS
Founder, Reign Ministries

In *Facing Danger*, Anna Hampton provides a thoughtful, practical theology and psychology of risk management from the crucible of "living on the edge." Drawing from a rich background of field experience communicated in breath-stopping and heartwarming stories, the author combines in-depth biblical exegesis about risk, current research, undaunted courage, and a mom's practical wisdom in the kitchen.

Well referenced with rich notes, checklists, diagrams, compelling personal stories, presentation outlines, charts, and other practical tools for risk analysis and management, this timely book may be read far beyond the intended audience of international humanitarian and global workers. It provides a rich treasure trove of practical, field-tested wisdom that should not be ignored by helping professionals, as well as organizational leaders and boards who are giving advice and making decisions impacting the lives of their people.

LEONARD J. CERNY II, PHD
Coauthor CernySmith Assessment

FACING DANGER

FACING DANGER

DANGER

A Guide *through* Risk

Anna E. Hampton

Zendagi Press

ISBN 978-0-9980544-0-7

Edited by: Ryan Adair (www.missiowriting.com)

Cover Design & Interior by: Sarah ONeal (www.evecustomartwork.com)

Cover Image Courtesy of Shutterstock.com/Vibe Images

ZENDAGI

ZENDAGI PRESS

NEW PRAGUE, MINNESOTA

I dedicate this book to all those of whom the world is not worthy.

HEBREWS 11:38

To the men, women, and children serving God in hostile places
where his name is not yet known, where his name is being sanctified
in dark and challenging places: you are called to endure faithfully.

Your deeds will follow you.

REVELATION 14:12–13

Then the dragon became furious with the woman and went off
to make war on the rest of her offspring, on those who keep the
commandments of God and hold to the testimony of Jesus. And he
stood on the sand of the sea.

—REVELATION 12:17 ESV

Keep your eyes open, hold tight to your convictions, give it all you've
got, be resolute, and love without stopping.

—1 CORINTHIANS 16:13 MSG

contents

foreword

Anna E. Hampton writes in her unique book, *Facing Danger: A Guide through Risk*, "If people knew (the) pain and deep grief I carry in my soul, then perhaps they would be shocked. Some might even think I'm too broken and flawed to be useful to the Master." But don't be misled by this frank transparency, for this is not another book in the genre "I was broken but praise God he healed me." This book is about the experiences of a young Minnesota girl and her husband who took their young children to Kabul, Afghanistan, and lived there for ten action-packed, hair-raising, faith-testing years of God-honoring cross-cultural service and sacrifice. More than that, it is a book born in deep spiritual reflection, matured by doctoral level research, and presented with a burning desire and determination to bring to the reading public some truths about living in an increasingly dangerous world that they may otherwise never hear.

Anna engaged in her doctoral research and later wrote *Facing Danger* because she was aware that cross-cultural workers are facing increasingly dangerous situations in their work environments. She knows that many of these workers arrive in challenging spheres of service with unresolved emotional problems, and she's painfully aware of high attrition rates among cross-cultural workers leaving their field of service prematurely. And remember these people belong to the brave minority who had already overcome the prevailing attitude of "risk aversion" in the Western world.

This book speaks to the issues of "risk management" and "insightful contingency planning," but it states that none of these necessary aspects of the planning and implementation of perilous ventures "can replace the Holy Spirit's leading. All plans may need to be laid aside when the Spirit asks us to stay and potentially give our lives."

The strong emphasis on the spiritual dimensions of *Facing Danger* is based on an intriguing, informative, and inspiring study of New Testament instances where men and women who served with the apostle Paul "risked their lives for the sake of our Lord Jesus Christ" (Acts 15:26 NIV). Detailed word studies and unusual exegesis based on rabbinical Hebrew methodology and deep delving into Old Testament studies of Israel's ongoing battles with Amalek took me personally into a depth of study on danger and risk taking into which I had never previously ventured.

The author states clearly concerning her book: "This is a suggested spiritual and practical understanding of biblical risk." If that was her goal, then Anna hit the target. And I would further suggest that, while this is not an easy book to read, it will repay abundantly the effort to delve into its insights, exhortations, and practical guidelines. Hopefully reading *Facing Danger: A Guide through Risk* will add to the numbers of men and women like the New York firefighters who climbed resolutely into the blazing Twin Towers as office workers escaped to safety. This kind of resolution should result in more and more people "volunteering" to serve the Lord, who faced the ultimate danger on our behalf, knowing full well the risks involved. The servant is not greater than the Master.

STUART BRISCOE

preface

It was the time when the Taliban controlled Kabul and much of Afghanistan. The world no longer seemed to care about Afghanistan and the plight of her people; all but two countries of the world had withdrawn their diplomatic ties. It was into this environment that I traveled with my husband and three-month-old baby boy.

We found ourselves in the wilderness of pain. Everyone around us was suffering, and as the years passed we suffered too. We experienced an evacuation, being held at gunpoint and robbed in our home by ten men, and seeing friends kidnapped and killed. We eventually became the leaders of a multinational team and strategic project. Unbeknownst to our upper leadership, Neal and I had agreed we'd leave as soon as the Taliban started killing humanitarian aid workers—which was our demographic.

In 2008, within just weeks of each other, a colleague was murdered in a distant city, gunmen raided the Serena Hotel killing hotel employees and guests alike and three American Red Cross women were gunned down in their humanitarian-marked truck. We realized that the time had come for us to leave based on our earlier pact we made with each other. The problem now was that we couldn't just pack up and leave—we were the leaders of a large team.

It slowly dawned on us that our understanding of biblical suffering needed to change because it didn't match the level of risk we were facing. We had no concrete biblical foundation for dealing with risk. As a husband-and-wife team sent out cross-culturally to serve among remote peoples, we had no substantive way to think about risk for our children, ourselves, or our team.

We needed direction to develop a biblical understanding of risk. Risk is different from suffering. All Christians are called to suffer for Christ's sake.[1] Suffering is also clearly part of the experience for all those who receive a special calling from God to serve him cross-culturally at great risk to themselves and their families. A theology of suffering systematically answers, "Why does God allow suffering?" However, suffering happens to the righteous and the unrighteous, in safe and unsafe situations, not just to those serving cross-culturally. In contrast, risk focuses on the moments leading up to potential suffering, and thus asks different questions. We began a journey to discover what those questions were.

In his book *Risk Is Right: Better to Lose Your Life Than Waste It*, John Piper defines risk as "an action that exposes you to the possibility of loss or injury."[2] While this definition of risk is simple and clear for all believers, the focus for this book is specifically on the cross-cultural risk taken for the sake of the gospel. Cross-cultural risk may be defined as "risk entered into for the sake of carrying the gospel cross-culturally with a high probability of experiencing great loss." There are numerous losses experienced when going into risk, remaining in a risky situation, and when leaving risk.

Piper also states that all believers experience risk. This simple definition wasn't helpful to us on the field, however, as there is a much greater degree of risk experienced by those going to an area where people are resistant to the gospel than our friends and family back home in the comfort of the North American culture. Only some Christians are chosen to risk their lives for the sake of the gospel.

We were well aware of what we were risking each time we returned to Afghanistan, and the feeling of loss became a constant companion, along with so many daily graces and blessings, but we needed a deeper biblical understanding of risk to know how to think about and understand our own feelings about the risks we were undertaking as a family. We delved deeper into the Major and Minor Prophets and asked God to show us his heart concerning risk. I started reading everything available on the topic of a theology of risk (that didn't take long). It soon became clear we needed to find or create a guide for reading and applying the Scriptures in the risk moment.

My conviction that a biblical understanding of risk is much deeper than a listing of various stories in the Bible has only deepened as I've studied the Bible. The majority of writing on risk has focused on stories in the Bible with no clear exegetical connection between them and between the Old and New Testaments. The continuity of the Bible between the Old and New Testaments is *both* relevant and consistent.

What Old Testament Scriptures was Paul thinking of when he mentioned the concept of risk? What Scriptures guided the early church in all the risks they took to spread the gospel? I wondered about Paul, a Torah-observant, first-century rabbi and Messianic Pharisee, and the connections he would have made between his life experience, as described in Acts and his writings, and the Old Testament text. These types of connections would have to inform a biblical understanding of risk.

Another question is, what are the necessary elements of a practical and biblical understanding of risk? In risk, how do we discern what God wants from our lives? To answer this, it seems we learn to discern God's heart, and in doing this, some of the wrong pictures of our Father's heart will be revealed. Next, it is imperative to discern how we hear the Holy Spirit's voice speaking to us during high-risk situations. Is there a guiding principle for applying various "risk" stories from the Bible?

Finally, the risk moment requires us to become increasingly self-aware of our responses to God, to others, and to ourselves. How do we work through our faith, emotions, and decision-making in risk? What would a guide look like for doing that when things seem confusing and the future looks dark?

It's important to understand as much as we can about risk ahead of time. Risk is categorized as an event. The "event" may be short- or long-term. However, the impact of a high-risk event is seldom a momentary experience; it may weigh heavily upon the survivor for a long period of time.

Typically, the risk moment occurs unexpectedly. One day in 2004 I was riding in our organization's humanitarian aid white van with my four-year-old son, Luke. My driver was just pulling away from a police checkpoint when a screaming mob started pounding on our van. (A mob is one of the most dangerous hazards possible.)

In a millisecond, several things occurred to me. Luke and I were at great risk, and worse yet, as the mom I could see that I was powerless to protect him. He was too big to conceal under my robes, and the shops across the road were too far away to make a run for it. There was no way I could "melt" into the crowds with my blond-haired boy.

The mama-bear part of me instinctively began to fight to protect my child. As the police officer began hitting my driver, trying to pull him from the van, I let my *chadar* (veil) fall so he could see that I was a Westerner. I punched in the number to my husband on my cell phone so he could hear what was happening. Then I flashed my American passport at the police officer and began pleading with him in English and Dari to let my driver go. As my driver slowly pulled away from the crowds, the trembling began. I couldn't stop crying and shaking for two hours afterward, even in the safety of my husband's arms.

I have also experienced long risk events. For eight months my family lived under almost total lockdown with my young children, with my husband going out to work on a planned, randomized schedule. There were daily threats of kidnapping since kidnapping expatriates was (and continues to be) a lucrative business. I left the relative safety of our home only when necessary.

Whether just a brief moment or a prolonged event, risk is often characterized as loud, scary, and confusing; a cacophony of voices and a mixed bag of emotions. The noise of the risk moment is like that surrounding Christian in John Bunyan's *Pilgrim's Progress* as he passes between two fearsome roaring lions. The lions roared loudly, their aim to distract him from his task, frighten him, and make him turn tail and run.

In that classic story, they appeared just when he most needed to get to Palace Beautiful for relief, care, and security. It took him awhile, but the porter, whose name was Watchful, appeared to help him realize that while they were large, fearsome-looking lions, they were chained. Watchful relates, "[The lions are] placed there for the trial of faith, to find out where it is and to reveal those who have none. Stay in the middle of the path."[3]

In risk, our enemy is just like these chained, roaring lions. He knows nothing bad has happened to us yet, but his aim is to distract us from our task, to roar so loudly we are paralyzed by fear and we lose our courage to move forward. He appears right when we are at our weakest and shows no mercy. We must learn to stand and fight the demons of paralyzing fear, confusion, and panic.

The result?

Mature courage helps us know whether we need to stand firm, move forward, or retreat to fight another day. There is a difference between courageous retreat and cowardly retreat, between courageously remaining and cowardly remaining. When we act courageously, our souls are enlarged and the fruit of the Spirit becomes increasingly visible in our lives. Our spirits become purified, full of power, and firm. In this God is glorified, and the peace that surpasses human understanding descends and guards our hearts and minds.

The need for guidance was never so clear as it was in the fall of 2008. In the face of an extremely threatening security environment, many agencies were leaving. Over a period of eight months, almost three-fourths of the Christian expatriate community left the capital city.

At that moment in October we were faced with overwhelming decisions. How could we responsibly steward a large project with a hundred expatriates? We received conflicting e-mails about the wisest course of action. The international board members of our company began to write personal e-mails to my husband: some board members wrote to say they thought we should all leave; others wrote that we should stay, that now was the time to press forward. One board member wrote one opinion one day and then sent the opposite opinion the very next day. The guidance needed to discern God's voice from a board providing one clear directive was missing in the flurry of contradictory e-mails.

Risk is chaotic. It appears as if danger and death are looming. We often feel threatened. It looks gray, gloomy, and dark. In the Hebraic worldview, the dark waters covering the earth in Genesis 1:2 speak of chaos, without form, no life, nothingness, darkness, no order, and no beauty. And yet Scripture reveals that the Spirit of God was hovering over those dark waters.

If risk feels just like the chaotic dark waters of looming nothingness and death, then we know God's Spirit is hovering over our risk situations. His Spirit is hovering over the chaos in our souls. Out of potential suffering, paralyzing fear, and daily threats of kidnapping and murder, God can bring life, beauty, wholeness, and peace.

The very next verb in the Hebrew after "God hovering" in Genesis 1:2 is

"God spoke." God *is* hovering and God *is* speaking in the risk moment. It is my deepest hope that through this book you would be strengthened in your capacity to see him hovering over the chaos of the risk moments you face in the journey of your calling, that you would hear him speaking to you, and that you would have complete clarity of mind and spirit as he faithfully guides you through.

ANNA E. HAMPTON
The Middle East
February, 2016

acknowledgements

I am grateful to my heavenly Father, the only one who is continually present, incomparably kind above all gods, unceasingly attentive, and unendingly merciful and caring. To my Infinite Beloved, because I am a thought in his mind; I am relevant, indispensable, and participatory in his divine secret.[4] He gently shepherds me.

The four theologians to whom I feel a personal debt for shaping my studies on risk, thinking, philosophy of religion, and biblical studies are Rabbi Abraham J. Heschel, Rabbi David Fohrman, Dr. Skip Moen, and Dr. Kenneth Bailey. Heschel opened up the Father heart of God for me in the Prophets like no other teacher has before, while Rabbi Fohrman taught me the beauty of comparative textual analysis in the Hebrew. From Dr. Moen, I continue to learn to harmonize Heschel's philosophy of religion approach with Jesus's work on the cross and the New Testament writings. Dr. Kenneth Bailey's "re-Semitization of Christology" has had a significant impact on how I read Scripture. Admittedly, mine is a theologically eclectic journey, to paraphrase Dr. Marvin Wilson.

It is risky business to propose thoughts on a Bible background on risk for cross-cultural workers. Three gracious men carefully checked over my exegetical discussion on risk and gave insight, correction, and excellent critical feedback. Your comments sharpened and enhanced my writing. Thank you to Dr. Lee Allison of Riverside Assemblies of God Church, Dr. Keith Missel of Friendship Church, and John Wile of Barnabas International, who helped during their busy ministry schedules. You are brothers to me. Any mistakes in exegesis are mine.

Thank you to two kind and humble Daves: They encouraged me from the very beginning and generously helped me get started by giving all their PowerPoints and notes they had already written on the topic and used with field staff. They shared organizational resources and expanded my resource network for this project.

Ten prominent humanitarian organizations magnanimously shared their risk and danger papers with me for further review and study. For security reasons, they are only acknowledged as "Organization A, Organization B, etc." I suspect many of these papers were written under great duress by home office staff when they had personnel in kidnap situations. The church owes a great debt of gratitude to those who went before in developing biblical statements on cross-cultural risk.

Words here cannot express my deep appreciation for the network of friends who have helped steward this project, gave kind and critical feedback, and encouraged me to keep writing. This book is much better because of so many friends taking the time to read, ponder, and enter the dialogue with me on this topic, assuming the best intentions of my heart in my early drafts. Thank you for helping me steward my pain through such gracious feedback and help in wordsmithing. Special thanks to Lisa W., Brian and Dr. Debbie Aho of Developing Shepherds International, Darlene Jerome of MMCT, and Drs. Charlie and Frauke Schaefer of Barnabas International.

We have over two hundred financial and prayer partners who have walked with us many years—some of you since I was thirteen! We are deeply grateful for your partnership. Your faithfulness in supporting us through so many challenges assisted the formulation of this book.

My children have had to find ways to snuggle with a mom who had books and papers everywhere while constantly on her computer, but hopefully always had some chocolate-chip cookie dough handy in the freezer for baking. I love being your mom and I'm so proud of each of you for your resiliency and deepening relationship with our Father.

Finally, I could never have done this without Neal. So much of this book is from you. Your support, encouragement, honest feedback, and theological debates over coffee and the dinner table stimulated and pushed my thinking forward. Together we faced heart-wrenching risk and were awed by what our Father did in, through, and around us. I daily experience his *hesedness* through you. Your love continues to deeply touch and heal my wounds. My beloved.

FACING
DANGER

chapter 1

The Enraged Beast

As a provider of pastoral care for those working cross-culturally, I talk with a lot of people who work throughout Central Asia and the Middle East. Without fail, when they learn my husband and I spent almost a decade in Afghanistan, I am queried if they should be concerned about security in their corner of the volatile region. And the general answer is yes, they should be concerned about security in their region. But security is not a feeling—it never is.

Our family *felt* unsafe back in 2000 when we lived under the Taliban rule in Kabul. In reality, however, we were very much protected by the Talib government of the time. Later, after the coalition forces liberated Kabul, everyone felt the freedom from tyranny and the ruthless living conditions that came from Taliban rule. As Americans, feeling "free" meant we *felt* safe. But freedom and safety are not necessarily related.

In 2002, almost a year after the liberation of Kabul, our home was attacked during the month of Ramadan by ten armed Afghan men. They had killed people in the two houses they had attacked before forcing their way into our home. Their eyes were wild with violence and material lust as they held us, with our toddler and baby girl, at gunpoint and ransacked our home.

A simple reading of the headlines in the Central Asia and Middle Eastern regions reveals that the physical war on the ground points to the cosmic spiritual battle waging all around us. The "enraged beast" is the enemy of our God, the one seeking to devour Christians and keep as many people as possible bound in darkness (Revelation 12:17). We need to read the headlines with spiritual eyes and hear the news with spiritual ears (2 Kings 6:17; 2 Samuel 5:24; 1 Chronicles 14:15).

We know that the battle is intensifying for several reasons. More and more unreached people groups are being engaged. The geopolitical war and unrest are displacing millions of peoples, thereby making them accessible to Christian workers. The increasing numbers of major natural disasters in the past decade have resulted in humanitarian aid workers being invited to provide aid in places formerly closed. The gospel has gone and it is continuing to go forth.

In our work as pastoral-care providers to global workers across Central Asia and the Middle East, we see that God's people are faithful to answer his call. We pastor people who are living in a variety of Central Asian and Middle Eastern settings—remote mountain areas where nomadic shepherds live, tiny villages, small cities, and dusty, dirty capital cities across the region. They are sharing the good news that Jesus has come to restore dishonorable people to our Father's house with honor (Luke 15). But this is not without paying a major price.

There are at least four major global trends making a comprehensive, practical, and biblical understanding of risk an urgent priority for all those serving on these remote front lines of cross-cultural efforts.

Four Major Trends

Increasing Danger and Persecution of Cross-Cultural Laborers

First, there is the increasing trend of danger and persecution affecting those who work in cross-cultural locations. Persecution of the current generation of Christian national and expatriate workers serving in resistant Muslim contexts has increased significantly. Many Muslim countries continue to make it extremely difficult for Christians to live, and, at times, brutal persecution results. Christians working overseas for faith-based organizations are paying a heavy price to carry the message of hope to the world. In Afghanistan, for example, over twenty Christian humanitarian aid workers have lost their lives.[5] In this way, foreigners have joined the Afghan members of the body of Christ who have paid the ultimate price.

The trends of the twenty-first century appear to be leading to increasingly severe risk to Christians wherever they are, but especially for those purposefully moving into cultures hostile to those following the teachings of Jesus the Messiah. With sadness I wrote in our monthly newsletter to our financial partners in 2010:

This past month I had a Skype conversation with a friend working in war-torn Central Asia. She related: "We are bracing ourselves for another wave of workers to leave. Since the murders, many global workers here are realizing they haven't fully counted the costs of giving their lives in a high-risk environment, even though many unreached groups remain. I am constantly crying. Our boys will have to say numerous good-byes during Christmas break and at the end of the school year."

My heart was heavy as I listened to Amy[6] share with me via video Skype. Since extremists executed our eight friends in August and another Christian woman just one week ago, numerous workers are facing intense spiritual warfare and the personal realization of the reality of what it means to be serving him in or near war zones.

Many are deciding the cost is too high and are leaving to return home. In this new world of global opportunity, those working among unreached people groups need additional member care support to sustain long-term effectiveness and resiliency.

Increasingly, Christians around the world are targeted by suicide bombers and terrorist attacks. Paul Borthwick describes a major global trend regarding the average age of the people in the world. He describes it as "young, restless, and uncertain." He writes:

> More than fifty percent of the world is under the age of twenty-five. ... There is a saying in the Middle East that poverty is the mother of terrorism. And hopelessness is the mother of a lot of violence in the world. If the choice is going to a great banquet in heaven with seventy virgins versus living a life of unemployment and poverty, some will be willing to blow themselves up to escape this life.[7]

However, there continues to be a great need to reach out to all peoples of major faiths. Up to "eighty-six percent of all Muslims, Hindus, and Buddhists do not personally know a Christian."[8] Converting from Islam to Christianity is costly. The majority will most likely get fired or imprisoned, but many are killed. It's become common knowledge that "Muslim regimes do not foster religious freedom. Conversion out of Islam is prohibited."[9] As anyone can see, there is an increasing trend of danger and persecution that is affecting those who work in cross-cultural locations.

The Trend of Increasing Attrition Rates

Second, there is the trend of increasing attrition rates among Christians working cross-culturally.[10] The harsh contemporary reality of cross-cultural service is contributing to the significant erosion of global workers. Many workers arrive on the field with vision, enthusiasm, and calling, but without realistic expectations, an understanding of risk and suffering, ample biblical literacy, and with ineffective interpersonal skills.

The World Evangelical Fellowship estimates that 30,600 internationally located laborers leave the field every four years. Of these, 71 percent leave for reasons that were preventable.[11] In one country in the Middle East, regional leaders from five different faith-based agencies report that merely one in ten coworkers remain for ten years. Most of them leave after three to four years. Another agency reported that the attrition rate for their staff in hostile, resistant contexts is 50–60 percent. This attrition means that more than half of all their workers leave for primarily preventable reasons and before they have become effective.[12]

A veteran pastoral-care leader responded to the problem of the attrition rate:

> The problem is that there's much more lost than money. Think of the damage to the family leaving a thriving work for either personal needs (depression; loss of funds; loss of vision) or other reasons (war in the country, needs of aging parents, etc.)
>
> Think of the sadness of a couple or family who have invested 8 to 10 years in a ministry and now have to leave it; they wonder if they misunderstood God's call; they wonder why their church is dropping them, etc.
>
> Think of the cost to the team left on the field (lessened

morale; overloaded work-loads for those still there who must pick up the task).

Think of the sadness of the people groups a team was ministering to. In some of our field locations, the translation project took more than fifty years, because for one reason or another team after team had to leave. The people wondered if they would ever get the Book. There's a loss to their donors who wonder if all that money they invested was wasted.[13]

Trend of Changing Sending Countries[14]

Third, there is the trend of expanding sending countries. In the past thirty years, approximately 75 percent of all Christian vocational workers serving around the world are coming from outside of Europe and North America. The twentieth century experienced the great shift of Christianity to the Global South, a trend that will continue into the future.

In 1970, approximately 41 percent of all Christians were from Africa, Asia, or Latin America. By 2020, this figure is expected to be almost 65 percent.[15] These global workers tend to be from poorer countries, where sending groups are often incapable of providing pastoral visits, and personnel are typically unable to afford supplementary restorative resources such as a yearly retreat out of the region where they minister. Newer sending country workers have much less member care from outside the country, and must find practical *and* spiritual ways to remain encouraged in risk and challenging cross-cultural contexts.

Trend of Increased Brokenness of Christian Laborers

Finally, there is the increased brokenness in the church that equates to bruised members going overseas. Dr. Stephen Sweatman, the president of Mission Training International, said, "If we describe the whole world as if it's one family, it is fatherless, abused, and hurting."[16] Christian workers who are called to serve internationally from all over the world tend to go to the field "softer" and more "bruised" due to many factors. Chief among these are the effects of dysfunction in our churches and families back home.

With high rates of sexual, physical, emotional, and mental abuse, divorce, and the accompanying trauma,[17] cross-cultural workers often carry to the field a variety of personal challenges. These may include unresolved past traumas, lack of skills in conflict resolution, dysfunctional interpersonal skills, issues related to manhood and fatherhood, or wrong conceptions of God and relating to him. These factors all contribute to problems of low resiliency and lack of endurance overseas, *especially* in high-risk and dangerous situations.

Are We Asking the Wrong Questions?

The problem of the high staff turnover rate has led to a proliferation of books and articles on suffering. One assumption seems to be, "If people only know and accept a correct doctrinal truth about God or suffering, then they will become more hardy and resilient. We just need to give the right information and they will be able to handle the 'dripping faucet stress'[18] of living in or near a war zone."

The difficulties internationally located staff have in not being able to handle the current risks are a significant criticism of the current generation of cross-cultural workers. Despite all the resources on suffering, there seems to be "an embarrassment of knowledge"[19] in how to handle risk and suffering. Abraham Heschel states, "We formulate and debate the issues while oblivious to and alienated from the experiences or the insights that account for our raising the issues."[20] Understanding the perspective of people who have lived the reality of front line overseas risk certainly would minimize the "alienation from experience" referred to by Heschel.

As far as I can tell, the discussion about a theology of risk has primarily been characterized by listing risk stories in the Bible and encouraging people to "have faith." For me, as a stay-at-home mom, anecdotal risk stories with little apparent connection to each other and no guide for how to think about the progression of risk in the Bible were not helpful. This approach did not touch my mind and heart, and it did not help me work through the chaos of living in a high-risk situation for days and years on end. I wanted to try to find out what Scriptures may have come into Paul's mind (he only had the Old Testament writings) when he entered risk and apply them to my own situation.

It's also crucial to recognize our own cultural "bent." Financial insurance plans and contingency planning can consume a great deal of time, energy, and finances in both secular and ministry organizations. The risk-adverse culture of North America does not lend itself to producing a generation of cross-cultural staff able to be resilient and withstand extreme danger.

If the assumption is that Christian laborers need to understand suffering, and agencies and leaders are asking, "What do frontline cross-cultural workers *not* understand about suffering? What do they need to know about suffering before going?" then is it possible the wrong questions are being asked? Are we giving the wrong answers to an extremely risk-adverse generation? Is there a key factor to increasing the resiliency of cross-cultural staff and reducing attrition rates in high-risk areas? If so, what is it?

The answer to the question must be relevant, not just in the North American church but also for workers "in moments of staggering cruelty and the daily threat of imminent disaster and death. The answer must work not just in the halls of seminary learning."[21] It must work for the Christian laborer who knows that by going to work tomorrow he is facing the risk of being hauled off to jail for being a Christian; or that she could be killed in the street on her way to work by a gunman firing a $15 Kalashnikov while riding his $125 motorcycle. The answers must work for a dying man or woman and the children who accompany them.

> Just as knowing about suffering is far different from the actual experience of suffering, so is *knowing* about risk far different from *the experience* of risking one's life.

Just as knowing about suffering is far different from the actual experience of suffering, so is *knowing* about risk far different from *the experience* of risking one's life. I propose that a biblical understanding of risk is a major contributing factor needed to increase steadfastness and firmness (clinicians use the terms "hardiness" and "resiliency") in risk situations.

Risk resiliency requires way more than mental assent to "correct" doctrine. A biblical understanding of risk is the prerequisite to a theology of suffering. Yet it is also a characteristic of the inner life. It includes cognitive assent *and* internal experiential heart response, as well as personal and community experience with the Lord. It is practical *and* spiritual, thoroughly grounded in Scripture. Having a firm grasp on this foundational requirement for followers of Christ planning to enter a dangerous, high-risk and hostile situation is crucial.

Hardiness and Resiliency

The majority of the people groups in need of transformation live in areas of the world where there has been a dramatic increase of persecution and murders of Christians. Greater resiliency is needed to withstand all manners and levels of persecution, difficulties, and dangers. But what is resiliency?

Resiliency is synonymous with mental toughness. It is what happens during and after hardship or suffering has taken place. Here is one definition of resiliency: *"Human resiliency is the ability to face reality, to engage with and grow through life's challenges and adversities via inner strength, social support, coping skills,* and core beliefs/values *including life purpose and spiritual meaning."*[22] How resilient are you?

Resiliency in member-care terms is often described metaphorically as being like a rubber band. It describes the elasticity of being able to be stretched and return to the same shape again. It's a good metaphor for us to keep in mind here. But rubber bands don't evoke much emotion in my soul. With all due respect to my psychologist and pastoral-care friends, I've secretly always pictured resilience more like having a spine of titanium. In other words, my convictions are so strong and so deep, it's as if they are forged in the strongest metal known to humankind and will not melt in the hottest fires of danger. I'm saying with David, "Therefore I will not fear ... though the mountains slip into the heart of the sea" (Psalm 46:2–3). I will not be moved from trusting God.

David formed and stated his conviction about how he would respond emotionally, physically, and spiritually *before* the reality of his greatest fear happened. This is what firmness of soul and strength of spirit look like, biblically speaking. Using David's words as a guide, we are to cultivate an inner toughness *before* trials come (hardiness), and as we turn toward God through the risk experience, hardiness will only deepen and increase after going through risk, resulting in a greater firmness of faith that is proven by our experience of God in that moment (resiliency).

In this sense, both rubber bands and "titanium spines" are incomplete pictures of resiliency because they don't demonstrate the picture of spiritual growth commonly experienced in risk. The Bible often compares faith to the image of a tree growing deep roots in the wilderness (Isaiah 41:19). A tree's roots grow deepest, seeking new areas of water and nutrients, when the circumstances above the soil are the most adverse—when it is the hottest and the driest above ground. Deep roots mean the tree is not toppled over in violent storms.

Risk faced in a cross-cultural environment forces us to confront our deepest fears, experience parts of ourselves we realize we are ashamed of (overwhelming rage, for example), admit and work out of our weaknesses, and recognize the reality of how little control we truly have over our lives. It forces us to turn to God or away from him. Risk often requires us to deal with potentially faith-shattering questions.

In risk we either grow deeper toward likeness and union with Christ, or we don't. Paul uses phrases like "the firmness of your faith" and "walk in him, rooted and built up in him and established in your faith" in Colossians 2:5–7. We take the firmness of faith with us into risk, which only deepens as our faith-thoughts are refined and we experience the truth of the reality of our Father's faithfulness through the risk experience.

So what Bible passages are relevant for moms, dads, children, and singles to develop firmness of soul and spirit? What will help increase hardiness and resiliency? And how do we integrate daily risk assessment with what the Bible says about risk?

Four Important Questions

I had a lot of questions on cross-cultural risk. For this discussion, I have framed them into four broad but important questions:

1. What can we learn about risk from the risk idioms used in the New Testament?

2. How do we understand stewardship and the Holy Spirit's leading in risk?

3. What components are necessary to consider and integrate into cross-cultural risk?

4. Integrating the findings identified in questions one through three, how do we calculate cross-cultural risk?

Answering these questions will lead cross-cultural workers to formulate their beliefs and develop a deeper biblical understanding of risk, integrated with what they have discerned the Holy Spirit calling them to do in the moment of risk. This includes the task of becoming risk literate (as defined in Chapter 8) and assessing what risk mitigation needs to take place for right stewardship in each unique risk situation.

Risk assessment and management are increasingly a daily necessity of the current fields of service. As a mom of young kids, I paid attention to risk assessment every day for almost ten years while living in Afghanistan. Was it safe enough for the children to ride their bikes on the street? Which bazaars were off limits due to kidnapping threats?

It's my desire that this book will strengthen internationally serving colleagues, and the children with them, to endure faithfully. This book will hopefully help identify crucial components of a biblical basis of risk and provide a biblical and practical framework for developing a personal conviction about risk for Christ-followers going to work in hostile, high-risk situations.

Part One discusses three specific references to risk in the New Testament and demonstrates their connection to an Old Testament story as spiritual background for preparing for risk. It includes a discussion of some of what Paul and the early church may have been thinking regarding risk as they moved forward to share the gospel.

One of the most common discoveries in risk are misconceptions we have about God. Often our Father uses risk to reveal to us those areas he wants to change in us as we follow him into it. God risks to bring us to himself, and as we vulnerably risk to bring others to him we become more like him, seeing him more truly as he is and gaining a greater understanding of his heart.

Part Two moves into risk assessment and management. All aspects of cross-cultural risk must be considered. Having a systematic way to work through a comprehensive risk assessment will increase the confidence of those working overseas, their families, partners, organizations, and teams. Especially helpful is the discussion of the mind and the emotions. Over a thousand studies on the psychology of risk by secular researches give insight to more effective awareness of how we are handling risk as individuals, teams, and leaders.

While it is crucial to thoroughly discuss risk management from a kingdom perspective of operating within one's calling of cross-cultural service, no amount of attentive study, effective framework, insightful contingency planning, and perceptive discussion can replace the Holy Spirit's leading. All plans may need to be laid aside when the Spirit asks us to stay and potentially give our lives.

Application

1. Analyze the country you desire or plan to go to or return to. What statistics can you find about attrition rates for the major Christian vocational organizations that are there?

2. Who can you talk with to find out what the real difficulties are on the ground and why cross-cultural workers are having a hard time staying there?

3. Who has stayed and what has helped them thrive in this challenging situation?

Chapter 1 Summary

1. Listen for the movement of the "marching on the trees" (1 Chronicles 14:15) as you read the news headlines. The spiritual battle is always waging behind the news stories, and there are almost always national Christians, Christian aid workers, and Christian vocational personnel among those events.

2. The four global trends are:

   • Increased persecution of Christians worldwide.

   • Increased attrition rates, a majority of which are for preventable reasons.

- Change of sending countries—more workers coming from the Global South.

- An increasing number of Jesus-followers going and serving "bruised." They are going into the field with broken relationships, from broken homes, with a lack of spiritual depth, and biblical illiteracy.

3. Four questions to ask are:

    - What are the passages in the Bible that are most helpful to begin building a biblical and foundational understanding of risk?

    - How do we balance stewardship and the Holy Spirit's leading in risk?

    - What components are necessary to consider and integrate into cross-cultural risk?

    - Integrating the findings identified in questions one through three, how do we calculate cross-cultural risk?

**Illustration 1.1 Theology of Suffering and Theology of Risk
Overview**

This illustrates that all believers experience suffering, whether living in relative safety or danger. Your theology of suffering determines how you respond to suffering, regardless of where you are. A theology of risk influences whether you move toward more risk or toward safety. What happens when a person responds with a theology-of-suffering answer to someone asking a theology-of-risk question?

part one

Bible & Spiritual Background

chapter 2

Three Risk Words in the New Testament

What Were They Thinking?

Is there any way to figure out what the leaders of the early church may have been thinking when they considered the risk of sharing the good news? The issue of risk is hardly isolated to the New Testament. If we look in the Old Testament, we see many times where people risked their very lives while facing enemies who seemed too big. One of those such times is in Exodus 17, in the battle between Israel and Amalek. There is a fascinating correlation between several New Testament passages and the Exodus 17 battle. It seems that these New Testament writers had this context in mind when they referred to risk.

There are three passages that use the word *risk* in the New Testament. Each time, the one English word is translated from three different Greek words. Clearly, while these three passages connect to each other by their use of the word *risk*, there must be different aspects to risk for us to understand and apply today. Here are the three passages where many translators have elected to use the English word "risk":

> It seemed good to us, having become of one mind, to select men to send to you with our beloved Barnabas and Paul, men who have risked their lives for the name of our Lord Jesus Christ (Acts 15:25–26).

> Greet Prisca and Aquila, my fellow workers in Christ Jesus, who for my life risked their own necks, to whom not only do I give thanks, but also all the churches of the Gentiles (Romans 16:3–4).

> Receive him then in the Lord with all joy, and hold men like

him in high regard; because he came close to death for the
work of Christ, risking his life to complete what was deficient
in your service to me (Philippians 2:29–30).

Luke and Paul, like all the New Testament writers, had memorized great volumes of the Old Testament in Hebrew, which had a significant influence on their writings. If we play a little "game" called "Where have we heard that before?"[23] We begin to see phrases, words, and concepts from the passages above pointing to the first battle between Israel and Amalek.[24]

We'll want to see more than one overlapping phrase to suggest that Exodus 17 is what Luke and Paul had in mind when they wrote about risk. We'll look at each connection and briefly consider Paul's overall view of spiritual warfare to better understand more about biblical risk and some spiritual principles of risk. There are four overlaps we will look at in this chapter: the use of "chosen men" in Acts 15:22 and Exodus 17; the priesthood in Philippians 2 and Exodus 17; the presence of the Father, Son, and Spirit through motifs and words in Acts 15:22–32, Philippians 2:27–30, and Exodus 17; and warfare and risk in Acts 15, Romans 16:4, and Exodus 17.

Idioms and Overlaps

Idioms are one of the major tools to understand the Central Asian and Middle Eastern cultures. The New Testament was written by Jews who had a Hebraic worldview. Thus, we see numerous Hebraic idiomatic phrases in the New Testament that are translated into Greek. Two synonymous idioms communicate the idea of risk in both the Hebrew and Greek in the Bible.[25]

Hebrew employs what is called "phenomenological language." This means it describes what risk looks like in the physical world and how it appears, using action verbs. The Greek language employs more philosophy and logic in its definition of words and ideas,[26] which means that we will see what risk looks like in action when we have our "Hebrew" glasses on but the precise meaning of the action when we have our "Greek" glasses on. Both perspectives are useful and will facilitate a more comprehensive understanding of how to respond to risk while engaging in faith endeavors.

Connecting "Choose Men" in the Old and New Testaments

The first question to ask when we read the Acts passage is, "Where in the Bible do we hear the phrase *choose men*?" Our probing will help us link the shared insights of both Testaments. We see here that the same type of men are chosen in Acts 15:22 as in Exodus 17:9 in the story of the battle between Israel and Amalek. "Choose men" is used the first time in the Bible in Exodus 17:9. Moses tells Joshua to "choose men" who can go out and fight the Amalekites with him. What kind of men should Joshua choose, and what kind of men do the apostles and elders choose?

We can sensibly speculate that Joshua chose many of the men who were known as elders among the people of Egypt while they were still slaves—the ones Moses and Aaron had to convince that God was on the move. The men chosen are the best men, those who are wise, discerning, and experienced.[27] They were men who had been examined through the refining fires of affliction (Isaiah 48:10; Job 34:4). These were mighty men, God-fearing men. Perhaps they even knew how to fight witchcraft and sorcery, because the Amalekites were known as sorcerers.[28] Moses clearly entrusted Joshua's discernment of the kind of men needed to enter into battle, and "choosing" means not all available men were chosen. Only some of the men, perhaps the most skilled warriors, were chosen.

Another aspect of these chosen men entering the risk of warfare was their motivation. They went into risk because they were chosen. There wasn't a group of Israelite men looking for an opportunity to take risks. We don't see Joshua coming up to Moses and saying, "Hey Moses, do you have any risky jobs I can take on to prove how much I love God and how special I am to him?"

Some cross-cultural workers have a misperception that pursuing risk is the highest calling, a demonstration of faith, and so they are motivated to pursue it. Very often, however, the motivations behind a person's behavior have a significant impact on how the behavior will affect that person or someone else. The New Testament points to the importance of the intentions of our hearts, rather than only evaluating the actions themselves (Matthew 12:33–35). To be chosen to risk, to be chosen to enter the battle, means one is chosen by Christ and risks for Christ for no other reason than being called. Men and women who have been chosen to risk do so because of being asked, either by leadership or because of a clear calling from God. They do not elevate risk as a value in and of itself.

> To be chosen to risk, to be chosen to enter the battle, means one is chosen by Christ and risks for Christ for no other reason than being called.

What Kind of Men Were They?

The leaders of the Jerusalem church needed to choose some men to go and help the Gentile church. Some Jewish folks had come from Judea and had gone to the Gentile church in Antioch and caused all sorts of trouble, pretending to be leaders sent by the Jerusalem church. They had disturbed the Gentile believers.

The Jerusalem church chose men—Judas and Silas—from among the brothers, adding that they were "leading men." Luke restates a few verses later that they "chose men." Why do we need to be told twice that certain men were chosen and not others? Repetition and amplification of words or phrases in the Bible narrative tell us to pay attention to what is taking place.

The leaders of the Jerusalem church sent a letter to the disturbed Gentiles, opening with these words: "Since we have heard that some of our number to whom we gave no instruction have disturbed you with their words, unsettling your souls ..." (Acts 15:24). Our contemporary Bible translations may not communicate the significant travesty of what these visitors were doing. The expression "unsettled their minds" is an idiom meaning "packing baggage into your soul."[29] They were putting oppressive regulations on the church, causing all sorts of distress and worry. They were upsetting the Gentile believers and dismantling the foundational teachings of Paul by harshly requiring circumcision and by ruling over the church with force. These men were stuffing harmful dogmas into the souls of the young followers of Christ; they were making minor issues major ones. In essence, they were the opposite of the men described in verse 22.

In contrast, Judas and Silas, themselves known as prophets, "strengthened and encouraged" the believers with their words. We see a notable difference of the presence and the impact of the teaching from these two types of leaders on the inner soul lives in the hearts of believers. I wonder if Luke and the elders had in mind Jeremiah 23 and Ezekiel 34 when comparing Judas and Silas with these men? In these chapters, the prophets convey God's view of the bad shepherds of Israel who neglected and devoured the sheep by causing fear and dismay and scattering the sheep.

They Risked Their Lives

Why would Luke contrast "unsettled their minds" with "risked their lives"? Those don't appear at first look to be related. The idiom "risked their lives" means "to hand over life" or "to expose oneself willingly to a danger or risk."[30] It means that these men were willing to die for their beliefs; they were men characterized by sacrificial love and were thoroughly trustworthy.[31]

I believe Luke is contrasting these two phrases because men who unsettle the minds of others are usually men (and women) who have too much time on their hands, who do not have a perspective of what is worth dying for, and who "major in the minors," as we say. It means they make minor issues supremely important, which damages Christ's body. However, men who risk their lives, knowing they can be killed, are men who are the exact opposite of "unsettled." This is something we understand by experience when we risk our lives for the sake of the gospel.

What happens internally is that there is a paring away, a simplifying, a narrowing of focus. The mind becomes settled on what is supremely important. Life is enjoyed in the simplest of terms. At that point, minor issues that were once important recede to the background, and men and women who have been privileged and chosen to enter this state are able to help others discern what is worth fussing over and dying for.

What is fascinating about this comment is that in typical Hebraic fashion, these four men are described with verbs, as men of action. The descriptions of these faithful servants were not concentrated based on their doctrinal knowledge, their degrees, rank, or their accomplishments, but on their righteous action. Judas, Silas, Paul, and Barnabas were to be entrusted to come and "strengthen the weak, heal the sick, bind up the injured, bring the strays back, seek out the lost, and gently teach and correct the sheep" (Ezekiel 34:4, my paraphrase). These are men whose souls are anchored and lead others to the same place as where they stand (Hebrews 6:19).

One Family's Experience

A family in a Central Asia conflict zone related that they had two pastoral leaders from different churches who offered to visit and minister to them through a period of crisis. Security had nosedived, and many people were fearful and anxious. The family thoughtfully processed both offers of a field visit and, in so doing, walked in the same manner as the apostles and elders of Acts 15. They chose men from a perspective of how they would impact their souls.

One pastor was from a church that seemed to predominantly value a formula of spiritual productivity that was unsuited for the Muslim context where the family lived. Additionally, the church leadership had communicated a ministry emphasis that was not shared by the family on the field. It didn't feel safe to have this pastor come and possibly add to the tension with a judgmental attitude, and so they declined his offer. To the other pastor who had offered a personal visit, they said, "Please come. You can help us." This pastor had experience in the Middle East, and the partnering church was 100 percent behind the family and the project they were involved in.

In the risk moment, it is *essential* to have leaders who will strengthen and encourage others, like Judas, Silas, Paul, and Barnabas. It is important to have leaders who have a calming influence on the sheep and who speak wisely, not ones who might add distress, worry, and fear to a crisis situation.

The Connection of Risk and Priesthood in the Old and New Testaments

There are two connections between the risk Epaphroditus took in service to Paul and the priesthood of Moses and Aaron. The priesthood in the Old Testament is an important emphasis in the story of the battle between the Israelites and the Amalekites (Exodus 17:8–16). Moses and Aaron are *both* priests of the people of Israel: "Moses and Aaron were among his priests" (Psalm 99:6; see also Hebrews 3:1–3). In this story, Moses and Aaron act as vessels for God's presence: Moses, through the lifting of his hands over the people of Israel, and Aaron, through helping to hold up Moses's hands when he became weary. The "lifting of the hands" over the people is how divine blessings were often mediated in the Old Testament.[32] Together, Aaron and Moses mediated God's power and presence to the people of Israel, which was part of their priestly role.

In the New Testament, Paul first describes Epaphroditus as a minister, using the same word for priestly service used elsewhere in the New Testament (Luke 1:23; Acts 13:2; Hebrews 9:21; 10:11). Next, Paul connects the risk Epaphroditus took and restated it as priestly service: "I have received full payment, and more. I am well supplied, having received from Epaphroditus the gifts you sent, a fragrant offering, a sacrifice acceptable and pleasing to God" (Philippians 4:18 ESV).

Christ's death is described by Paul in Ephesians 5:2 as a "fragrant offering." "This was a common phrase to describe the sacrifices of the Tabernacle and Temple,"[33] writes Tim Hegg. Paul considers the practical action of risking one's life for the sake of the gospel as acting in priestly service. He regards the action of risk as profoundly spiritual![34]

When we put together what Moses and Aaron did in Exodus 17 and the high commendation of Epaphroditus given by Paul in Philippians 4:18, we see risk in a new light. Moses and Aaron were helping the Israelites win that day through their actions, while Epaphroditus ministered to Paul through his risk and what he brought to Paul.

We see in Abraham's willingness to offer his son to the Lord as a sacrifice, that he "risked" his son's life in obedience to God. The Lord met him at the "risk moment" by pointing Abraham to a ram caught in a bush.[35] Risk is priestly service in battle and it is also spiritual care to those who are engaged in battle. This priestly service is described in sacrificial terms; risking our lives for another and God's kingdom is inherent in sacrifice.

Finally, we see here the community of those who engage in risk. Paul calls Epaphroditus "a fellow worker, a fellow soldier." There's a special relationship between those who have risked together, and Paul gives the highest commendation for these risk takers for the gospel.

Seeing the Father, Son, and Spirit

Looking through the eyes of Paul and the early church leaders, there are several places in our three passages (also in Exodus 17:8–16) revealing the presence of the Father, the Son, and the Spirit. Evidence of the Spirit of God's unifying activities revealed in the unity of the choosing of the men include:

- Acts 15:22: "It seemed good to the apostles and elders ..."

- Acts 15:25: "It has seemed good to us ..."

- Acts 15:25: "... having become of one mind."

The apostles and elders demonstrated what unity of the Holy Spirit looked like in action (Ephesians 4:3–4). They showed this by how they arrived at agreement over a significant decision of selecting which men to accompany Paul and Barnabas, as well as the decision of picking what requirements to ask of the Gentile churches.

The Father and Son are mentioned in both the Acts and Philippians passages. In Acts 15:26, it is only the second time in the New Testament when "Lord" and "Jesus Christ" are combined into one title for God.[36] Paul says in Philippians about Epaphroditus that "God had mercy" and "receive him in the Lord," which are both translated from Old Testament titles for Jehovah God. Finally, he gives the reason they should receive him in the Lord—he almost "died for the work of Christ."

How are these passages connected to the Exodus 17:8–16 story? In Exodus 17, God the Father is on his throne (vs. 16), Moses sitting on the stone with his shepherds' crook prefigures Jesus, who is our Good Shepherd, and the Spirit is empowering the Israelites to fight the battle and win through Moses's outstretched arms.

For those of us in the middle of a risk situation, it's common to feel alone and isolated. Sometimes it can even feel like God has abandoned us. But in the three risk passages in the New Testament and the story of Exodus 17, God the Father, the Son, and the Spirit are present and active. We must hold on to these living pictures and grasp tightly the spiritual reality that Jesus will be with us always, even to the end of the age (Matthew 28:20).

Risk and Warfare

All three uses of the word *risk* in the New Testament connect risk to warfare. Let's look at the three Greek words that make this connection.

Paradidomi

Paradidomi means "give over to," and the tense used in Acts 15:26 means that these men have actively chosen to deliver over their hearts and souls and *remain* in that position. It's like they aren't just setting themselves up for the possibility of difficulty, but that they have decisively placed themselves into the center of the difficult place—that's where they choose to live, so of course awful things may happen.

This word used in Acts 15:26 is frequently used in the context of betrayal and war with God's enemies in the New Testament. For example, it is used in Matthew 26:45, where we learn that Jesus was "given into the hands" of sinners. Jesus, the one who will "crush Satan's head," is engaged in warfare. It also means there is potential for being betrayed[37] and for giving up one's life into the hands of one's enemies as part of the cosmic battle being waged between God and Satan.

Other ways this word is used includes stewardship,[38] delivering the Word to others,[39] and cosmic battle.[40] Jude tells us that followers of Christ are to battle as in a war for the faith "given (*paradidomi*) to the saints" (Jude 3). Earlier I mentioned *risk* in Acts 15:26 means "to hand over life." This same phrase in the Hebrew—"given into the hands"—is used in the Old Testament regarding warfare over a hundred times![41]

Parabaleusamenos

The way this word is used in Philippians 2:30 means it is an action willfully, knowingly chosen by Epaphroditus; it's "I've thrown aside my life." The risk is having decided to do it, so yes, there may be awful things that come, but, of course, they would—it's where Epaphroditus decisively placed himself. When Paul describes Epaphroditus as one who risked his life (*parabaleusamenos*), he amplifies the description of Epaphroditus with five nouns, including "fellow soldier." Paul describes Epaphroditus as a warrior who suffered with him.[42] Later he reminds Timothy, "Share in sufferings as a good soldier of Christ Jesus" (2 Timothy 2:3). These all tie *parabaleusamenos* (risk) to warfare.

Hypotithemi

Finally, in Romans 16:4, the word for *risk* (*hypotithemi*) connects the concept of risk in the New Testament with the battle between the Israelites and Amalekites in Exodus 17. Prisca and Aquila essentially "risked their necks," which is a second idiom used to translate *risk* in the New Testament.[43] It is stated, "mortgaging their necks."[44] What a picture of vulnerably laying oneself open to whatever may come!

It is the same tense used in *parabaleusamenos*; it means to have decisively chosen this action. To risk is to expose one's neck to the boot or the sword, so of course it may be cut off. It's not that they were ready to "place their necks under," but *they did do this*. The sword may or may not fall, but the neck is exposed nevertheless. They had in a sense fully given their lives for the sake of the gospel; it's just that their lives weren't taken at that point. Prisca and Aquila had staked their very lives on Jesus Christ, laying their necks on the line because of the solid foundation of Christ under them.[45]

The Greek word Paul used to describe what Prisca and Aquila did is also used in the Septuagint (the first Greek translation of the Old Testament) for "placing under" (a rock). In Exodus 17:12, the rock is what Moses sat on when he became tired of standing and holding his hands up. Each time *hypotithemi* is used in the Septuagint, it is used for the "placing under" in covenant agreement and God's help. Throughout the Bible, both God the Father and Jesus are described as our rock: "he will become a sanctuary and a stone of offense and a rock of stumbling ..." (Isaiah 8:14 ESV).[46]

In risk, we've seen that we are choosing to lay our necks on the line, exposing ourselves to and giving our lives over to danger. We do this as priestly service because of what Jesus suffered for us through his death on the cross.

Risk and Danger

What is significant about the concept of risk in the New Testament is that none of the three words used in the Greek for risk are synonyms to the Greek word for danger. Risk is used in all three contexts for laying down one's life for the sake of Jesus Christ and sharing the good news. Biblically speaking, there seems to be a nuanced difference between risking one's life and the dangers we are exposed to when we go cross-culturally. Logically and obviously there is a connection between risking life, reputation, health, physical safety, and more when traveling and working cross-culturally.

To be sure, Paul was exposed to various dangers on a constant basis, as are all those who go cross-culturally to share the gospel. The two words used for danger in the New Testament reveal that there are many dangers experienced when obeying the call of God. Paul lists these in 2 Corinthians 11:26–27:

> I have been on frequent journeys, in dangers from rivers, dangers from robbers, dangers from my countrymen, dangers from the Gentiles, dangers in the city, dangers in the wilderness, dangers on the sea, dangers among false brethren; I have been in labor and hardship, through many sleepless nights, in hunger and thirst, often without food, in cold and exposure.

Paul's reality is our reality. These are real dangers we still face today. As previously stated, for the purposes of this study cross-cultural risk is defined as "risk taken for the sake of carrying the gospel cross-culturally with a high probability of experiencing great loss." The dangers Paul lists are what we often experience in risk too. Perhaps we need to ask ourselves if we are willing to risk our lives, the lives of our children, *and also* to risk with courage the dangers listed above and those outlined in later chapters.

When our home was invaded by ten armed men and we were held at gunpoint by the robbers, at one point the situation was dangerously escalating out of control. I was refusing to do what the robbers wanted until they let me go retrieve our baby girl from the nursery. Due to the heated argument, they had my husband on his knees with Kalashnikovs touching each of his temples, their fingers on the triggers. I recognized I was only milliseconds away from becoming a widow.

Yes, the danger of robbery meant we were risking our lives, and we were there in that situation facing danger for the sake of the gospel. I'm not minimizing the dangers we faced, but only pointing out that there are exegetical differences in how the Bible talks about risk and danger. Logically, we risk many dangerous things when we go into cross-cultural service—it is to be expected.

Application

1. What kind of leader are you? Would you be one of the "chosen men or women"?

2. When you leave a room, do you leave a "fragrant offering," a calming and peace-filled presence to those in stress?

3. What has been your perspective on risk compared with the idea of "risk as priestly service"?

4. Where do you sense the Father, the Son, and the Holy Spirit's presence in your risk moment?

5. Read Matthew 10. There is a progression of opposition in six stages: "Prevented (vs. 14); rejected (vs. 14); detained (vs. 17–19); abused (vs. 17); pursued (vs. 23); and killed (vs 28)."[47] Which of these are you facing, based on the dangers Jesus relates here? How do you sense the Holy Spirit leading you to respond to this opposition at this time?

Chapter 2 Summary

1. Three key Greek words for risk are:

    *   *Paradidomi*: to hand over life, to choose to expose oneself to danger (Acts 15:22–32).

    *   *Hypotithemi*: to risk one's neck; to mortgage one's neck (Romans 16:4).

    *   *Parabaleusamenos*: to gamble one's life (Philippians 2:30).

2. The three passages on risk are connected in four ways to the Old Testa-

ment story of the battle between the Israelites and Amalekites (Exodus 17:8–16). These are:

- Chosen men: the same phrase is used in both Acts 15 and Exodus 17.

- Risk, priesthood, and sacrifice: risk is associated with the service of priesthood to those engaged in cross-cultural ministry. Moses, Aaron, and the priests of Israel all served in battle.

- Risk and the Father, Son, and Spirit: risk is associated with God the Father, Son, and Spirit in both the New Testament passages and the Exodus 17 passage.

- Risk and warfare: the same word used for *risk* in Romans 16:4 is used for *stone* in Exodus 17. Risk involves laying our lives on a firm foundation in battle.

3. Risk and danger are different Greek words and concepts in the Bible. Are we willing to risk our very lives, and are we willing to face danger for the sake of the gospel?

chapter 3

The First Israelite War

Amalek from Generation to Generation

I've suggested that the three Greek words for risk and their surrounding verses point to the war in Exodus 17. Now let's take an in-depth look at a few of the highlights of this passage and see what more we can learn about Luke's and Paul's reflections on risk after studying this story. The text is Exodus 17:8–16:

> Then Amalek came and fought against Israel at Rephidim. So Moses said to Joshua, "Choose men for us and go out, fight against Amalek. Tomorrow I will station myself on the top of the hill with the staff of God in my hand." Joshua did as Moses told him, and fought against Amalek; and Moses, Aaron, and Hur went up to the top of the hill. So it came about when Moses held his hand up, that Israel prevailed, and when he let his hand down, Amalek prevailed. But Moses' hands were heavy. Then they took a stone and put it under him, and he sat on it; and Aaron and Hur supported his hands, one on one side and one on the other. Thus, his hands were steady until the sun set. So Joshua overwhelmed Amalek and his people with the edge of the sword.
>
> Then the LORD said to Moses, "Write this in a book as a memorial and recite it to Joshua, that I will utterly blot out the memory of Amalek from under heaven." Moses built an altar and named it The LORD is My Banner; and he said, "The LORD has sworn; the LORD will have a war against Amalek from generation to generation."

Moses reminded the people of this experience in Deuteronomy 25:17–19:

> Remember what Amalek did to you along the way when you came out from Egypt, how he met you along the way and attacked among you all the stragglers at your rear when you were faint and weary; and he did not fear God. Therefore it shall come about when the LORD your God has given you rest from all your surrounding enemies, in the land that the LORD your God gives you as an inheritance to possess, you shall blot out the memory of Amalek from under heaven; you must not forget.

The Amalekites made a surprise attack and ruthlessly killed the elderly, the weak, and the sick—all those who were straggling behind. "Israel was forced to fight its first defensive war for survival."[48] It's possible that the Israelites viewed the attack as one with genocidal intentions, as described in Psalm 83:4–9.[49]

The Amalekites, first introduced as descendants of Esau's grandson, are distant cousins of the Israelites. The Israelites are repeatedly commanded to never forget what the Amalekites did and to utterly destroy them.[50]

Ancient Background

"In Jewish tradition, Amalek represents pure evil,"[51] which was demonstrated in the actual spelling of the word. Before the modern Hebrew script was developed, the Hebrew language used to be written with letters that were pictures. Each letter had a meaning. This form of Hebrew writing is called "Paleo Hebrew." Understanding the meaning of the letters augments the understanding we get from doing Hebrew and Greek word studies.

The first letter of Amalek, the *ayin*, is drawn as an eye in Paleo Hebrew and still represents an eye in modern Hebrew writing. This is probably where we get the phrase "the evil eye." "Malak," the second part of the word, is a verb that means "to chop off, to sever." Thus, the word Amalek means the "severed eye" and "represents spiritual blindness acting arrogantly in the world ... the lack of fear of God, and, therefore, represents the powers of darkness and evil."[52] William Braude and Israel Kapstein write:

> "Amalek" is at its root, the kind of locust which swoops down

swiftly, or to suggest a hound that licks up blood, or a fly greedy to get at an open wound. But the remembrance of Amalek is also meant to remind Israel of their moral breach at Rephidim shortly after their departure from Egypt, a breach that served to bring on the hound—Amalek, who thereupon resorted to all kinds of evil tricks.[53]

What is particularly evil about this war is that the Israelites were not on Amalekite territory, nor were the Amalekites in danger of the Israelites invading their territory. The Amalekites attacked Israel because of their ancestral hatred of Jacob. The Israelites were so deep in the wilderness that they could not simply return to Egypt to get away. No matter which direction they went, the Amalekites would have attacked them. They *had* to enter battle.[54]

Moses's Hands

When reading the story of Israel's battle with the Amalekites, we see that Moses was subject to human frailty; he could not hold up his hands all day long on his own. But there is a great deal more symbolism in his hands. The Israelites are given a living word picture of what steadiness and faithfulness look like. Moses's hands were *emunah* (faithful), meaning that with help they had the quality of being steady until sunset. This is the only time *emunah* is used in the Old Testament in the physical sense; elsewhere it refers to the steadiness, reliability, faithfulness, and trustworthiness of God and faithful God-followers.[55]

Apparently, Moses at first did not realize the role he was to play in the battle. He had planned to go and stand at the top of the hill overlooking the valley where the battle was to take place. It seemed there must have been a process for him, Aaron, and Hur to realize the significance of Moses's hands remaining lifted with the staff of God in them. So they found a rock for Moses to sit on and assisted in battle by helping hold up Moses's arms. He discovered during the day that God's Spirit was working through him to help the Israelites prevail. Through the steadiness and the faithfulness of Moses's hands, Yahweh was experienced as trustworthy and present with them, in answer to the question of Exodus 17:7, "Is Yahweh with us or not?"

There are many well-known symbols for the Holy Spirit in the Bible, but one of the lesser-referenced ones is the hand of God for a symbol of the Holy Spirit.[56] Some examples are "the hand of the Lord was on Elijah," "the hand of the Lord came upon [Elisha]," and "for the hand of the Lord my God was on me (Ezra)." God demonstrated grace toward the Israelites by demonstrating the power of his Spirit through the hands of Moses upraised over the battle.

Progression of Hands

The place where the Israelites angrily challenged God was called Rephidim. This name means a place of "trying and strife," but it also means "slothful hands." It is significant that the first half of chapter 17 has "Rephidim," meaning "slothful hands," and the second half of the chapter we see Moses's "faithful and steady hands."[57] In his commentary on Exodus, Nahum M. Sarna writes, "Rephidim signifies the moral lapse of Israel, because right before the battle they had angrily quarreled and confronted Moses and God, almost in judicial overtones, levying charges at God with his lack of care of them."[58] Six times in 17:1–7 it says that the Israelites grumbled, resisted, or quarreled; they "journeyed in strife." Their lapse of trusting God resulted in warfare and death.

There's a progression of "hands" in this chapter. From Israel's slothful and pride-filled hands in Rephidim to Moses's steady hands empowered by the Holy Spirit and the help of the community, to the last verse we see God's hands on the throne in a picture of permanence, sovereign rule, and certainty of the outcome.[59] What is so comforting is that God is sitting on his throne; he's not wringing his hands, worried about the Amalekites. He knows the end plan.

Sitting implies rest. Psalm 110:1 is one of my favorite verses on risk. The psalmist says that God is sitting and the victory will result in his resting his feet on his footstool (earth). In the Turkish language, the word for footstool is *puf*, which is pronounced like the English "poof." That seems to be appropriate here. Someday, the enemies, the injustice, and the evil we see all around the world will go "poof." The tears and the pain will all be gone.

The Rock

Moses sat on a stone. As noted earlier, "stone" is used as a title for God and the Messiah. The word *eben*, which is used here in the Exodus passage, is spelled *aleph bet vav*. In Paleo Hebrew, the letters are pictures and they have significance. These three together say, "The strength of the house secured with a nail."[60]

Moses's sitting presents aspects of the Godhead. Sitting on the rock with his hands outstretched prefigures verse 16, where we see God sitting on his throne with his hands on his throne. Jesus Christ, the representative of Yahweh, was nailed to the cross, securing victory in the battle with Lucifer over death. The Holy Spirit mysteriously flowed from Moses's hands to those in battle, empowering them to win.

I find comfort in this picture. Even though the Israelites who were fighting the battle didn't know all the particulars of what was happening up on the mountain or in the heavenlies, they knew they were winning when Moses did his job (had his hands raised), and they knew their job was to battle their enemy and leave the results to God.

Looking Up

However, leaving the story with the emphasis on Moses's hands and suggesting that the main application is the powerful action of the Holy Spirit and the need for a community of faith praying for us in risk would be to misrepresent an important spiritual principle at stake here. In the very first battle the Israelites as a nation experienced, they were given a living word picture for all time. Moses, with his outstretched hand with the staff of God in it, represented Yahweh. By looking up to Moses/Yahweh, they were submitting their hearts and the battle to God[61] and were strengthened to keep on fighting.

Moses represented the meeting of the heavenly realm (the place of God) and the earthly realm (of battle). God's existence, relationship to, and covenant with the Israelites was being experienced in winning the battle only when Moses's arms were upraised with the staff of God and with the help of Aaron and Hur.[62] They were to look up to the heavenly Father and rely on him for strength in battle.

Later in their history in the Promised Land, they would interact with Asherah, literally meaning "staff, rod, or pole." The Asherah was placed in high places that were easily seen as the territorial god giving a blessing over that particular area. Commonly, "the Asherah was a nude woman between two lions or a tree between two gazelles."[63] Hosea 4:12–14 pronounces the sin of Asherah: "My people inquire of a piece of wood. They sacrifice on the tops of the mountains ..." They looked up to the wrong thing.

Later, David wrote, "I will lift up my eyes to the mountains; from where shall my help come? My help comes from the LORD, who made heaven and earth" (Psalm 121:1–2). And Paul continued the importance of looking up when he taught, "Therefore if you have been raised up with Christ, keep seeking the things above, where Christ is, seated at the right hand of God" (Colossians 3:1–2). Look up! And in Ephesians 2:4–7, he said (Aramaic Bible in Plain English):

> If therefore you are risen with The Messiah, seek that which is above, the place where The Messiah sits at the right side of God. Feed on that which is above and not that which is in The Earth, for you have died to yourselves and your lives are hidden with The Messiah in God.

Notice I *didn't* say "just have faith." If I had a dollar for every occasion I've heard this phrase, I'd be able to take all my friends out for coffee. This has never been a helpful phrase for me in times of risk or danger. How does one "just have faith" anyhow?

Who or what do you look up to when things get stressful? This is an indicator of how you will respond in risk situations. It may not be a nude woman on the mountain in the form of a wood pole, but is it a nude woman on the Internet? Is it overeating food? How about alcohol? Whatever our coping mechanisms for normal "stress" in our home cultures, those will automatically be magnified a hundred-fold in risk situations.

Memorial

Toward the end of the story in Exodus 17:14, Moses is told to write everything that happened that day as a memorial in a book and recite it "in the ears of Joshua." The Lord is not simply telling Moses *not* to forget the day; one commentary said, "The Hebrew stem means much more than the recall of things past. Rather, to be mindful, to pay heed, signifying a sharp focusing of attention upon someone or something. It embraces concern and involvement and is active not passive so that it eventuates in action."[64]

Do not forget! Looking upon leads to remembering, and remembering leads to action. God does not want the Israelites to slip back into accusing God of not caring for them like they did at Rephidim.

I Will and You Shall

There's an interesting incongruity between the Exodus 17 and Deuteronomy 25 versions of this story, which reveals a guiding principle in risk and spiritual warfare. In the Exodus passage it states that *he*, meaning God, will war with Amalek forever, but in the Deuteronomy passages it states "you (the Israelites) shall blot out" Amalek. So which is it? Is the Bible contradicting itself here?

The two versions are complementary, *not* contradictory. In Exodus, we learn God will war; he will do it. When God says what he will do it, it is an invitation to examine and understand the actions of Yahweh. We can stake our lives that there will be one day, ultimate, permanent, realized, and complete victory over the enemies of God. But in Deuteronomy it says that we will war with Amalek for generations to come. It seems that Amalek, the enemy of our God and of all humanity, will be finally destroyed as we fight *alongside* God. We are called to action, to battle, to endure in the fight until our last breath (Matthew 10:22; 24:13; Romans 5:1–5). And because the Exodus text says that the Lord will war with Amalek from generation to generation, it means *each* generation is called to fight the enemies of our Lord. We are all called to spiritual battle.

This spiritual concept that God invites us to participate with him in the battle against the Amalekites for all generations until his final victory comes into its fullness means that we can look up to him and trust his control over our risk situations. Our risking, our facing danger, and the resulting suffering we experience is all part of the ongoing battle that has a purpose and meaning given by God himself. While we may not feel in "control" of our situations, God is, and in this awareness we can draw strength of soul to press on.

Yah

There is another significant insight into the battle from generation to generation in verse 16. This verse reveals the spiritual battle waged until the end of Revelation. The actual Hebrew is "Yah's hand on the throne." However, many translations say something like, "The Lord has sworn ..." The phrase "hand on the throne" carries the meaning of permanence and absoluteness of future events. In the future, Amalek will be obliterated permanently.

However, we learn something else incredibly significant in the spiritual realm in the Hebrew spelling. Looking at the Hebrew spelling of "Yah" and "throne" at the beginning of verse 16, we see they are both missing the letter "aleph." What is the significance of this? Using the Bible to interpret the Bible, Psalm 9:4–10 explains about Amalek: "You have uprooted their cities; the very memory of them has perished." What does it say next? "But the LORD abides forever" (vs. 6–7). Here "LORD" is spelled in full, the missing aleph inserted. "He has established His throne for judgment" (Psalm 9:7). Now the word *throne* also is correctly spelled with aleph and is therefore complete.[65]

It signifies that Yah's name and throne will be complete but they are not yet complete. This is because the battle is still going on. The Lord is still fighting, and we are called to fight alongside of him. When Amalek is finally and permanently defeated, Yah's name and throne will be complete, and there will be peace.

Four Spiritual Principles

This story, along with the amplification from the three New Testament illustrations, demonstrate four spiritual principles experienced by the Israelites that are applicable to us today.

Steadiness of Actions

Strength of soul in battle comes from steadiness of acting in faith. In this sense, risking looks like resting on the rock and basing our lives on the rock, which is the faithfulness, the unfailing love, the holiness, and the power of God in his promises and intentions for his people. Sometimes strength of soul looks more like doing the dishes because it is the right thing to do in the chaos of risk. I'm not talking about mystical spiritual activities. Often, more prayer meetings and Bible reading are *not* the answer. The answer is doing the right thing in the moment, and it's often physical and very practical.

Stay in Community

Just like Moses, we cannot win the battle on our own. We need the help that comes from two sources: the power of the Holy Spirit and the practical and spiritual help from the community of saints around us and those back home praying for us. The enemy often operates like a pack of wolves, picking off the weak and isolated. We need to stay connected to the Spirit and the praying family of God around us.

Understanding our Enemy

Like the Israelites opened the door to attack by the Amalekites, we also open the doors for the attack of the enemy by allowing personal relationships to be characterized by strife, quarreling, anger, and rebellious distrust toward God's faithfulness. This doesn't mean that if the Israelites hadn't grumbled they wouldn't have been attacked. We are not exempt from attack in the world where evil exists, but the level of rebellious distrust toward God opened the doors to the enemy and removed God's protective, restraining hand.

Underestimating our enemy is probably one of the most common issues I see in cross-cultural service. People don't see the "coincidences" of when gossip, betrayal, slander, and outright persecution happen. We rationalize, minimize, and just blame "sin" and get accustomed to a "normal" that is anything but normal. I can't underscore this enough. Demons are real, our enemy studies us and knows us, and the enemy attacks when we least expect it and are least ready. In my experience, he more often attacks women and children before he attacks the men. If he can weaken the family serving cross-culturally, then he can destroy the ministry.

Look Up

The most important spiritual principle in this story is to look up to our heavenly Father, submit our hearts to him, and trust the one[66] with the strength and power to save us, depending upon and trusting in him. He is gracious to forgive us and rescue us, but we have to fight our way out and through.

Warfare Preparation

So what does this war in Exodus teach us about risk? John J. Parsons notes that this attack by Amalek "symbolizes all subsequent spiritual warfare in the lives of his people."[67] Warfare in the context of the Israelites was an act of worship and obedience to God.[68] The cosmic battle focuses on who humans will worship: either Lucifer or God.

Since risk is a part of warfare, we wonder what standards for facing risk there are in the Old Testament. What would Paul have been thinking about as he wrote on risk? Now that we see risk is connected to war with Amalek, which we are to engage in every generation, we need to know how to prepare for this war. Paul may have been thinking of the teachings in Deuteronomy 7 and 20, which are the two key passages on warfare prescribed for the Israelites.

Paul, a rabbi, wrote several key passages on spiritual warfare. He interpreted the spiritual meaning of the war in Exodus 17 with how Christ-followers are to think and act in risking their lives in the war with the powers of darkness. Our enemies now are not flesh and blood but the forces of chaos in the spiritual realm: principalities, powers, sin, flesh, death, and the man of lawlessness.[69] Some key themes he may have considered from the Deuteronomy passages include:[70]

1. When you see your enemy and wonder how you can defeat such a great enemy, do not walk in fear but remember what the Lord has done in the past, the great trial, the signs, the wonders, the mighty hand, and the outstretched arm (Deuteronomy 7:17–19; 20:1).

2. Know your God. He is in your midst, he is great and he is awesome (Deuteronomy 7:21).

3. Remember that the Lord will do it (Deuteronomy 7:22).

4. When you draw near to battle, pay attention to your internal life. Are you afraid or panicking? Remember the Lord goes with you, he will fight for you and give you victory (Deuteronomy 20:3–4).

5. Reasons listed in Deuteronomy 20:5–8 for not going into battle are that there is unfinished business back home with the house or work responsibilities, engagement to marry or a new wife, or being fear-filled and faint-hearted.

All of these warfare principles apply to the modern cross-cultural worker today. Even the main principles behind the three reasons for not going into battle are wise and have not lost their relevance in our own day and time.

For example, we experienced two of the reasons listed on our own journey. We could not go "into battle" (work cross-culturally) due to unfinished business back home with the house or work responsibilities. Neal and I found that we did not have the mental and emotional capacity to handle life in Central Asia and responsibly manage to rent our home back in the States. Some can do this, but we simply aren't made that way. We had to sell our home so we could focus on living where we were.

We also were simply not ready to move to Afghanistan right after we married even though we were older than most. Our courtship was long distance (over several continents!), and our company required us to stay home for the first year. We appreciated the time to have our first year of marriage in our home culture together.

There are additional reasons why we don't go to work cross-culturally or leave the field earlier than anticipated. However, the issues of family-related responsibilities (i.e., aging parents, struggling adult children, educational challenges, etc.), are not specifically listed in the Deuteronomic text. The spiritual principle demonstrated here is to discern what is impeding them from fully entering service to the Lord at each stage of life.

The Israelites were also required to prepare spiritually for battle.[71] There were numerous actions they had to do before going to war, which were designed to help the Israelites experientially understand that God was present with them in battle but also cared about their internal lives. Just as they needed to have spiritual vitality to go into battle, so we need to prepare ourselves to risk our lives as well.[72]

Perhaps David was thinking of the battle with the Amalekites in Exodus when he wrote, "Blessed be the LORD, my rock, who trains my hands for war, and my fingers for battle; he is my steadfast love and my fortress, my stronghold and my deliverer, my shield and he in whom I take refuge, who subdues peoples under me" (Psalm 144:1–2 ESV). Finally, Revelation 19 and 20 give a detailed picture of what the final battle with "Amalek" will look like: all the powers of darkness will be entirely blotted out from the face of the earth once and for all.

Putting It All Together: The Old Testament and New Testament on Risk

In Chapter 1, the first major question I wanted to answer was, "What can we learn about risk from the risk idioms used in the New Testament?" To answer that question, I discussed three risk words. In Chapter 2 we saw where those risk words fit into the story of Exodus 17, and I also mentioned the differences between the Greek and Hebrew ways of viewing the world. We can overlay the Greek idiomatic structure with the Hebrew action words depicting risk. What I love about this picture is the integration of the spirituality and practicality of it.

Physically, Moses needed help. Aaron and Hur both had to have physical stamina to hold up Moses's arms all day long. Moses was in his eighties; he needed to sit down (okay, at my age, I don't think I'd want to stand all day either!). The "chosen men" needed to know warfare skills before they went into the battle. I can imagine them practicing their sword fighting the evening before as they prepared. It took physical strength to kill enemies all day; they would be hot, sweaty, covered in blood, and tired.

The community supporting the men fighting are Moses, Aaron, and Hur. These three are engaged in priestly service by the lifting up of their hands and representing the people to the Lord and the Lord to the people. A rock was placed beneath Moses, representing the firm foundation we rest on as we move into risk. That foundation stone is Christ. And finally, those chosen to engage in the battle are doing what chosen men and women always do—they get on with it!

Conclusion

Israel is commanded in Deuteronomy 25:17–19 to remember what Amalek did to them and to blot out their memory. This is a call to spiritual warfare—from generation to generation there will be war, as Exodus 17:16 states. When we view our callings in these terms, it means we understand that the battle between good and evil, God and Satan, while ultimately won by God, is not over yet.

Through God's power in the lives of believers, God's followers can fight the adversary and win. Still, there is training and preparation that must happen in every believer's life to prepare him or her to battle the spiritual blindness and arrogance in that generation. Jeremiah 12:5 declares, "If you have run with footmen and they have tired you out, then how can you compete with horses? If you fall down in a land of peace, how will you do in the thicket of the Jordan?"

How do we become chosen men and women who live like great warriors? We do so by living with our spiritual eyes, seeing the spiritual realities of the physical world around us, and listening for God calling us into specific risks. When the Lord is with us and when we depend upon him moment by moment, we win the battle against Amalek we have been assigned to fight.

Application

1. Which aspect from the story related in this chapter challenged or touched you the most? Why?

2. Look for everything possible to be thankful for, and keep adding to the list.

3. As the Lord told Moses, choose to remember (with your family) all that the Lord does during the event or season of risk.

Chapter 3 Summary

There are four spiritual principles we can learn from this story:

-   Steadiness in actions: Strength of soul in battle comes from steadiness of acting in faith. In this sense, risking means resting on the rock and basing our lives on the teachings of Scripture.

-   Stay in community: Just like Moses, we cannot win the battle on our own. We need the help that comes from two sources: the power of the Holy Spirit and the practical and spiritual help from the community of saints around us and back home praying for us.

-   Understanding the enemy: The enemy is allowed to attack us, allowed access to us, and weakens us when we are characterized by quarreling, strife, and angry disbelief in God's faithfulness.

-   Look up: We need to submit our hearts to our Father, and he will give us peace as we go through the battle.

chapter 4

Custodians of the Alabaster Vase

When we risk our lives for the sake of the gospel, there are many resources that we have been given for this purpose. Risk implies a loss, which includes not only for ourselves but for all the people impacted, as well as many physical resources. However, it seems teaching on stewardship in the church is most commonly limited to the context of money. But a careful word study of stewards and stewardship throughout the Bible demonstrates it encompasses a totality of life.

Beginning in Genesis 2, humankind was given the responsibility to steward the earth and all that is in it. Throughout the Old Testament, a steward is one who oversees all of the affairs of a household. From the Greek word used for stewardship in the New Testament, we derive the English word "economics."[73] In an article entitled "Stewardship in the New Testament," William Hendricks writes:

> Stewardship belongs in the larger setting of all the world, caring for it, building homes, nourishing families, being aware of the community of faith, and the broader community of mankind, being wise in caring for possessions, having wisdom in supervising the work of God's kingdom, being liable for life and its opportunities, and being grasped by the plan of God itself. Total stewardship is total responsibility of all that man has and for every relationship and experience of life.[74]

What is fascinating is that in the New Testament Jesus seems to have two opposing views of stewardship that result in two different approaches to risk.[75] There are two extremes of stewarding in risk in kingdom economy, depending upon the situation and the person. By listening to the Holy Spirit's leading, he guides in stewarding people, cars, offices, money, and even time, energy, and emotions.

Pour It All Out … Or Maybe Not

Calculated Risk

The first scenario is our word *paradidomi* (risk) from Acts 15:26. This same Greek word is used twice in Matthew 25:20 and 25:22 in the story of the talents. In the parable of the talents, the stewards who took calculated risks to increase the master's resources were commended, while the one who took no risk was not.

In this story, all of the servants had the correct desire: to please their master.[76] However, the servant who hid the talent and did not attempt to risk increasing the master's money listened to his internal fear and buried the money. This servant had the wrong understanding of his master: "I knew you to be a hard man," he responded (Matthew 25:24). His misunderstanding of his master resulted in wrong choices. Brad Young writes in *The Parables: The Jewish Tradition and Christian Interpretation*, "He misunderstood the essence of his master. The servant had good intentions, and the proper desire, but the wrong picture of his master, and so had insufficient vision to use his resource wisely."[77]

What is especially uncomfortable about this parable are the consequences experienced by the one-talent servant. That servant lost everything, even to the extreme of being cast out of God's presence. Stewarding is serious business!

We are to enter into risk with the right intentions and desires to please our Lord. But even more than that, our God desires us to know him as he truly is. He uses the circumstances of risk to remove the wrong pictures we may have of him. When we experientially know him deeper, we spiritually see how we are to wisely steward ourselves and the resources entrusted to us to bring him glory in that risk event. He wants us to steward his resources with a heart that loves and fears him, *not* with a heart that only fears him.

If we stop here, we will draw the conclusion that stewardship is all about increasing the master's resources. If there is only one "right" answer, we'll conclude that risk analysis and risk mitigation are imperative, for we must preserve his resources at all costs. But this doesn't seem to be the view of Scripture.

Pouring It All Out

The other risk word, *parabaulos*, which is used in Philippians 2:30, is used in the context of the fragrant offering that Epaphroditus risked his life in order to bring to Paul. Paul probably coined this word because there is no reference to it in any Greek writings before his time. He used a word apparently created from a verb that means "to throw down a stake, make a venture," and the noun that means "gambling, rash, reckless," or "persons who risk their lives to nursing those sick with the plague."[78] Epaphroditus "gambled" his life to bring gifts to Paul that are called a fragrant offering. How can this be considered responsible? To find the answer to this question, let's again play the game of "Where have we heard that before?"

Where have we smelled a liberal fragrant offering given to the Lord? Not only do we find fragrant offerings pleasing to the Lord in the Old Testament, but in the New Testament all four Gospels share a story of a woman with an alabaster vase filled with expensive perfume (Matthew 26:6–13; Mark 14:3–9; Luke 7:36–50; John 12:1–8). Perhaps it was two separate women and two different events, but we see that in all four occasions this woman liberally "wasted" an expensive resource to honor her Lord. Imagine the fragrance wafting through the room that evening!

What does our Lord say about this so-called "waste"? He said that what she did would be remembered forever, her sins were forgiven, her faith saved her, and she could go in peace. What she did was beautiful, and she loved him much. It took extreme courage for this woman to do what she did in the presence of others. Jesus received her gift and commended her. Likewise, sometimes it seems when we risk for the Lord and lose everything, including precious lives, the Lord receives the risk as a fragrant offering that is honoring to him.

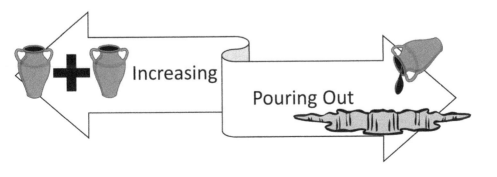

What's Your Final Answer?

How shall we reconcile these two views on stewardship? We are individually and corporately custodians of the same "alabaster vase." How are we called to steward what we have been given? Do we increase the Master's talents, or do we break the vase and pour out our lives for him? Both take risks, but one appears calculated and responsible and the other is more like gambling, wasteful, risking it all recklessly. In the Hebraic mind, however, both are suitable responses ... for those situations. Those in the West are from a cultural worldview that demands a formula, a process, or a three-step guide.

As Neal and I studied the Prophets, we saw that they faithfully took risks to preach repentance to the people. Prophets like Jeremiah were faithful their whole lives, but in the end the stewardship of his ministry, if measured by Western church metrics of investment and return on investment, would have virtually nothing to show. Sadly, I suspect Jeremiah wouldn't have been able to pass the modern Western church's threshold for success. He lost too much of the time. His stewardship did not result in any apparent "success."

Yes, responsible stewardship demands we do risk analysis, mitigation, and management (see Chapters 11–13). However, having done all of that ahead of time, life in the Spirit means we walk into risk with gratitude and thankfulness for all the Lord has entrusted to us. We faithfully steward those resources to the best of our abilities and then give them all back to him in the risk moment to do with as he directs.[79] The final answer is yes. Pray about what you are to do, and then steward as you have been led for that risk situation.

What Do We Steward?

Opportunities and Physical Resources

From Matthew 25, we see that we need to steward physical resources, which implies nonphysical resources too. In cross-cultural project work, "opportunity" includes the opportunity to stay in the country (visa and resource acquisition), and it also includes future opportunities to share the gospel.

For those working among unreached people groups, if the government kicks all the expatriates out because of foolish risking, then the light is no longer there in that unreached setting to share the gospel. Opportunities must be stewarded so light can remain in proximity to the peoples waiting to hear the good news.

The Local Body

We also need to steward our impact on the local church, whether we go or stay in the risk event. It's relatively easy for expatriates to leave a dangerous situation. What happens to all of the believers left behind who can't simply fly or drive out? Leaving dear friends in the face of danger is painful, and some even say irresponsible. Our local brothers and sisters may develop bitterness from our leaving, but at times they may be in greater danger if we stay.

We demonstrate honor for them by inviting them to give input on whether we leave or remain. We also demonstrate honor by letting them make the choices they need to make to steward themselves and their families, not legislating their response in risk. We demonstrate honor for them by how we act in *their* risk situation.

My friend Farida[80] asked me to come and visit her in her home one day. However, she gave me some stipulations. I had to walk in the manner she walked, carry my purse the way she did, and wear what she picked from my closet. In this way, I appeared as an Afghan woman and socially she would have much less risk since it was dangerous for Afghans and outsiders to be seen together.

How fun it was for her to come into my bedroom and pick out my *peron* and *tumban* (long shirt and baggy trousers) and teach me how to walk and carry my purse! We laughed as I learned from her how to "be" Afghan. And I thoroughly enjoyed my visit in her new tiny home a few days after that. I was never so proud of my newfound skill of cultural contextualization some weeks later when I was walking in the bazaar by myself, and I heard local men mutter in Dari, "KharejI ya DakhelI?" ("Is she an outsider or a local?")

Fruit

Matthew 25 teaches that when we steward, there will be something more to steward when we have done well. The servants increased the master's talents, which means they had more to steward. Oftentimes eternal fruit grows during the riskiest times. In other words, after almost two-thirds of the community left Kabul in 2008, we had more opportunities than we'd ever had to share why we stayed. This resulted in the fruit of locals opening up to the good news. Then we had even more to steward! It was an exciting time and continues to be (the dangerous places always are!).

Business risk analysis will always talk about risk as an opportunity, and the same is true in risk associated with a cross-cultural calling from God. Risk *is an* opportunity, and in the power and leading of the Holy Spirit amazing things we cannot predict or control will happen. We need to steward this fruit.

Not only do we see the eternal fruit of new lives following our Messiah, but we also experience the increasing fruit of the Spirit in our lives as well. We learn perseverance, patience, and even kindness in the face of evil. Risk teaches us to learn to wait, and in the quiet waiting for something to happen we learn to trust. As we trust and keep giving our fears continually over to God, we become stronger in faith. When one or more of us is strong in the faith, it encourages and challenges the rest of his body simply by our example in risk. Every generation needs to see this. God said he would have war with Amalek in every generation, and every generation needs the remnant of courageous warriors who will stand strong and teach others how to do that.

Pain

In all three uses of the word *risk* in the New Testament, there were dangers and hazards associated with it. The church acknowledges the personal cost paid by Paul, Barnabas, Prisca, Aquila, and Epaphroditus. How they handled the pain in risk revealed something about their character, for which they were all commended. What they did is called the stewardship of pain. Sometimes risking touches past pain in our lives, and sometimes risking for Christ causes new pain to enter our lives. How do we steward the pain we feel?

There are several different ways we can steward the pain of risk, or the pain revealed through risk. Using Frederick Buechner's outline[81] of stewarding pain, we can see several ways *not* to steward pain in risk:

1. Pain from our past gets uncovered in the risk, or pain happens to us, and we want to forget, hide (through spiritualizing), cover up, and pretend it never happened. It is unsettling to remember and too hard to process,

and so we simply don't deal with the pain uncovered in risk. The problem with this is that when we ignore the pain, when we push it down, our souls stop growing and the pain becomes an abscess, a bitter root, that infects everything and every part of our lives. We become cynical and jaded.

2. Another way we avoid stewarding pain happens when we use the risk or our pain to win sympathy. We point to the risk we took to get people to give us attention but ignore the blood seeping from our souls. The sympathy feels good for a while until people get tired of listening and the next great risk story comes along.

3. We use pain as an excuse for failure: "I'm always going to be like this," or "Sorry, I can't give you the response you want, this is how my culture responds." Yes, Neal and I have heard this one (as if one culture gets permission to break biblical standards simply because it claims to be superior).

4. Allowing bitterness and unforgiveness to seep into our souls because we experienced pain. God didn't "measure up" in risk and neither did our teammates. Whole teams have blown apart because people didn't respond in risk in the way others thought they should.

The question then is, how can we steward pain in such a way that we grow in our understanding of God's desires for us when we face risk? There are several factors to keep in mind here. First, Satan is no gentleman. He often seems to attack women and children first. He sends hurt and trauma to the exact areas already wounded to distract us from our calling. And those times of pain in crisis are exactly the places God wants to heal.

I recall another expatriate woman viciously attacking me and accusing me of all sorts of prideful behavior. We even had mediation to try to work through all the things of which I was being accused. A few years later, she told me that she never really forgave me at that mediation meeting or after, nor did she ever respect my husband and me. As I reflected for years on this painful event, I realized that this woman attacked me just a few weeks after my mom died. She attacked me in my grief. (She was only a few years younger than my mom.) I began to see the spiritual reality operating behind her; she experienced real hurt from me and needed to confront me. But she was hurting not just from me but I suspect from some prior event as well.

As a woman on the path of sanctification, I did have some things to ask forgiveness for, but the level of cruelty in her words and e-mail was out of proportion to what I had done. I think the enemy used her to try to savagely discourage me when I was at a weak point in my life.

Strangely, our God wants to heal us even as we go into battle in the event of risk. What we can prepare and work on, what we have some choice over, is how we deal with the pain in our lives and in the lives of our friends and teammates. How will we choose to respond to the pain of memory that crisis brings up? Buchner interprets the parable of the talents in Matthew 25 to mean that the one who hid the talent buried his life, covered up the pain, and in doing so, he shrunk, he became less, he was diminished, and he was ultimately outside of God's presence.

The way out of the pain is through it. What I mean by this is that when emotional pain becomes overwhelming, the path to healing is usually much clearer when we remain aware of it, rather than covering it up. When aware of our pain, the hard times in our past, we can open up the deep places of our souls to trust others for help in healing. This is when we become most alive. When we are in touch with our pain, we are aware of our powerlessness to truly do anything without God's help. When we know our pain intimately, we know deep joy and peace because we know exactly how amazing it is that God uses us anyway. Our pain does not become our identity we hide behind, but it becomes a tool to change us and heal us.

There are multiple sources for depression, and I've experienced several of them. I've been clinically depressed twice in my twenty-five-year ministry career and experienced deep woundedness, mostly at the hands of other Christians. I've been diagnosed with panic attacks and healed from this "disorder." God allowed all of this pain into my life, some of it right when we were in the middle of the risky times in Afghanistan, to strip away areas of my life through pain and to heal me from past pain.

If people knew my pain and the deep grief I carry in my soul, perhaps they'd be shocked. Some might think I'm too broken and flawed to be useful to the Master. But the secret is, and I'll whisper it here, *he delights in using me.* And I delight in his delight of me. And I am continually healed on deeper and deeper levels the more I walk in his presence.

Myself

By implication, I must steward myself so that I can steward the opportunities, physical resources, the pain, and the fruit that is entrusted to me. Stewarding myself includes the emotional, spiritual, mental, financial, relational, and cultural energies needed to persevere and endure in whatever risky situation entrusted to me.

What does it mean to "steward myself"? This is a crucial part of stewardship that has to be addressed for us to maximize what God is doing in and through us during risk. Stewarding myself includes learning discernment about what is happening inside of me (see Chapter 4), where I am at in my spiritual journey (see Chapter 6), what my core questions are (see Chapter 7), and what my emotional and thinking patterns are (see Chapter 10). I describe this in Chapter 11 in terms of what is happening between God and me, how I am handling my relationship with others, and what is happening in my inner life through my thought patterns and emotional life.

It sounds complicated, but it's really not. I summarize it like this: Stewarding ourselves brings glory to God as our minds, emotions, and wills become increasingly like the image of God created before the foundations of the world were laid. It's not rocket science, and it's also not new. I've simply taken what most of us already know about following Christ and apply it to the risk moment as a guide, especially for those who feel isolated and alone.

Isaiah 22

One final word on stewardship: Isaiah 22 is one of the saddest pictures in the Bible of God's anger toward a negligent and unwise steward. The steward, Shebna, lived as if all was well and did nothing to prepare for the day of judgment. The Lord violently hurled Shebna away and put Eliakim in place of Shebna, giving him great honor. Isaiah describes Eliakim as a father to the inhabitants of Jerusalem who lived in a terrifying time. This is what the risk moment needs—men and women who will be as fathers and mothers to those in risk.

We had such a man as this. The pastor of our church in Kabul and his wife were dear people who were God's chosen man and woman for a difficult time. Neal and I have rarely felt "pastored" during our years living in "risky" countries, but under this pastoral couple in Kabul for just a few short years, not only us but many in our community felt loved, affirmed, and pastored.[82]

One Pretty Big Admonition

I mentioned that there is one major caution when it comes to authority and stewardship. Earlier I stated that if you fit the profile of the greater faith community, even if you don't socialize with that community, you and your agency still have a high risk of being deported or having your visa denied. I also mentioned a strong admonishment to obey your leaders. Don't disobey them. If you cannot obey them, then remove yourself from their authority, nicely.

Here is where we've had numerous discussions on what it means to steward the opportunity and God's leading in risk. It has to do with the tension of obedience to authorities, stewarding your felt call on your life by the Holy Spirit, and the risk impact on the community. If you leave one agency to go to another visa-providing agency in the same city because you want to do what you feel called to do by the Holy Spirit, please take a few minutes to think through a few issues:

1. Recognize and assess the risk impact on your former agency. Do you honestly think that going with a different agency in the same city will make your previous agency immune to your "risky" behavior? It is a myth to think that they will not be at risk anymore when you leave.

2. Consider the impact on the broader community. If the majority of the community is acting one way but you are engaging in the opposite behavior, even for the sake of the gospel, reconsider what you sense God is calling you to do. They are not insulated from your risky behavior; your actions will likely impact the entire community.

3. People may be more likely to be biased toward what they think they "hear from the Lord" when not involved in healthy community (dialogue)

with other mature believers (who do not necessarily share the same perspectives they do). I think this is especially a danger for people from individualistic cultures. It seems that the lack of healthy dialogue can result in reduced quality of everyone's thinking—those who "jump ship" as well as those who don't.

Yes, God *does* work out all things for his glory. As Paul says, some preach Christ out of envy and rivalry but others from goodwill (Philippians 1:15). He then concludes his thought: "In every way, whether in pretense or truth, Christ is proclaimed; and in this I rejoice" (Philippians 1:18). Thankfully, God still works through us, he works in spite of us, and his kingdom goes forth.

Application

1. Make a list of everything God is calling you to steward.

2. How do you tend to deal with pain in your life? What do you need to change?

3. How have you been challenged by the two extremes of stewardship discussed from the Bible? On a scale from 1 to 10, with the alabaster vase gambling situation being number 10 and the calculated risk being number 1, which number do you think God is calling you to live out? What is the risk impact on others?

Chapter 4 Summary

1. Stewardship involves much more than finances. It also includes physical resources, opportunities, pain, fruit, and even yourself.

2. Steward yourself carefully if you feel called to disobey your leaders. Do risk analysis of your behavior on the broader community and prayerfully discuss it again with the Lord regarding your calling.

chapter 5

Listening for God's Voice in the Risk Moment

War is the realm of uncertainty; three quarters of the factors on which action in war is based are wrapped in a fog of greater or lesser uncertainty. A sensitive and discriminating judgment is called for; a skilled intelligence to scent out the truth.
—CARL VON CLAUSEWITZ

In 1832, Carl von Clausewitz's book *Vom Kriege* was published and has been credited with giving us the concept of the "fog of war." Although he never technically used the term "fog of war," the Prussian military expert so clearly described the misperceptions and false information associated with warfare that the term is used to this day to describe the difficulty associated with decision-making in the midst of conflict. How much more distorted is our understanding when we consider that our warfare is also waged in the spiritual realm! We need a supernatural advisor to cut through the fog of the celestial battlefield.

The good news is that Jesus sent us such an advisor. The Holy Spirit is our Advocate, our *Paraclete*, the one called alongside to help us (John 15:26; 16:13–15). As we gain confidence and correctly hear his voice, we'll have more clarity into how to steward the resources entrusted to us in the risk moments. How do we hear the Holy Spirit's leading to stay, to leave, or to move forward into even more danger?

Hearing the Holy Spirit through Seven Sources

There are at least seven ways through which the Holy Spirit may choose to speak in the risk moment. You may experience others, such as in nature, but the first six are the primary ones I experienced in Afghanistan. (We were unable to get out in nature since that was considered too risky!)

Occasionally, when you can't hear God's voice speaking quietly to you, balanced input in the risk moment from some combination and emphasis of the other six ways may make the way clearer. I advocate that no one source be the only basis on which risk decisions are made. Let's take a look at the seven sources through which we are able to hear the Holy Spirit.

Security Consultants: Christian and Non-Christian

Let's start with security consultants. My husband had multiple streams of security reports coming in to his office every day to help him in risk assessment and management. These included Christian security agencies like the Korean Crisis Management Service, Crisis Consulting International, Emergency Planning College (UK), Fort Sherman Academy, and also security reports from our passport country, independent security firm reports (think tanks), nongovernmental organizational (NGO) security reports, host country security reports, national friends, the community of nongovernmental organizational leaders, and security officers providing information to each other. There also may be interagency reporting where information is shared from the respective embassies and other sources that agencies have.

When the Spirit is moving, it's true—we stay despite our government's warnings. Even when they cease diplomatic relationships, we may still continue to stay. Sometimes, your passport government asks you to leave due to the disintegration of security, and you may need to leave.

It's crucial to know you have a clear calling from the Holy Spirit to stay when your government doesn't want you to remain. In these situations, when we do not have our government's support, we must have a clear, written-down recognition of all the risks and potential losses and help our families and partners understand. For example, our families will do better when they are equipped with the knowledge that our government will most likely not bend to help rescue us when there is no diplomatic mission in the country.

The Community Around Us

Second, by mentioning the community around us, I mean that we need to pay attention to and listen to the Christian and non-Christian locals and expatriates.

The input of the national and expatriate community is a significant way the Holy Spirit speaks in risk situations.

Locals

The wise and informed leaders in the local community were a strategic resource of security information for my husband and me. It is also wise to ask local leaders for their risk advice and risk theology. The truth is that they have unique biblical and cultural insights to add to our understanding of risk. To our dismay, they were often underutilized and went unasked for their thoughts on risk, both biblically and practically.

It is wise to have trusted friends from within the culture relating to you what is being said in the bazaars, the government, and local religious services or regular public gatherings. While rumors abound, pay attention to factors like the tone, frequency, and level of violence being communicated. These factors are like a barometer, gauging the atmosphere. If you are able, it is wise to have friends from a variety of socio-economic sectors sharing with you on a regular basis what they believe is happening.

One of the oldest Christian agencies working in Afghanistan seemed to have recognized the value of obtaining information from trusted locals. Information obtained from leaders who wisely sifted through news events from their own instinctive cultural insights were key sources of credible information about the reality on the ground. All too often we saw expatriates putting too much "weight" on the information from outside the country as well as government security reports (we were frequently told by our government to leave as soon as possible).

The insight from our local friends was often superior to all of our security analysis. They were simply the insiders and saw the cultural cues most of us missed. The Holy Spirit spoke through them, even in unexpected times. For example, one day a colleague and I were walking in a nearby bazaar, orienting a new staff woman to the types of supplies available, when a shopkeeper leaned over and whispered in English, "It's not safe; you shouldn't be here right now." Having an insider tell us the security situation, which I absolutely had *not* sensed, immediately raised all my red flags and shot my adrenalin to high.

My instinct in that moment was to move myself and the other two women to the middle of the street where as Western women we were highly visible to all, get on the cell phone to my husband, and maintain connection with him until we were out of there and found a taxi to drive us home. I breathed a sigh of relief when we were a couple of kilometers away from that area.

Expatriates

Additionally, the expatriate community is an essential aspect of balanced input. A community of wise veterans who have weathered the storms of the ups and downs can provide a needed balanced perspective. Sometimes we need help from guides who have walked the risk path before and understand discerning the spirits and the leading of the Holy Spirit.

A major mistake many workers or organizations make is to think that what they do doesn't impact others serving God cross-culturally, even when socially not seen together. The reality is that all too often people who fit the profile of humanitarian aid workers are considered religious threats and are grouped together when it comes time to deport workers or deny visas, even when we live across town from each other and don't attend the same community events.

During the years we were in Afghanistan, the expatriate leaders of our community regularly met together to discuss security and the physical safety of the broader expatriate community. These meetings enhanced the spirit of unity for all of us. As leaders, they modeled "chosen men and women." They prayerfully considered the Lord's leading of all of us as a community.

An area of temptation for leaders is one mentioned in Isaiah 5:21: "Woe to those who are wise in their own eyes, and clever in their own sight!" Warren Wiersbe comments on this, "Instead of listening to God, the leaders consulted with one another and made decisions based on their own wisdom."[83] It's important to remain sensitive to God's leading and not be pridefully filled with our own importance and experience.

We saw this when leaders of teams in the community did not consider the broader impact of doing what was "normal." Sometimes we forget to consult with other leaders to assess the impact of our actions on the broader community. For example, one group worshiped loudly at the annual conference hotel. The other group worshiped in whispers, but locals still assumed that both groups were connected due to the first group's "loud" worship. The first group possibly had not considered the need to worship differently to minimize the consequences others may face.

Families

Third, our families are another key way the Holy Spirit speaks to us. It may be through your immediate family, like your spouse and your children, it could be through your extended family back home, or it could be through your spiritual family, those with whom you have cherished friendships and who truly know you in your ministry context.

If your children aren't doing well in the environment, this is of utmost concern. You know your children better than anyone else, and they pick up on your stress. Are they stressed because you are stressed? Do they need to be stretched to learn resilience? Or is it time for you to leave and get them to a more secure place?

How about your spouse? How is your spouse handling the long-term stress? What changes can you make to help your spouse have greater resilience in the situation, or do you need to consider leaving for the other's long-term mental, emotional, and spiritual health? These are all areas where we need to discern the voice of the Holy Spirit.

Our family also includes our extended family. Just as Simon of Cyrene was conscripted to help carry Jesus's cross to Golgotha, we who go must keep in mind what it costs others, especially our families, when we choose to obey God's call on our lives. It's hard for me to imagine what my mom must have felt like when, as her youngest, I took my three-month-old baby boy to Afghanistan. Of course, our families wanted us to follow the path God had for us, but it was and continues to be a big sacrifice for families and parents to give their blessing to a few years or a lifetime of being separated.

Some of us come from cultures that are community oriented, and so leaving the community has much greater meaning in these situations. You may have family responsibilities or expectations that you will be unable to fulfill as you follow God's leading to serve him in another culture. You yearn for your family's blessing and even release from fulfilling these responsibilities in the traditional way. But before they can do this, they need us to clearly share our call and our understanding of risk as we see it in Scripture. In some instances, your family may not even share your faith, in which case the cost for you will be high as you choose an individual path that does not allow you to meet your community responsibilities.

Your choice to please God means you may disappoint them and they may choose not to support you relationally. It will be challenging to find ways to demonstrate your love and respect for them and your culture as you leave them and enter this risk situation.

Ideally, every time you leave your family, your parents and siblings and extended family will bless you and give you the freedom to go in peace. As the ones who are leaving, it may be important to bless them back and release them from any guilt they may feel about not going themselves. There is repeated deep loss every time we leave our families in every stage of life. I think of my friend Patti, who sent her firstborn off to college. As the mom, she was ten thousand miles away, unable to be there for the challenges of her daughter's first year. She was grieving new losses as a mom of an adult-aged child.

As the ones going into risk, we also need to gently walk with our families on their journey to a deeper understanding of what it means to follow Christ into high-risk situations. They will have questions about our calling. Be ready to answer the question, "Are you *sure* this is what God wants you to do?" and "How do you justify taking little ones into such danger?" These and other questions are important to be able and ready to answer. From who else can our families learn about living through risk if we don't find ways to communicate with them about it? They can be some of our biggest advocates, so give them the words to say so they can accurately represent you and Christ's calling on you.

I have been comforted on numerous occasions through Jesus's words in Matthew 12:50, when Jesus states, "For whoever does the will of My Father in heaven, he is My brother and sister and mother." Imagine, I am Jesus's sister, I am his mother. He is my brother. So many times as I've lived cross-culturally or been away from "home" for much of the past twenty-five years, he has sent the brother, sister, father, and mother I needed.

The Bible

Fourth, the Bible speaks to us about what the Spirit wants us to do in the risk moment. Is there a particular section, story, or phrase in the Bible that keeps coming to your mind? Is there a song from a certain Bible story that you can't stop humming? Is there a certain picture from the Bible that comes to mind right when you wake up in the morning? Was there a burning in your heart like the disciples on the Emmaus Road when you heard a story repeated at the weekly worship service (Luke 24:32)? These are just some ways the Holy Spirit speaks to point us to God's Word for direction. How does the Word speak to you?

In the reality I faced, a listing of "risk" stories was not helpful to me. What was more helpful was when I began to meditate on the lives of the prophets.[84] A careful reading of the Prophets gave us a guide to understanding not only our emotions in risk and God's emotions in risk, but also the path forward for Neal and me with our children. What we learned was that when the prophets preached repentance to the people, when they proclaimed the nearness of God's judgment, they and their families did not leave when judgment fell. They stayed and experienced the awful events unfolding. The Spirit spoke to us through the careful study of his Word.

The Holy Spirit's Voice

In John 14–16, Jesus spends an extensive amount of time teaching his disciples to depend on the leading of the Holy Spirit, especially in times of difficulty, persecution, and the "fog of war." The prophet Isaiah assured us in Isaiah 30:20–21 of access to the leading of the Spirit, saying:

> Although the Lord has given you bread of privation and water
> of oppression, He, your Teacher will no longer hide Himself,
> but your eyes will behold your Teacher. Your ears will hear a
> word behind you, "This is the way, walk in it," whenever you
> turn to the right or to the left.

He also may speak quietly and directly to each one of us. However, sometimes it may just be an impression of what we are to do; it doesn't always "feel" like the Holy Spirit. Sometimes there are no accompanying "feelings" whatsoever, but you just "know" the next thing to do. You can't explain it. It will almost never contradict your God-given authorities and, even if it does, there is a blessing in obeying authorities the Lord has put in place over you, even if or when they make a decision different from what you believe the Lord is telling you.

There are times when God speaks in that quiet voice, just like we read about with Elijah (1 Kings 19:12). He speaks in numerous creative ways. He speaks differently to Neal than he does to me. But what God says and his leading is *always* in line with his character. We can recognize the Holy Spirit's activity through the fruit in our lives and in the lives of those around us (Matthew 7:16–20).

Those in Authority Over Us

Sixth, and extremely important, is the designated authority and leader of the Christian worker. There are numerous verses about obeying authorities, and only a couple of places in the New Testament where Christians disobeyed authorities (Acts 4:19; 5:29). In those places, they disobeyed authorities who were charging them not to teach at all about Jesus. The high priest wanted them to stop completely, give up, and end the movement about Jesus. That is a different situation than the times on the field when we use caution and maybe "take a break" from showing certain films or meeting with people due to security risks.

Paul repeatedly writes in his letters to the churches and Timothy to obey their leaders.[85] Hebrews 13:17 states, "Obey your leaders and submit to them, for they keep watch over your souls as those who will give an account. Let them do this with joy and not with grief, for this would be unprofitable for you." These verses teach us to obey; they don't say, "Obey only if you agree with your leaders."

Why are Jesus, Paul, Peter, and the writer of Hebrews so strong on this issue? It is because leaders have been given the responsibility to steward their staff and resources. They are responsible to God for their good and not-so-good decisions. And we, as followers, are responsible for obeying them.

If your leadership, after much prayer and consideration, decides it is best for you to leave, then it is time for you to leave. Let's not make their responsibilities more difficult for them than they already are. There are pain-bearing aspects of leadership, especially in risk. Our leaders are watchers of our souls and will give an account for that, and that is a heavy responsibility. However, if your leaders give you the freedom to decide to stay *or* leave, then you will need to discern what the Spirit is asking you to do.

Dreams and Visions

As I've written this book, I've listened to many Central Asian brothers and sisters talk about risk and how they hear the Holy Spirit. Neal and I gave our first complete Risk Assessment and Management (RAM) workshop to Central Asian Bible students. When we asked them how they hear the Holy Spirit's voice and leading, their first response was, "Through dreams and visions." The fruit of the Spirit was evident in their faces and in what they shared as they revealed the details of their visions. For many Westerners, this is outside their normal experience of God.

The reality is that God gives many dreams and visions and reveals himself much more in this way to people outside of the Western culture. Admittedly, this is at times hard to accept for those steeped in a Word-based interpretation of truth. I have heard many stories of how God worked through dreams and visions, how he has brought many in Central Asia to himself in this way, and increasingly there are more books that testify from Christ-followers around the world to him working in this way. A simple test I always apply in these situations is from Jesus:

> Beware of the false prophets, who come to you in sheep's clothing, but inwardly are ravenous wolves. You will know them by their fruits. Grapes are not gathered from thorn bushes nor figs from thistles, are they? So every good tree bears good fruit, but the bad tree bears bad fruit. A good tree cannot produce bad fruit, nor can a bad tree produce good fruit. Every tree that does not bear good fruit is cut down and thrown into the fire. So then, you will know them by their fruits (Matthew 7:15–20).

I'm not a "dream and vision expert," but I generally look for what kind of fruit is evident in the life of the believer, in the story itself, and in his or her face as he or she shares it. My experience has been that the dreams and visions are consistent with biblical principles and the story of Scripture as well as the character of God revealed in Scripture. When we open ourselves up to the mystery of life in the Spirit, we experience the unfathomable greatness of God in the creative way he communicates with and gently leads his people.

One Guiding Principle

We still need to know how to apply scriptural stories and spiritual principles to each unique risk situation. I can recall as a young mom in Afghanistan being sent a list of "risk" stories, and being told this "theology of risk" was the guide. Perhaps I am slower than others, but I couldn't see the connection between those stories and how I was supposed to apply them to myself and the situations I faced with my husband, little children, team, and community.

Often I see the emphasis in theology-of-risk discussions focusing on what Paul did in a variety of situations. It would be easy to tell someone that since Paul fled a situation, they should also flee. Likewise, to tell someone to remain because that is what Paul did is equally inadequate. Instead, our primary focus here needs to be on *how* he heard the Holy Spirit. While Paul sets for us an excellent example in Christian vocational risk, his guide and ours always is the Holy Spirit. Without fail, Paul relates what life in the Spirit led him to do. Sometimes the Holy Spirit spoke to Paul through his friends and the locals in the community, and at other times he spoke through visions.

> The Holy Spirit's leading is the one overarching guide in risk analysis and management.

The Holy Spirit's leading is the one overarching guide in risk analysis and management. This is why it is so important to know how we each uniquely hear his voice and discern how he is speaking in each situation. One of the ways God matures us is that he creatively speaks to us differently in different situations and at different stages of life. He wants us to learn to pay attention and to develop the eyes of our hearts. He may even speak through our emotions.

How do we learn to hear God's voice? The answer from the saints of the past two thousand years of church history are unanimous and unequivocal on this.[86] Through solitude and the discipline of silence in prayer, we learn to hear his voice. If our prayer times are always characterized by us talking to God, and we never stop our inner dialogue and sit in silence, meditating on his Word, giving him an opportunity to speak, then we are our own obstacles in learning to listen and identify his voice.

I imagine some young moms reading this wonder how they can ever find a moment of silence in the busyness of caring for little children, especially in high risk. I remember at that stage of mothering that "moments of silence" were my times to sleep! This is why I encourage utilizing the times you do have—at the kitchen sink, in the shower, when you are walking on the way. Use these as "throne moments"—times where you come before the Lord's throne in the silence of your heart and meditate on him. Even though it is a battle, it is possible to cultivate these moments.

One example of how the Holy Spirit may speak through emotions may involve feeling overwhelming unrest and anxiety when thinking about a certain plan. The emotions of unrest and the lack of peace are his way of saying, "Stop, don't do that." But sometimes we know he wants us to move forward despite our fears and anxieties. So how can we tell? Differentiation between the two scenarios requires prayerful listening and discernment, and possibly even consultation with others.

For example, not long ago I was tempted to apply for a job in my field. I talked with my husband about it, but every time I pictured myself in this job a sensation deep inside of me of not being well and unrest arose. It was more than a "pit in my stomach"; it was a feeling totally devoid of peace. On the other hand, numerous times I considered not going to church due to high-risk factors (e.g., a suicide bombing, etc.), I immediately "knew" that despite my fears I needed to attend and be there. As leaders in the church, we had done extensive risk mitigation already, as much as humanly possible and was appropriate for the situation. This is why the writer of Proverbs says, "Without consultation, plans are frustrated, but with many counselors they succeed" (15:22), and again, "For by wise guidance you will wage war, and in abundance of counselors there is victory" (24:6).

Discernment in Risk

Distinguishing good from evil can be especially challenging in the risk environment. There is a significant spiritual principle often unacknowledged here. We learn that it takes practice to distinguish good from evil. Hebrews 5:13–14 (ESV) teaches that "everyone who lives on milk is unskilled in the word of righteousness, since he is a child. But solid food is for the mature, for those who have their powers of discernment trained by constant practice to distinguish good from evil."

Definition

The key idea in discernment is "to know what we see rather than to see what we know."[87] Henri Nouwen's definition is "spiritual discernment is the art of recognizing God in the many events, meetings, and situations we experience in daily life."[88] Additional phrases describing discernment include "perceiving clearly, judging accurately, sifting through the illusory, and discovering what is real."[89] Strengthening the "muscle" of discernment and seeing the spiritual realities increases resiliency and clarity in the risk moment. We clue in to what is happening.

In his book on discernment, Nouwen states, "The presence of God is often subtle, small, quiet, and hidden."[90] Then he points to Isaiah 11:1: "Then a shoot will spring from the stem of Jesse, and a branch from his roots will bear fruit." God is working, barely noticeably, in small, tender, and vulnerable ways. Not seeing him in these small ways is spiritual blindness.[91]

I remember a time in Afghanistan when I was very confused. I asked the Lord to help me figure out the darkness and confusion inside, not knowing how he would choose to help. The discussion below includes some of what I learned on my path out of darkness and inner confusion through the people he brought to help me, the books I read, and what he taught me from his Word. Thibodeaux's discussion is the most practical in understanding and applying mature spiritual principles to individual discernment.[92] I am indebted to him for the following discussion where I weave highlights from his book with our focus on discernment in risk.

Discernment uses a combination of faith and reason. It means much more than making a choice. It includes an awareness of what is going on inside of me, an honest assessment of my situation. Deepening discernment means I am becoming increasingly self-aware of my inner life. It involves every aspect of my person, my emotions and mental analysis, my will and prayer life, my desires and what I am resisting. It's asking, "What is the source of my thoughts, emotions, and actions?"

It's a process; not a "doing" but a "being," an increasing awareness of moving closer toward God or moving further away from him. It's learning to be in tune with the movements of my spirit that lead toward God, and through knowing this righteous action results. The premise in Thibodeaux's book is that "all of our thoughts, feelings, and actions are moving us either closer to God or further away from God." What does this look like?

Moving Away from God Inwardly

What happens in the risk event can be a combination of the perfect storm potentially moving us away from God. The devil, plus the potential trauma of looming tragic circumstances, plus our past woundedness, plus destructive behaviors, plus psychological baggage, plus emotional weakness, all mixed with risk, and we may negatively respond to God and others in the risk event. The feelings arising inside really lead us internally on the path toward death. Then, because of our negative response, add in the guilt we feel from being a cross-cultural worker and what we think our supporters expect from us, and we cycle down into depression and increasingly addictive patterns of coping. We become increasingly less resilient and more psychologically/emotionally unstable and depressed.

Moving Toward God Inwardly

The opposite, however, looks like this: Allowing the energizing power of the Holy Spirit to work in us, plus seeing the good in the world even in the smallest circumstances, plus choosing life-giving thought and emotional behavior patterns, psychological well-being and emotional strength, then we respond to God and others positively. The feelings inside, even when experiencing the conviction of the Holy Spirit, lead us internally on the path toward life.

We still may suffer from depression and have coping challenges (long-term risk events are hard), but overall we know we are moving forward with his power and help. We become characterized as people walking in the Spirit.

One simple guide for assessing what is going on inside of us is asking a question based on 1 Corinthians 13: How am I increasing or decreasing in faith, hope, and love?

1. Faith: Did my actions today give me greater trust in God, in the church,

and in the people in my life, or did they lead to unproductive and paralyzing doubts?

2. Hope: Have the feelings I've been experiencing lately led me to increased focus on the day of Christ's return? Am I being encouraged on deeper levels that my destiny lies in the sure foundation of God's providence (1 Thessalonians 4:18; Hebrews 10:23)?

3. Love: Have the things preoccupying me led me to greater love for God and others?

One note about the question above on hope. I remember a meeting in Afghanistan when the main topic involved risk analysis of the security level that week. A colleague reminded all of us that we are to hope in the day of Christ's return. His point was well said.

However, if the house is burning down, we need to manage the risk of what we are about to lose and get out of the house. Risk analysis and management are responsible stewardship. If the situation is deteriorating all around us, we need to make an assessment and plan for our course of action. However, overlying and underlying all of our risks is the hope that we grasp tightly to the day when Christ returns to make everything right once again. There is a difference between the internal hope and the reality of evil around us to which we are required to respond.

Discernment of Demonic Spirits

There is also the spiritual aspect of what is happening. From Genesis to Revelation, the Bible assumes the presence of evil and heavenly spirits. Overspiritualization is one of the most common tendencies of those immature in the faith or those unwilling to face their sin. Those with the spirit of pride will often blame the demonic realm instead of accepting their sinful contribution to the problem.

It may be helpful to know the names of some common demonic spirits whose goal is to add to the havoc of risk. The following specific demonic spirits can attach or be more active in risk. We personally have encountered some of these but most likely there are others too. The list doesn't account for the territorial spirits and is not intended to be complete.

- *Spirit of "voices of deception."*[93] These voices are a combination of distraction, intrusion, confusion, layers of thought, and repeated nagging thoughts. These voices include intruding thoughts like, "I'll never get beyond this; I don't understand; I'm confused; you're stupid; you should know better." It's different than the psychological terminology for negative thought patterns. It is a cloudiness of mind and an inability to cut through the confusion, even for those who are normally logical and quick decision makers.

- *Spirit of jihad.*[94] This spirit is active in many Muslim environments today. It strengthens those intent on waging war against all those who do not believe in the "correct" form of Islam. It may be found at the major Islamic shrines in the region.

- *The choking demon.* I've known and heard of this demon doing its dirty work in Afghanistan, Pakistan, Central Asia, the Hindu-Indian areas of London, Turkey, and in the USA harassing folks preparing to go to Turkey. I do not know if it has another name, but its main job is to harass and create fear through choking. It doesn't seem to kill—it seems to press on the air pipe so that it is hard to breathe and call on the name of Jesus. It seems to feel and sound like choking.

- *Spirit of pride.* This is common among those serving cross-culturally who have experienced many risks. In the risk moment, it is worse, causing a skewing of discernment on which direction to go.

- *Spirits in items dedicated to Islam.* Demonic spirits have been known to attach to items dedicated for Islamic use through Qur'anic prayers. Amulets, clothing, pottery with evil-eye designs—all these have been known to allow evil spirits to manifest in the home.[95]

The enemy is not terribly creative. He does a similar thing in other religions as well: Shamanism, Voodoo, Hindu gods, religious syncretism like the Folk Islam in Bulgaria that mixes Christianity, Islam, and animism; even at times Eastern Orthodoxy all use icons as a talisman. The enemy is no dummy either; he studies us. Our nanny was a local girl who became a follower of Jesus during the first year she worked for us. After seeing her struggle in her local school situation during that year, we invited her to live with us for a year so I could help her with her studies. We had already gone to bed one evening when she came upstairs to ask us to pray for her. She related that she was seeing things moving in the room, the curtains were being disturbed, and she felt an evil presence.

I intuitively sensed that if I were to go down and stay in the room with her, the enemy, if he were bothering her, wouldn't manifest himself in my presence, and she would feel foolish. I also knew that she would never learn to trust the Holy Spirit's power inside of her to be able to confront the spiritual realm and win. So we first asked her to consider if she had any unconfessed sins and to ask the Lord to reveal them to her. Then we prayed Ephesians 6:10–18, admonished her to speak aloud to the harassing demon trying to frighten her, and then to go to sleep.

After she went back down and tried this, she came back up a second time, and we strengthened her again in the Lord, and she returned to do battle in the room. She finally won and went to sleep, and that harassing demon never bothered her again.

Making Decisions in Risk When Confused

It is not uncommon in risk to be confused. People's emotions are running high. Fear is pervasive. Sometimes it's bewildering to know what is the right and good thing to do. Confusion becomes a desolating experience when we allow ourselves to be upset about not knowing what's going on, and when our uncertainty or lack of knowledge leads to disturbances within.

The antidote to this is to praise, reverence, and serve our Lord however he wants in the risk moment. There is usually just enough light to take the next step (Proverbs 20:24). The answers to the following questions are not meant to be primarily or only spiritual activities; sometimes I just needed to be faithful to joyfully serve my children and make a fun snack for them and keep up the laundry even when I had great anxiety and fear for my husband's safety. I often remained in continual prayer as I went about my daily business. Here are some questions to ask and hopefully help cut through the confusion:

- What is the most loving thing to do?

- What is the most hopeful thing to do?

- What is the most faith-filled thing to do?

- Are my decisions in risk moving me toward God or away from God?

- Am I relying on false gods of my own making?

- What is the most strategic thing to do at this moment for the kingdom of God?

For example, when things were at their riskiest for us (meaning the scariest), and the majority of the community was leaving, my husband took the time to study the focus of our project. He learned that 80 percent of our project efforts were *not* going to the unreached people groups. The moment of risk is a time of change and opportunity, and so he was able to flip the priorities of our project and slowly put the majority of our energies and focus on helping reach the unreached people groups. It was a hugely strategic time that is still reaping benefits to this day.

Conclusion

Just as Jesus walked unrecognized on the Emmaus Road with two of his disciples, so he walks with us in risk, often unrecognized, and "joins us in our sadness and despair."[96] He understands the smell of suffering and death:

> He listens to our story of confusion, disorientation, deep grief, loss of direction, human failure, and inner darkness. He is with us in our lostness. Jesus speaks, revealing that God knows firsthand our lostness and that his love is stronger. The experience of recognizing and remembering him leads to the burning heart experience. He is eternally present to us though we cannot physically see him. Knowing him through remembering him and through the burning heart experience, we realize he is found in our heart. The problem is that in times of crisis, it's hard to remember Christ because our pains are being experienced in the moment. The hurt, the failure, the remorse, the pain of the past bites at us.[97]

We may work through all of the risk and danger analysis and then pray together, and through that a gentle "knowing" of the next step seems to come into plain view. There isn't a formula for this, but a careful and prayerful discussion of stewardship and risk, and weighing the potential outcomes with our callings in light of the goal of extending his kingdom, is helpful.

Sometimes, however, we simply don't know what to do. He calls us to trust in the "unknowing," and he calls us in our unknowing to believe in his goodness.[98] It is imperative to still trust him, even when we don't understand him.[99] There are no processes or formulas to guarantee ahead of time that we've made the right decision. But as we look to the Lord, making him our priority to know and to love, and as we openly trust his leading that is rooted in his love for us, we will begin to see the next step and his peace *will* come.

In terms of comprehensive risk analysis, we have to consider and balance multiple ways the Holy Spirit is leading. I discussed seven sources to incorporate into discerning the Holy Spirit's leading. We cannot ignore what spiritual forces may be impacting the situation. Additionally, discerning God's leading internally is also a major factor.

Application

1. How has the Holy Spirit spoken to you in the past and in what type of situation?

2. What negative circumstances did he use to speak to you?

3. If you are unable to find times and places of solitude to hear his voice due to safety concerns, then get creative. Make one of your daily tasks a place where you enter the throne room of heaven (e.g., in the shower, while you wash dishes at the kitchen sink, as you walk on the busy, dusty streets—wherever it is, cultivate times of silence in your heart and listen to the Holy Spirit's voice).

4. Make a list of the positive things that have happened today. Thank God for them. Then do it again tomorrow. Keep doing it every day as you

move through the risk event, looking for and then thanking him for all the positive little things he does in your life, including the sunrise and sunset, the food you eat, etc.

Chapter 5 Summary

1. The seven ways the Holy Spirit speaks in the risk moment are:

   - Security consultants

   - The community around us

   - Family

   - The Bible

   - The Holy Spirit's voice

   - Organizational or spiritual authority

   - Through dreams and visions

2. There isn't one formula that works for everyone for discerning the Holy Spirit's leading; his voice is consistent with the character of God and discerned through the resulting fruit in the life of the person listening to him.

3. Be sensitive to discerning the spirits that may be playing havoc in the risk situation.

   - Faith: Did my actions today give me greater trust in God, in the church, and in the people in my life, or did they lead to unproductive and paralyzing doubts?

   - Hope: Have the feelings I've been experiencing lately lead me to increased focus on the day of Christ's return? Am I being encouraged on deeper levels that my destiny lies in the sure foundation of God's providence?

   - Love: Have the things preoccupying me led to greater love for God and others?

4. Discernment when confused:

- What is the most loving thing to do?

- What is the most hopeful thing to do?

- What is the most faith-filled thing to do?

- Are my decisions in risk moving me toward God or away from God?

- Am I relying on false gods of my own making?

- What is the most strategic thing to do at this moment for the kingdom of God?

chapter 6

The First Question of the Bible

A Spiritual Journey

Thus far we've looked at some Bible passages on risk. We've seen the absolute necessity to discern the Holy Spirit's leading into or out of risk, and the direct bearing his leading has on stewarding all that is entrusted to us in risk, including ourselves. To better understand where God is spiritually leading us in risk, it's helpful to know the starting point.

The first question of the Bible is, "Where are you?" God asks this of Adam and Eve after they had covered themselves with fig leaves because they had sinned. In Hebrew, there are two different words for *where*. It is the difference between *ayyeh* and *'eypoh*: *ayyeh* (short form *'ay*) is "where" as a statement of surprise, like, "Why aren't you here where I expected you to be?"; *'eypoh* is "where" like, "Where is the exit?" "Surprise versus location. Unless we know the difference between the two, our translation will hide something from us."[100]

What word do you suppose God used in the garden? Was he asking the location of Adam and Eve? No, he uses the word *'ayyeh*. Not only that, but in Genesis 3:9 it is spelled with an added *he* at the end.[101] This reveals God's emotions about what the first two humans did. In pain, he howled the question, "Where are you? Why are you hiding from me?" from the depths of his heart. He was communicating the devastating grief he felt over the separation that now existed between humans and himself. It's similar to the screaming pain in our souls when the love of our life has died.

He didn't ask because he didn't know where they were; he asked so they would acknowledge where *they* were, both spiritually and physically: they were separated from him and so they hid. He wanted them to name the problem and honestly admit what they had done. In the same way, he wants each of us to see

79

our separation from him and wants us to *want* to return to him as much as he is grieved that we left.

Where are you on the "return journey" back to God? The journey of faith has been mapped out in a variety of ways over the past two thousand years of church history, asking, "What are the stages of maturity in faith and the characteristics of each level of intimacy on the journey with Christ?" Maturity can't be defined by a checklist. How spiritually aware are you of where you are at right now in your relationship with God? In preparation for risk, we also want to consider how we can help people become more aware of where they are in their faith journey.

Spiritual Maturity

Maturing faith is decribed by Henri Nouwen as movement in five characteristics.[102] The first is that one moves from opaqueness to transparency. This means that one begins to see the reality of the world and oneself, not the false masks and illusions, but the reality where the transcendent is seen in common places, things, and people. It's moving toward more transparency and authenticity. It's being able to be aware and honest of where you are in your relationship with God and with loving others.

The second movement is from illusion to prayer. Moving from self-dependence, the illusion of control and self-reliance, to prayerful dependence, validation, and reliance upon the Spirit results in deeper union with Christ. A deeper prayer life moves beyond lists to constant prayer in the inner heart with an attitude of acknowledgement and dependence upon God for everything.

Third, moving from sorrow to joy. This is working through how one lives with loss and choosing to mourn the losses as a way to joy, as Jesus taught in the Beatitudes. It is a regular cultivation of joy and gratitude in all things, while at the same time being able to name losses and hardships for what they are.

Next is the change from resentment to gratitude. In this movement, one is being freed from resentment, from cold anger that results in suspicion, cynicism, and depression. It means cultivating living with gratitude for every moment. As we gain increasing clarity of discernment of the subtle differences between good and evil, we are more and more thankful to God for everything.

Last, we move from fear to love. In the earlier stages of faith, fear controls one's actions, self-definition, and self-perception. Maturity comes in increasing recognition and ability to articulate the fears and "default" patterns we each have in our lives and bring into the cross-cultural team situation. Moving into love means participating in the divine love of intimacy within the Trinity. There is a congruence of what people feel and the spiritual fruit in their lives regarding their growing love for God and others in their hearts and minds.

A person who is not filled with fear but love is consistently grateful and joy filled, not complaining or criticizing others. This person can share appropriately and transparently and vulnerably demonstrates spiritual maturity. In maturing people, there is increasing dissatisfaction over a lack of intimacy in prayer with God; there is frustration over not being able to be alone with him more often.

A spiritually mature prayer life is not characterized by praying through lists; when people pray it feels like they are experiencing God sitting right next to them. Conversations with others may actually be described as prayer. Maturing folks focus on constantly praying, as Paul writes, "Pray without ceasing" (1 Thessalonians 5:17). Rabbi Abraham Heschel, seen in the front line with Martin Luther King Jr. in his famous march in Alabama in 1965, later wrote, "I felt my legs were praying."[103] His prayer life resulted in righteous action.

How would you describe yourself in each of these categories? How would your spouse or your closest friend describe you? If you were walking in the halls of heaven and overheard God talking about you around the corner, what would you hear him saying about you in each of these categories?

The Need for Community

A major point of agreement from all faith traditions within the church is that moving on the path toward spiritual maturity does not happen without help. It demonstrates a lack of wisdom to live in isolation, not seeking input and advice, or not being spiritually accountable to someone. In risk, it is even more dangerous to choose to isolate ourselves, as we are major targets of the enemy and our own negative emotional and thinking patterns seem to "turn up" the volume in these times.

Risk also affects our relationship with God. I mentioned that stewarding ourselves includes our personal relationship with God and asks, "What is our current experience of God in risk?" There are three parts to how risk affects us in our relationship with God. Spiritual maturity is the first part I have addressed. In the next section I discuss a second aspect of how our relationship with God is affected by risk, and in Chapter 7 I discuss the third part.

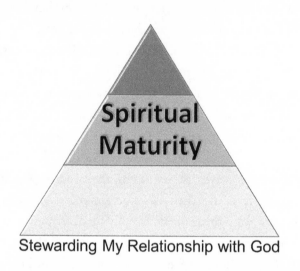

Stewarding My Relationship with God

Diagnosing Our Awareness of Spiritual Maturity

It would be understandable to think that we must have spiritually mature people going into risk areas. But sometimes spiritual maturity is wrongly equated to age, experience, and educational degrees. Older age does not automatically indicate spiritually mature or spiritually self-aware workers. Just because someone has been "on the field" for a couple of decades doesn't automatically mean that person is wise. If age and experience aren't the key, then what is?

While a focus on spiritual maturity is helpful, a more helpful indicator may be the awareness a person has of where he or she is at on the stage of his or her journey with Christ and union with God. What signs are indicative someone (myself?) is on the path toward deeper spiritual maturity? How aware am I of where I am on the journey? How aware is my teammate of his or her journey? And what will a new staff member do—how will they respond once they arrive cross-culturally and begin to experience the challenges of living in a risk situation? There are least seven areas to keep in mind in regards to our own or someone else's spiritual maturity.

Personal Responsibility

I can remember one staff member coming to Neal and sharing that he had an unmet expectation of the organization. When queried, he related that he understood the organization would invest in his spiritual development. It's safe to assume that the resources we invest in personally are the ones that we will pursue with more diligence. What priority do you make on having an awareness of where you are on your personal spiritual journey? Awareness is indicated through some combination of "inputs."

For example, "What books are you reading? Do you journal or process your life with someone? What teachers do you sit under? Do you engage in one-on-one mentoring/pastoral counseling or coaching? What plan have you developed for personal spiritual growth?" There is no shortcut to the deeper life, and life-on-life discipleship is still the Master's way.

Describing Your Spiritual Journey

How do you describe your prayer life and your understanding of spiritual warfare? What spiritual disciplines do you regularly cultivate? If asked, do you have specific, recent examples for each of the five movements described above? How do you describe your experience of the Father, Son, and Spirit? Answers that are primarily on one extreme or the other indicate potential areas of concern.

For example, if your experience of God is exclusively described with emotional terminology, you may not have enough foundational biblical literacy. By contrast, if your relationship with God is described only with cognitive, theological factual descriptors, you may need to work at becoming more aware of your emotions, or, at the very least, God's emotions.

Are your spiritual disciplines disconnected from spiritual awareness? In other words, do you go through the motions of spiritual disciplines instead of doing them as an outgrowth of an intimate relationship with God?

We hear the "I have an accountability partner" phrase quite a lot. One woman I was coaching through a difficult marriage revealed her husband had an accountability partner, but over the months I walked with her he continued to be spiritually, verbally, and emotionally abusive to her and the children. An accountability partner is not a "magic pill" to spiritual maturity; an accountability partner must be someone with the backbone to confront us when necessary.

Recent Stories

Real-life recent stories of experiencing God are indicators of someone on a journey to deeper union with God. What kind of stories come to mind? Do you have stories of failure and redemption to tell, or are all the stories positive? If so, it may reveal a lack of an awareness of struggle.

By Fruit

Jesus's one simple guide is that by their fruit we will know whether or not someone is his disciple (Matthew 7:15–20). What kind of fruit is evident in your life? This is both internal and external. This does not pertain solely to outward activity. Jesus was not trying to "Christianize" productivity. He refers to the fruit of the inner life, more and more with the Father's heart in us, and the fruit of a life lived under his direction, not based on the Western definition of success.

> Our Father doesn't want our productivity. He wants us to abide in him so that he can work his fruit in and through us.

He describes a fruitful life that enters into activities based on his leading and our abiding in him (John 15), which results in the fruit of the Spirit and faithfulness that is expressed through obedience. It is not asking, "How productive are you?" This is probably one of the biggest challenges cross-culturally—people are busy spinning round and round from one meeting to another, keeping track of all their activities so they can report back home to partners. The enemy is quite happy when we are so busy in our work that we don't have time for prayerful solitude with God to hear him speaking to us.

Our Father doesn't want our productivity (1 Samuel 15:22; Psalm 51:16–17; Hosea 6:6; 1 John 5:3). He wants us to abide in him so that he can work his fruit in and through us. He wants us to obey him and do as he asks. When this happens, our behavior will be consistent with the reality of our inner lives. "How I live today is a reflection of how I am living my life."[104] How we act in relation to our families, teams, national believers, and the culture match the reality of a heart and mind increasingly feeling and thinking more like our Father in heaven. We won't need to hide like Adam and Eve.

Discerning Another's Spirit

Part of discerning spiritual maturity in another is based on what God has been individually dealing with us. Watchmen Nee taught that "our ability to know the spirit in another person does not come from books, nor from the experiences of older saints, but from our personal dealings before God."[105] Despite what some modern preachers teach, there are no shortcuts for this. When God allows pain in our lives, it will take time to work out what it means for us. Pain *is* painful.

Watchman Nee writes, "We need a workable spirit by which to diagnose another's spirit."[106] He goes on to say that we obtain a workable spirit by our dealings with God. As we learn to sense our faults, explain them, and heal from the cause of those faults, we have discernment into the spirit of others. For example, when someone is crying, we need to consider the reasons behind their tears. Nee teaches that tears result from either self-love, pain, or being broken by God. Why are we crying? Are we embarrassed we've been found out? Or are we ready to be broken enough to make the changes needed to conform to God's standard of behavior? When we understand why we cry, it is easier to discern the source of tears in another. At times, being in pastoral care requires tough love.

An Awareness of What Is Too Hard to Deal With

It is a false belief that cross-cultural service is no place to deal with growth. We all deal with issues in our lives. We are all on a process of healing and sanctification, so it doesn't necessarily mean a person can't have any issues to be able to go into the risk environment. Sometimes the internal issues are revealed in the risk environment, and that is when God wants to work. Oftentimes, it is the cross-cultural community going through the risk moment that understands us the best and provides a loving, secure place for us to share the "shadow areas" of our lives.

However, sometimes our inner pain is too great. We need to be honest with ourselves when we need to step away for a little while to deal with past or current traumas and heal before stepping back into the battle.

The Awareness of How to Strengthen Oneself in the Lord

Both Ephesians 3:14–20 and 1 Samuel 30:6 teach the principle of being strengthened in the Lord. What ideas do you have of how you will do that in the risk situation? Don't wait for the risk situation to decide on regular habits.

There were several practices we began early on as a family in Afghanistan and continue to this day. One is to have a family worship evening on our Sabbath day. It was protected—we rarely had guests over or accepted invitations to go out. We planned special snacks and worship videos our kids enjoyed. We also invited our home church in the USA to help provide Sunday school curriculum to systematically teach the Bible to our children. We had so many cancelled church services due to security; we needed help to make sure they were getting a biblical education.

Another way to strengthen oneself in the Lord is to arrange a community worship service. Our community would often get together and sing songs and hymns, share testimonies, and share struggles. All of that was a major factor in strengthening the community, both adults and children.

Six Foundations of Faith

All too often much of the attention on risk has focused on "just having faith." The answer is often boiled down to talking about the "conclusions of faith"[107] to cross-cultural workers who may not be sure they possess *enough* faith. This leads to another difficult question: How much faith is enough? Before going into a high-risk situation, a cross-cultural worker who has never been tested wonders if his or her faith will stand up under pressure. Too many frontline, linguistically competent personnel have lost their faith and turned their backs on God.

These dear folks do not lose their faith over the lack of correct theological beliefs, but more often because of a lack of integrating dogma with lived experience. They lose their faith because of misunderstanding the human and divine emotional responses to massive disappointment, relational wounding, and the reality of living where the trauma and the "smell of death" are constant. God simply doesn't measure up to their expectations.

What if we asked a different question that leads us to focus on what is necessary *before* faith? Are there essential ingredients leading to faith, elements to cultivate that develop, nourish, and grow faith? Psalm 37:3 teaches, "Trust in the LORD and do good; dwell in the land and cultivate faithfulness." The JPS 1917 version says "cherish faithfulness." What does it mean to cultivate or cherish faithfulness? One way is by focusing *not* on the content of faith but on what qualities give rise to faith. By looking at how to cultivate faith, we access what Heschel has termed "depth theology."[108]

Depth theology asks, "What are the internal practices in the depths of the heart that are actively cultivated and give rise to faith?" These practices are not feelings but attitudes and perspectives cultivated on a regular basis and frame our perspective on risk. Depth theology focuses on religious insights and the prerequisites to, and the act of, faith. In contrast, theology deals with "the beliefs and dogmas born of faith."[109]

What is necessary to be in place for faith to develop? In Exodus 17, Acts 15:26, Romans 16:4, and Philippians 2:30, it is seen that risk and faithfulness are directly related to the qualities and characteristics of what they are being placed upon. If faith is defined as "an act of man who, transcending himself, responds to him who transcends the world,"[110] then the essentials introduced by Abraham Heschel for being able to do this are wonder and awe, indebtedness and praise, and remembrance and doing rightousness.[111]

Wonder and Awe

Wonder

Risk takes courage, and "courage [is] impossible apart from a commitment to the transcendent."[112] The fact is that God, the one who is matchless, unparalleled, totally above us but passionately in love with us, is the source of wonder. When we cultivate the perspective of God's power and faithful love for us, we can have courage. The problem with our modern era is that we tend to try to objectify and reduce everything—including God—but a person can never be fully objectified.[113]

If we are truly cultivating wonder of God, we will cultivate a wonder of his divine image stamped on our teammates. Perhaps there will be less conflict if we are in wonder of the image of God in the people he has brought to our ministry teams!

Wonder is radical amazement that is completely unrelated to simple curiosity. But ultimate wonder stands amazed that we exist, that our God *wants* to be in a relationship with us. Wonder is not taking everyday things for granted; it gives rise to humility: "To God ... I would commit my cause, who does great things and unsearchable, marvelous things without number" (Job 5:8–9 ESV). Wonder is the beginning of awareness of the presence of the divine in everything: "Wonderful are your works, my soul knows it very well" (Psalm 139:14 ESV). The wonders of God are so numerous that they cannot be told (Psalm 40:5).

There are two ways to cultivate wonder and at least one major obstacle. The obstacle is expediency. Time-oriented cultures value speed, control, efficiency, and productivity. However, wonder unfolds in other ways. The fruit of wonder grows by beholding the beauty and grandeur of the universe. It also grows by cultivating an appreciation for that which is majestic, magnificent, and matchless.

It takes time to stop and behold the beauty all around us. Some days I looked up and realized I couldn't remember the last time I had stopped to admire the audacity of the majestic one-hundred-foot straight pine trees surrounding my Kabul home, trees that had dared survive so many decades of war. Noticing them took time. They reminded me to wonder at the magnificent God who made such beauty.

Awe[114]

Awe is a response to God and it precedes faith. Without awe, there is no reason for faith to develop. It is the antithesis of fear, the way to wisdom, and it is the spark of awareness of the divine presence in the mystery. The mystery is all that we cannot comprehend about God and his essence because of his greatness and our finiteness. We cultivate awe of both God and the mystery surrounding him.

Both awe and wonder take time to develop, and expediency is a disaster to developing these crucial heart perspectives leading to faith. Awe is more than just a feeling, an emotional reaction; instead, it is "the act of insight into a meaning greater than ourselves."[115]

Where is this spiritual wisdom found? Awe is described in Psalm 111:10, Proverbs 1:7, 15:33, and Ecclesiastes 12:13. Proverbs 9:10 says, "The [awe] of the LORD is the beginning of wisdom, and the knowledge of the Holy One is insight." Awe of God is wisdom; it is a way of being in rapport with the mystery of reality. Again, Abraham Heschel says, "The beginning of awe is wonder, and the beginning of wisdom is awe."[116] Out of this, faith can begin to form.

A lack of awe is revealed in the approach to the world. The world becomes a place to control, dominate, calculate, and use for one's gain. Diminished awe means increased conceit and the lack of ability to revere that which is worthy of awe.

Wonder and Awe in Relation to Risk

Doubt is a Greek idea that is based on rational knowledge. Hebrew does not have a word for doubt but has many expressions for wonder. Wonder is the biblical starting point to face reality and is the beginning of true knowledge and thus is a way of thinking.[117] "This is the LORD's doing, it is marvelous in our eyes," said the psalmist (Psalm 118:23). Job was told to "stop and consider the wondrous works of God" (Job 37:14–15 ESV). And Psalm 66:5 declares, "Come and see the works of God, who is awesome in His deeds toward the sons of men."

Moses stood at the top of the hill and considered the effects of raising and lowering his arms. It took time for him to watch the battle and see what was happening.[118] He had to watch the physical battle to realize the spiritual reality taking place through him. Moses realized the wondrous reality of what God was doing through him, so he entered into the mystery of the supernatural outworking of God's power to save the Israelites in the face of a brutal enemy (Exodus 17:11–12).

I remember the feeling of awe that came over me when I realized the risk-level we were choosing to remain in together as a family. We had agreed to be one of the three families to stay through the eight-month "lockdown" and reevaluate security in the spring. I experienced wonder and awe that God would ask us to do such a thing. We joyfully stayed, not knowing the (short-term) outcome. Would we all still be together in the spring?

I gathered our elementary-aged children and sat on a rug by the old Russian heater in the kitchen. Together, we recited Psalm 23, a chapter they had each memorized at the age of four. That fall day in late 2008 I taught them that we were living verses 4 and 5 from that psalm. They listened wide-eyed and then went back off to play.

Praise and Indebtedness
Indebtedness

With the realization that the living self is a gift, then one experientially knows indebtedness. The awareness that the world has an origin outside of itself, and that God is present and gives life, gives rise to the awareness of being indebted to him and the realization of a demand to live in a certain way. John Merkle writes, "I am what is not mine. We owe not only what we have but also what we are."[119] Indebtedness is the concept that will, freedom, and life are all given as gifts, and there is worth and meaning beyond what it is that I can conceive.

There is a connection between indebtedness to him and the call to live significantly. Indebtedness can be summarized as, "What is required of me?"[120] Not only does an awareness of indebtedness include the requirement of response, but it also includes a sense of embarrassment from the evil inside of me and my lack of awareness of God's presence. When I am embarrassingly aware of and acknowledge these things, my embarrassment leads to a broken heart and repentance.[121]

This leads to the next question: To what are men and women called? This question has to do with being concerned with God's concerns; ultimately, it has to do with his concern for good and evil. In this case, indebtedness gives rise to the sense of owing gratitude to God and, therefore, responding to the challenge of God. So faith is the *expression* of indebtedness, not just the sense of it. Indebtedness continues to inform faith, becomes one of its essential features, and nurtures it.[122]

I recall one particular moment in Afghanistan when everything inside of me screamed to take the children and leave. "Let Neal finish our current contract!" I thought. I was filled with fear and I didn't want to do what I knew the Lord was asking of me. He whispered directly to my heart, "Will you drink the cup I am handing to you?" The cup meant obedience to stay and face with Neal whatever God had in store for us. When I looked at the cup with the eyes of my heart, its contents were bitter. I knew he wanted me to drink it—whatever our future held—only if I could do it joyfully.

I saw the nail-scarred hand holding the cup and realized how little he truly was asking of me because of how greatly he had suffered to redeem me from the kingdom of darkness. I felt, at that moment, the indebtedness I owe him for my very life. It was during that moment of indebtedness I realized I could step forward in faith and say yes. I drank the cup with a commitment to battle for joy whatever it cost me and was stunned at the peace that enveloped us during that time.

When we experience the great indebtedness we have toward our heavenly Father, it leads to gratitude. Gratitude is simply thanking God for every good thing that he gives us, and thankfulness for all the bad things he protects us from. Gratitude leads to praise, the next attitude of the heart we must cultivate for our faith to develop and grow.

Praise

For Heschel, praise is the expression of indebtedness, a response to the glory, transcendence, and especially the presence of God to whom we are ultimately indebted. However, praise is also the climax of one's faith. First we sing, then we believe would be stating the priority of praise. There is a crucial distinction in faith and faithfulness and the role of praise. Praise is the initial response to God, an experience of faith, for faith is an event, a moment in which "the soul of man communes with the glory of God."[123] Being ready to "have faith" means we express faithfulness in praise as an initial response to the demands of God.

Indebtedness and Praise in Relation to Risk

Indebtedness and praise must be cultivated on a regular basis. In response to the wondrous works of the Lord for saving them in Exodus 17, Moses built an altar and named it The Lord is My Banner. This was an act of worship and recognition that all of Israel was indebted to the Lord's mighty saving power. The tangible reminders and the written record reminded the Israelites for all time what he had done.

Remembrance and Doing Righteousness

The Bible reminds us throughout to remember what the Lord has done. Remembering is a spiritual exercise to discern all the instances of God's care, as Heschel says, a cultivation of "an inner attachment to sacred events." To believe is to remember, but it is not merely accepting truth as a set of beliefs. The concept of faith includes the concepts of commitment and loyalty, so it includes the memory of commitment of the past years, even generations, including those in the Bible.

For Heschel, a soul must constantly drink from the stream of memories before one can enter the realm of faith.[124] What he means is that we need to remember how God has worked in the past, including the stories of our biblical family all the way back to the beginning of Genesis. How much do we recite all the times we know God has worked in our lives? Do our children know those stories?

Moses was commanded by God to write down what had happened and recite the words in the ears of Joshua. Writing, remembering, understanding—this is the sequence of steps commanded by God to Moses as a command for the Israelites to follow for all time.

Doing Righteousness

The doing of righteous deeds and righteous actions are two activities God and humans have in common.[125] These are commonly thought of as expressions of faith but they are also pathways to faith development. In Exodus 24:7, the Israelites were responding to God's commands, and the order of the verbs in Hebrew is "do" and then "hear." Translators translate "hear" with "obey," but it is really the Hebrew verb "to hear." So the people respond with the order of how faith in action looks: "We will do, and then we will hear." This is a Hebrew idiom for understanding and discerning God's Word.[126] As the Israelites engaged in right response, which are righteous deeds to God's commands, they more deeply understood God's Word (Isaiah 42:20; Matthew 13:15). This is Heschel's "leap of action," responding as an act of faith based on God's truth and will.

What this means is that first we obey, and then in our obedience we begin to understand the outworking of God's plan in that situation. We cannot always understand *before* we obey. This is where a "leap" of faith is needed so that understanding will come. It is not unlike parenting young children.

When our children were little, we knew they were too young to understand some of the boundaries we set in place for them. But they were required to obey, the first time, immediately, with a happy heart. We always tied this definition of obedience to God's requirement of obedience from us. As they grew and matured, they began to understand why some of those boundaries were in place and why they were required to do certain things. Obedience comes first, and then understanding follows.

Remembering and Doing Righteousness in Relation to Risk

For the Israelites in Exodus 17, remembering and understanding what God had done demonstrated faith. When we accurately understand and interpret God's works, and actively work at remembering God's works, then we have given an adequate human response to God's activity. Faith for the Israelites was not an agreement to correct doctrinal belief, but understanding genuine spiritual reality—God was with them—and the truth of who God is—their divine military leader who had saved them once again.

These six foundational aspects for developing faith are crucial in our relationship with God. Instead of suggesting that field workers need to "just have faith," a better question to ask instead is, which of the six foundational components do you need at this time to begin cultivating on a regular basis for your own faith to grow?

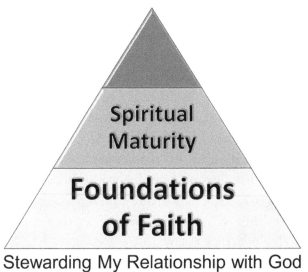

Conclusion

Knowing the reality of God's presence was the crux of the problem in Exodus 17, and it is still the main issue for those of us in risk situations today. The problem isn't, is he there, but how aware are we that he *is* there? The essentials for faith to develop are to cultivate a sense of wonder and awe for the transcendent meaning and presence of God in all things and events; to cultivate an awareness of one's indebtedness to God, resulting in a heart filled with gratitude and praise; and finally, to actively remember and see God's actions and presence in the past and present, and to cultivate unshaking hope in his actions and presence in the future. This results in experiential knowledge of the true God and choosing to do righteousness as an act of faith even when God "feels" concealed. It results in a faith that will stand the worst hell throws at us.

Faith is more than words of beliefs; it is the action of personal consent to the reality believed and hoped for. The consent is living God's way according to God's Word, and this is responsiveness to God.

In Exodus 17, Moses chooses to do what was necessary to keep his arms up, with the aid of the community, Aaron, and Hur. He could not fulfill God's call on his life at that moment without help from others. God directed him to write down the events of the day and then recite them to Joshua (Exodus 17:14). Joshua was to understand, to have insight and discernment about the supernatural events of the day, that it was not his superior military leadership and fighting skills, but a transcendent God who was working out the end of the battle in good and evil, of which that battle was just one of many.

Joshua and Moses were to see that their lives were caught up in a story much larger than their own. By obeying God that day, and each person doing his part, they had a firsthand experience of all six elements leading to faith that resulted in a personal experience of a transcendent yet present God.

The two areas I focused on in this chapter are answering the question of "Where am I?" and "What areas do I need to cultivate to grow my faith?" A personal God, desiring to be in an intimate relationship with each one of us, uses every aspect of risk to "chip off" the rough areas of our natures and increasingly make us like him. He doesn't waste any experiences or any hardships. Answering these two questions will help you discern what God desires to do in your life through the experience of entering, remaining, or leaving risk.

Application

1. How would you describe the state of your current relationship with God? What are you still hiding from him?

2. Which essential of faith is the Spirit whispering to you to begin cultivating on a regular basis?

3. If "discerning where we are on our faith walk" requires increased skill of discernment, how can your organization and leadership team learn to grow in this? What if your leadership goals were not, "How can we be more effective?" but instead, "How can we increase discernment of how God is leading us personally and corporately?" What would need to change in your organization?

Chapter 6 Summary

1. The spiritual journey means increasing awareness of where I am in relationship with God. It is described in five sets of categories of:

   - From opaqueness to increasing transparency
   - From illusion to prayer
   - From sorrow to joy
   - From resentment to gratitude
   - From fear to love

2. Depth theology is paying attention to six foundational essentials—six attitudes of the heart—to cultivate regularly so enduring faith results:

   - Wonder and awe
   - Indebtedness and praise
   - Remembrance and doing righteousness

chapter 7

Finding Our Core Question in God's Heart

There are two spiritual growth points commonly experienced going into the risk situation: The first is a core-question issue, and the second is the wilderness experience. In between and through those two we experience God's heart. When we experience one or both of these tough spiritual challenges, we experience the reality of God personally reaching down into our lives to uniquely reveal part of himself to us. He desires to reveal himself to us in the part of our souls that need healing. And he often uses the risk event to do this.

Core Questions

Part of going through risk is personally experiencing the firm foundation we are laying our life upon. Sometimes, we have questions about that foundation, about God himself. We often need a realignment of our understanding of God's heart, who he is, and what he thinks and feels about us and our risk situations. These questions and fears in risk have an underlying theme. They aren't just random but are connect to our sin nature and past pain.

These questions, called core questions, are where God is speaking to us in our inner life. They point us to where we need to focus our attention. As we work through the core questions, wrestling in our relationship with God, we are healed, strengthened, deepened, and better prepared for whatever is on the other side of risk.

A spiritual principle that emerges during a significant time of risk is that our fears often reveal a related weakened view of God. "When I face challenges in life, which attribute of God do I tend to distrust?"[127] We don't always realize or word our core questions like the ones below, at least in our minds, but when we uncover the root of our fears it usually leads to one of these questions that we are sometimes ashamed to admit we are asking.

We are ashamed because we think we are "supposed" to be mature cross-cultural workers, and we wrongly think, "What would our partners think if they knew I was questioning God?" So the question never gets addressed. Instead, we bury it and try to limp on for as long as possible, but our growth is stunted and we slowly lose our risk resiliency like air leaking from a balloon. I want to assure you: God can handle these questions. He longs for us to ask them, because then he has the joy of answering them and showing us part of himself now that we are asking.

Some examples of core questions we ask of God in risk are:

- Do you care?

- Are you just?

- Are you going to let the wicked win?

- Are you going to let them violate me with no justice in sight?

- Do you remember me?

- Are you good?

- Do you know me?

- Do you understand what I am facing?

- Do you see what I see?

- Are you weeping for me and with me?

- Do you love me?

- Do you approve of me?

"What big events impacted your life before risk? Reflect on these big moments, especially the ones which were painful and the lessons you learned from them."[128] It may be that God is continuing those lessons but from a different angle or depth. God gently leads us into the risk event so our experience of him moves from the "what" we know of God to the "how" we know of him, through experiencing his faithfulness, presence, and love.

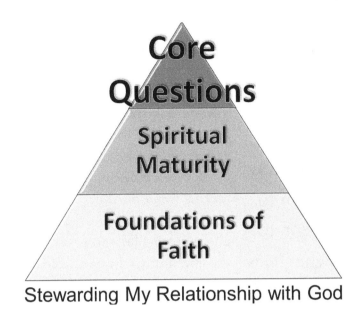

The Pathos of God

Most books on suffering jump immediately to how God will act after the risk is taken and how he will help a person through suffering. God's emotions are almost never addressed, and commonly there is a narrow focus on doctrinal truth.[129] However, emotions felt by God are mentioned considerably more times in the Old Testament than concepts about God.[130]

Church history of studying God has almost exclusively examined the timeless attributes and ideas of God. The resulting image reveals concepts of God like goodness, justice, wisdom, and unity. Heschel notes that "timeless notions detached from God's being are not how God or the prophets speak." They spoke of God's attributes as "drives, challenges, and commandments." He is personal and intimate. God is moved and affected by human response to or rejection of him.[131]

Whether it is the inheritance handed down to us from previous generations of Bible teachers or what we have created in our own generation, we learn our God is a remote and rather austere unemotional God whom we mix up with our own cultural values: health, wealth, vending machines, and Santa Claus. These wrong values lead us to think that because we sacrificed (put into the vending machine),

> When we discover that the god of our making is not our Rock, that he doesn't act the way we expect him to, then we begin to question what he is truly like.

we should get a little reward out. God should be answering our prayers. Why doesn't he bless us with results when we've sacrificed so much? (This is the Santa Claus part.) Compounding this wrong image of God, we easily confuse our heavenly Father with our sinful earthly father, and we are left with a god of our own making.

When we discover that the god of our making is *not* our Rock, that he doesn't act the way we expect him to, then we begin to question what he is truly like. This is exactly the question God *wants* us to ask so he can reveal to us the truth of the reality of his heart. He reveals his reality to our "true selves," not the false self being concealed with masks and illusions. God's knowledge of us precedes our knowledge of him (Jeremiah 1:5). So when he asks us to do something hard, risking for him or leaving a risk situation, we gain knowledge and comprehension of him. I discover my "true self" in light of experiencing his care for me.

From the perspective of seeing God's emotions through the Prophets, we begin to understand how our hearts are being formed in his holy image in the moment of deep wrestling with him.

View of God and His Inner Life

We learn about God's inner world throughout the Old and New Testaments. The prophets describe his heart repeatedly, showing the entire range of emotions with which we are familiar. They were sent not only to preach a message of repentance and coming judgment but also to "strengthen the weak hands and make firm the feeble knees" (Isaiah 35:3 ESV). They did this by sharing God's words with the people, which most often described his feelings.

God's emotions and his passions are not directed toward self but are emotional responses defined as acts formed with intentions. His are changing concerns, directed toward others, which do not define his essence. "Emotions can be reasonable just as reason can be emotional."[132] God's passion is not unreasoned emotion, but is imbibed with ethos—its inner law is ethical. In other words, not only do his emotions righteously respond to good and evil, but his mercy, his anger, and his wrath show us what is good and what is evil.

God's pathos is a form of relating to people; his emotions are acts of how he responds to humankind. The prophets continually preached repentance before God's judgment fell, because God's anger arises when there is injustice and no mercy. When the people repented, when their conduct was in line with covenant living, the Almighty could change the proclaimed word (Hosea 11:9; Isaiah 48:9; Jeremiah 19:7–8; Deuteronomy 9:19; Exodus 32:7–11).

"In genuine Hebraic thinking, self-sufficiency is the sense of the self being unaffected or unmoved by realities outside the self, and this is no ideal."[133] In other words, he is not self-sufficient but is moved by what we do and what is in our hearts. We affect God! Humankind is seen as God's bride, a partner, and a factor in the life of God that is necessary to accomplish God's plan.

The prophets, speaking for God, reflect a God raging, with an acute sense of right and wrong in their words. The prophets' words disclosed attitudes of God rather than lofty ideals about him. Meditation on God's words drove the prophets in increased sensitivity to the presence of God, not to impersonal head knowledge about him. They had experiences of the revelation of God's heart that became theirs.

We gain knowledge of God by living together with him in every detail of our lives (1 Chronicles 28:9). But God's emotions are never separated from his love but are born out of his love. His anger and wrath are not at all like human wrath. His wrath and justice more often give way to mercy than the inverse.

The prophets were constantly communicating how God presently felt about a situation. Rather than viewing God by ascribing human feelings to him, it would be more biblically accurate, as creatures made in the image of God, to understand humans reflecting God from God's perspective, and align one's emotions with the heart of God.[134] It's easier to see when we feel sadness, grief, rejection, or righteous anger, how we are reflecting his heart. He is not detached from what is happening in risk, just as we are not detached, but wholly involved.

Sharing Faith with the Prophets

What gave the prophets faith? "Prophetic faith is sympathetically sharing the heart of God and how He feels toward humankind. Since biblical faith includes faith with the prophets, the revelation of [God's emotions] is one of the sources for biblical faith."[135]

Understanding God's emotions in situations in the Bible is a primary source that nourishes and grows our faith. We see throughout Scripture, and especially in the Prophets, that God chose to disclose his feelings and thoughts to humankind.[136] God spoke and shared his feelings always in relation to us, his grief at our betrayal and rebellion. Unlike the ancient pagan gods and the Greek and Roman gods, the God of Abraham, Isaac, and Jacob chose to reveal to us his thoughts and concerns through numerous events.

From the prophets' perspectives, because they experienced God's love for his people and themselves, they suffered right along with the people they were trying to save. The prophets did not send their families to safety; they experienced God's judgment along with the people, taken captive or dying at the hands of their countrymen or enemies.

We base our risking for Christ on the absolute certainty of God's love, care, and concern for us. He feels anguish and righteous anger over the evil and injustice reigning in the streets. It is God's love and holy justice that enables us to face real adversity. God, the one dwelling in the high and holy place, also dwells with us. He desires to revive our spirits and our hearts so we heal and have peace with him (Isaiah 57).

The Message of the Wilderness

"I'm in the wilderness. I'm tired of being in the wilderness. It's so hard and lonely, and I can't hear God's voice." It's fascinating that we often just naturally equate the wilderness with not being able to hear God's voice or sense his presence. These are phrases Neal and I often hear as pastoral-care providers. Most of us have been in the wilderness at some time or another. Since we all have been there, what exactly does it mean to be in the wilderness? What is God doing by leading us into the wilderness and allowing us to stay there, sometimes for years on end? The wilderness has several overarching characteristics.

The wilderness is the place of bewilderments, a place of chaos. Without God's restraining hand, it naturally and spiritually is the place of death. *Wilderness* and *language* share the same root letters, the same Hebrew root: D-B-R. When looking at the spelling in Paleo-Hebrew (the ancient form of writing Hebrew), wilderness is spelled *mem dalet bet reysh*, meaning "from the chaos there is a door or way to the house of the Source (Head)." There is a way home, even when we feel like our lives are filled with fear and out-of-control circumstances. "Home" is finding our place in God who is the source of our lives. And the root letters used for *spoken* and related words like *language* are *dalet bet reysh*, which means, "our language is the door leading us to God."

God's language communicated in the Word leads us to him; at the same time, like the sons of Korah in their rebellion, our language can lead us away from God as well. What words are we repeating to ourselves? And are these words leading us to God or away from him? What are we speaking out loud?

The wilderness is where we learn to hear God speaking to us. It is significant that the very first phrase, the first verb in the book of Numbers, is God speaking. Numbers only talks about the experience of the Israelites in the wilderness. When we are in the wilderness, it feels like we can't hear his voice. However, almost every single chapter of Numbers has the phrase or synonym "and God spoke," except the few chapters when God spoke through Balaam and Moses. God spoke throughout the entire time the Israelites journeyed through the wilderness so that they would know he was with them.

The wilderness is the place where God resided in the middle of the camp. Specific instructions were given so that God could dwell with Israel. God resided in a temporary hut and he designated the Feast of Booths (the temporary Succah hut) for the Jews to remember every year of the wilderness experience. All of us who are grafted into Abraham's family are not to forget the transience of the wilderness, the rebellion of the wilderness, and the miracles of God's sustaining presence in the wilderness.

The wilderness is the place where the Good Shepherd finds us (Luke 15). It is the place God longs to take us, for he wants to be alone with us, to speak tenderly to us, and make the valley of our woundedness a place of hope (Hosea 2:14–15). How is our speech characterized in the wilderness areas of our lives?

Are we speaking the reality of awe because of God's care for us, his constant presence with us? Are we sanctifying his name in all that we do? And how carefully are we paying attention to his presence?

Finding God in the Wilderness

Risk may be a wilderness experience. Even when we go through it as a community, it can still feel lonely at times. We wonder what God is up to. Just as the Israelites feared the wilderness and wanted to go back to Egypt, we don't know if we will survive the wilderness, and we can't just escape the wilderness.

We wonder where God is at. He seems absent, hidden. The common phrase, "I don't *feel* God anymore," is right, and it makes one ready for growth. Why is this? God is stripping away our old ways of hearing him, the ways characterized by the young in the faith. He strips away our wrong concepts of him, our wrong ideas of what he is like and how he feels.

The result of this stripping away often feels like dryness, boredom, emptiness, even as if our spirits have died. At this stage cross-cultural workers may give up on God, on marriage, on ministry, on cross-cultural work altogether, and just go home. They can't pinpoint their real fears, and so there is a disintegration and annihilation of all they held dear, the expectations of life and God, and the loss of "feeling God." Earl and Elspeth Williams write in their book *Spiritually Aware Pastoral Care: An Introduction and Training Program*:

> All extreme suffering evokes the experience of being forsaken by God. In the depth of suffering people see themselves abandoned and forsaken by everyone. That which gave life its meaning has become empty and void; it turned out to be error, an illusion that is shattered, guilt that cannot be rectified, a void. The paths that lead to this experience of nothingness are diverse, but the experience of annihilation that occurs in unremitting suffering is the same.[137]

But for those who "stay in the game," who wait on God, who endure and persevere through, they find on the other side of the darkness, confusion, and stripping away a genuine hope, maturity, renewed vision, and love.

This is where our enemy likes to tell us God has abandoned us, and it surely may feel that way at times. But we cannot trust our feelings. In the bewildering confusion and darkness of the wilderness, the real truth is that God is actually closer than he has ever been before. In the physical realm, when we step from deep darkness into extremely bright light, we are blinded by the light. We cannot see with our eyes, and so we have to stop and let our eyes adjust.

In a similar way, when we enter into risk, it is not uncommon for our spiritual life to feel like we've entered the wilderness. It feels like darkness has descended and God is not responding in familiar ways. It very well could be that what feels like darkness is actually the blinding presence of God's nearness, and that he wants us to learn to live in his presence in new ways. This possibility is best discerned with a trusted Christian guide who has walked this path before and can help point out the signposts in our lives and help us confirm this is the reality that we are not being deceived.

"Darkness is the place where egoism dies and true unselfish love for the 'other' is set free."[138] In the wilderness, he is asking us to learn to listen to his tender voice speaking Spirit to spirit. We won't "feel" him in the same way as before because human feelings are just that—human. We learn to discern him spiritually with the eyes of our hearts.

Application

1. Pay attention to your inner dialogue for the next twenty-four to forty-eight hours. What seems to be a common fear? Which core question of God does it seem to lead to?

2. Draw a picture of how you think God feels about you—not the "church" answer, but the reality of what you picture in your mind. Does this picture represent the God of the prophets and the one Jesus Christ came to reveal?

3. In what ways is God not living up to your expectations in risk? In what ways is he delightfully surprising you in revealing himself to you?

4. If you feel like you are in the wilderness right now, what does that feel like? What does God seem to be stripping away from your experience of him right now?

5. Do you want to be alone with God? What aspect of being alone with God do you fear the most? What aspect do you enjoy the most?

Chapter 7 Summary

1. Core questions: A spiritual principle at work at this time is that what I fear the most often turns out to be the characteristic of God I have the hardest time trusting. When you face challenges in life, which attribute of God do you tend to distrust? Some examples of core questions we ask of God in risk are:

   - Do you care?

   - Are you just?

   - Are you going to let the wicked win?

   - Are you going to let them violate me with no justice in sight?

   - Do you remember me?

   - Are you good?

   - Do you know me?

   - Do you understand what I am facing?

   - Are you weeping for me and with me?

   - Do you love me?

   - Do you approve of me?

   - Do you see what I see?

2. God's pathos: God's emotions reveal his will and concern for us. He is not detached or removed from what we are feeling. On the contrary, our emotions reflect him because we reflect his image.

3. The wilderness is often God's tool to get us alone where he can chisel away all that is dross and all that is impure. God refines us and teaches us to listen to his voice in our spirits, not with our human senses.

part two

Assessing & Managing
Cross-Cultural Risk

chapter 8

What Is Cross-Cultural Risk?

Dealing with risk in cross-cultural situations requires both a spiritual *and* a practical response. While I am not a risk expert, I've tried to cull through several significant books on risk and define the most applicable areas of risk needed for a practical understanding of those serving cross-culturally in high-risk areas because of a special calling from God.

I have defined cross-cultural risk as "potential loss for the sake of the gospel." There are a lot of different terms being used for risk today; words like "crisis response," "crisis," and "danger assessment." These all tend to be used synonymously. Often a discussion is labeled with a theology of risk, but then the majority of the content is really about a theology of suffering. The Bible uses different terms for risk than it does for danger. Any endeavor, including risk assessment and management, begins with defining terminology.

What We Are *Not* Talking About

The focus of this book is on the risk taken by those who purposefully go to a high-risk situation in another culture due to a special calling received from the Lord. I am not entering the discussion of whether or not God risks,[139] nor am I addressing issues of God's sovereignty.[140] I am not talking about suffering or a theology of suffering here either; it is also not my intention to imply a "leap of faith" as a basis of risk.[141] The term "leap of faith" implies not knowing because we're not sure if we can make it to the other side. What are we leaping from or to?

We know the long-term outcome by faith, for the Bible is clear about the outcome. God's rule will eventually extend throughout a new heaven and a new earth. At the end of Revelation, we read God's answer for humanity's and the cosmic problem: evil *will* be banished. Our souls are anchored in that future reality:

This hope we have as an anchor of the soul, a hope both sure and steadfast and one which enters within the veil, where Jesus has entered as a forerunner for us ... (Hebrews 6:19–20).

Key Risk Terms

Cross-Cultural Risk

Risk taking is depending on Christ's resurrection power; we choose to go or remain in a situation where we are willingly exposing ourselves to persecution or suffering or laying our lives down, which we do for the advancement of God's kingdom. We do this because of what Christ did on the cross to break the power of death and redeem us from the enemy's kingdom. This is faith-based risk, one that is experienced in the context of one's calling.

In this definition, we see that we *value* our lives but lay them down. We anticipate certain *outcomes* we *value* because of our *beliefs* about those *outcomes* and their *values*—these are key features of faith-based risk.[142] "Defining risk is an exercise in value-focused thinking. People value different outcomes, and so define risk differently."[143]

> Faith-based risk refers not just to the external aspects of danger, but must include what is happening internally about God, others, and oneself.

Faith-based risk refers not just to the external aspects of danger, but must include what is happening internally about God, others, and oneself. It refers not only or even primarily to the content of what is believed in risk, but it must interact with the act of risk: "What is happening to and in me during risk? What am I choosing to believe in risk? How am I choosing to act in risk?"

For faith-based cross-cultural risk, the starting point of all assessment begins with discerning God's presence. From there we proceed to hear what God is saying to us in the risk moment, which hearkens back to Genesis 1:2: there we read first of God's hovering presence in risk, then we hear him speaking. Then we move to risk assessment and management, incorporating the elements of stewardship and the leading of the Holy Spirit. Next is risk assessment and management, which has several key parts, as I explain in Chapter 10. Finally, there is the implementation of the decision made for that risk event.

Secular versus Biblical Risk

There are some key differences and similarities between the cross-cultural risk definition above and aspects of most other types of risk. An example of one standard definition is: "Risk-taking is any consciously or non-consciously controlled behavior with perceived uncertainty about its short-term outcome and its possible short-term benefits or costs for the physical, missional, economic, or psychosocial well-being of oneself or others."[144]

The history of risk has almost without exception included the concept of insuring oneself against the concept of loss and calculating the probabilities of loss—the costs and the benefits involved.[145] Even Solomon advised risk mitigation by engaging in calculated risk-taking behavior in Ecclesiastes 11:1–2 (CJB): "Send your resources out over the seas; eventually you will reap a return. Divide your merchandise into seven, or even eight shares, since you don't know what disasters may come on the earth."

Commentators have given various opinions on these two verses, but they seem to follow Hebraic parallelism, where the author presents one idea on one line, and either the repetition of that idea or the opposite idea on the second line.[146] If we view Ecclesiastes 11:1–2 in line with the two proposed extremes on stewardship in Chapter 4, we see the same extremes in these two verses. Sometimes we take calculated risks, and at other times we liberally pour out our lives and resources. Biblical risk is approached somewhere on the continuum between these two extremes, based on the Spirit's leading for that risk event and our lives.

Long-Term versus Short-Term Risk

Stewardship implies the probability of loss, loss mitigation, and consideration of the benefits in the outcome. Thus, these are components of biblical risk. Just as secular risk is always viewed for its short-term and long-term outcomes—costs and benefits—so also is faith-based risk viewed in the same way.

Short-term costs for the Christian worker and organization must always be analyzed. This is exactly where the Father wants us paying attention to his leading. "Short-term" for this purpose is defined as this side of eternity, whereas long-term is defined as the other side of eternity (after death). This is based on the long-term view taken in the Gospels in the discussions of separating the wheat from the weeds in Matthew 13. But unlike secular risk, the eternal benefits we are often looking for may not be immediately visible.

There are those who say "we aren't risking" when we go into dangerous cross-cultural situations for the purpose of sharing his love, but this is simply a myth. There is a lot we risk short-term. When thinking about cross-cultural risk, "short-term" may be a bit longer than months or even years. With that definition in mind, we can further divide short-term into manageable segments: the next day, week, month, or thirty years from now.

I think of the story of two Christian aid workers in Central Asia who ran to the home of a house on fire because a bomb had landed there. At great risk to their lives, these two women went in to rescue those inside the home. Afghans were out on the street watching the whole story unfold and marveled at the foreigners who would risk their lives to rescue poor people they did not know. They never forgot that and wondered what made those women risk their lives. Later, they learned that those women were Christians. The seeds planted in the hearts of these Afghan men through the risky, righteous action of these women grew until years later the men chose to follow Jesus. We often never know the outcome of what happens through our risk!

Measuring Short-Term Reward: Faithfulness and Fruitfulness

There are two aspects of reward especially encouraging on this side of eternity, which I would describe as rewards or benefits. One is the experience of knowing that I have been faithful to God in the risk situation—I did all he asked me to do with joy, even when I felt afraid. I held nothing back from him. I was faithful, even if criticized by others who didn't think I did well. God is my judge (1 Corinthians 4:3–5; 1 Peter 2:23), and I hear the Holy Spirit's commendation, "Well done, good and faithful servant."

Another extremely rewarding part of risk on this side of eternity is hearing stories of eternal transformation. Stories are one key way to measure the benefits of cross-cultural risk. Time must be delegated to draw out, remember, and record stories of God working and drawing people to himself through the risk situations. Because of security issues in much of Central Asia and the Middle East, it will take time to build trust with folks who are willing to relate the stories of transformation and retrieve this data.

Long-Term Reward

We also see that there are rewards given in heaven. However, the emphasis in Scripture is not so much the reward as looking for the day when Christ will return to give the rewards. Scripture always seems to talk about "the Day." Our endurance and faithfulness are key when waiting for that day—Jesus makes this clear in each of the messages he gave to the seven churches in Revelation. The reward is based on a love relationship with Jesus, and out of his gracious kindness he chooses to give a reward.

Josef Ton has written extensively on a theology of martyrdom and rewards, so I refer to his book *Suffering Martyrdom and Rewards in Heaven* for additional discussion on rewards. Unlike secular risk, from the perspective of a cross-cultural worker, the risk is uncertain only in the short-term. Long-term one can argue by faith and his Word that there is no risk, for the Christ-follower has eternity in the presence of the Lord (John 17:3; Philippians 1:20–23).

Risk as Event: Conceptual and Situational Thinking Required

As already described, cross-cultural risk is best understood as an event. This means we will be more effective in understanding, assessing, and managing risk using conceptual *and* situational thinking.[147] Why is this? I have already suggested that the wrong questions have been asked. I wonder what would happen to the resiliency of staff on the field if we approached each risk event both conceptually and situationally, addressing both the issues of the mind and the heart?

Another reason risk is better approached with conceptual and situational thinking is because each risk event and the circumstances surrounding it are unique to each situation. No one risk policy or procedure fits all situations. This may be one of the biggest mistakes organizations make—instituting programs and policies on risk to try to cover all situations—because this may lead to false confidence that comprehensive risk management has taken place. We need to be equipped in understanding both forms of thought so we use the right tools at the right time for assessing and mitigating risk.

Conceptual Thinking

Conceptual thinking refers to broad theories, generalized spiritualized principles, and general laws of nature. Thinking conceptually about risk means we are using logical, rational thought. It includes applying spiritual principles in balanced ways. In conceptual thinking, usually we are more detached from the actual problem. This is helpful, but it is one-sided.

We use conceptual thinking when we want more knowledge, when it is some idea or thing we are not part of and need to describe, deduce, and reduce. With this approach, we arrive at an answer that is general enough to try to cover all situations. The problem with only utilizing conceptual thinking is that the answer too often crystallizes into dogma and remains in the domain of the mind; it does not take into account the arena of the inner life of the person and unique situations in risk that are complex.

Situational Thinking

Situational thinking is based on what is happening in the risk event and also how that staff person and the team are doing in their journey and maturity. It assesses each risk event with its unique contributing factors, including all the various causes to the risk event, all the possible risk events, and the totality of the possible consequences—both good and bad. There are numerous and complex factors to take into account here. Situational thinking employs common sense, discarding what is unhelpful or in apparent opposition at the moment from conceptual thought.

Differentiate between Suffering and Risk Answers

A major breakdown in both pastoral encouragement and leadership communication is when a field-based worker shares a risk-based problem or question, and the answer is given for a theology-of-suffering problem or issue. For example, when I was struggling with my confusion in risk, how to process my feelings, whether I was called to stay or go, to be told that in whatever happens "God works everything together for his good" (a truthful concept based on Scripture) was a suffering answer to a risk problem. It wasn't helpful because it was answering a question I wasn't asking.

When someone asks a risk-based, situational, and empathetic-seeking question, and all he or she receives in return is a suffering-based, conceptual, and head-level response, there may be unnecessary miscommunication and misunderstanding. To be sure, sometimes the situation requires a head-level response. But I am arguing here for a thoughtful dialogue that addresses the issues at hand, not a preconceived theologically dogmatic answer to suffering.

Well-intentioned, sending country–based colleagues and leaders are advised to use care and humility to communicate their thoughts to those out on the front lines possibly facing kidnapping or death that day. Telling field-based persons in high-risk situations that they should remain because "now is the time God is going to act" is a conceptually-based statement with a "this is how you should act" response. Don't do this. This statement doesn't strengthen the spirit and could prompt additional burdens.

Do, however, give a response. If supporting leadership from home doesn't respond, the field-based colleagues may feel isolated and unsupported. Give help, give input, and give supporting perspectives. Ask some good coaching questions. Acknowledge the challenges that the field staff are facing. The emotional, psychological, and spiritual impact must be factored in here as well. Sometimes leadership has to model integrated risk assessment and management for their staff to feel emotionally free to do so as well.

Each risk event requires its unique assessment and management. There *are* "best practices" in risk assessment and management that are important to be considered; most of the time we assemble the security information and then need to make a decision based on a combination of factors, including the Holy Spirit's leading. Because each risk is a situation we are a part of, we must use a balance of conceptual and situational thinking because risk "involves an inner experience; in uttering judgment about an issue, the person himself is under judgment. [Con-

ceptual thinking will help us move into risk, but situational thinking is necessary]
when we are engaged to understand issues on which we stake our very existence
and potential death."[148]

Practical Application

Crisis response preparedness is not a one-size-fits-all policy. Common sense
should prevail here, along with situational thinking. Not (re)doing risk assessment and mitigation when the threat level has increased dramatically is unwise.
The truth is that most theology-of-risk statements are purely conceptual thoughts
and do not address situational responses. Many organizational policies utilize a
biblically anecdotal approach and do not provide a way of thinking and feeling
through risk. Evaluate your organizational policy and consider how to more effectively address the minds and hearts of your field people in risk.

Not only that, but find out what trainings are available close to you. There are
organizations that offer crisis response training and danger mitigation. Practical
situational awareness and risk mitigation training is helpful and builds resiliency.
However, recognize that a military approach adapted and utilized for cross-cultural
risk policies and risk mitigation will be more effective when incorporated with the
holistic cross-cultural risk mitigation approach explained in Chapters 10 through 14.

What *is* helpful from folks outside of the situation is acknowledging and
addressing the totality of what is being faced. One partner back home sent an

e-mail that has continued to minister to us to this day. Notice in this e-mail the conceptual *and* situational thinking that was thoughtfully applied here in a way that deeply touched our souls at a time when we were afraid:[149]

You mentioned walking through the Valley of the Shadow. "I am the rose of Sharon, and the lily of the valleys." Song of Songs 2:1. There are times in life when we can admire the beauty of the Rose of Sharon. The word *Sharon* means "a plain." These are times when life is good. We can see where we are going. Our vision is unobstructed; the weather is sunny and bright. The plain is flat and easy to walk through, and much can be accomplished. During these times, if we don't become so busy, we can stop the activity and appreciate the beauty and fragrance of the Rose of Sharon. What a joy these times are.

But He is also called the "lily of the valleys." The lily grows in the shadow of the valleys. When we are led through the valley, our first impulse is to try to quickly get out. Valleys are dark, narrow, and foreboding. Danger lurks around every corner. We can't see very far and it is difficult to make decisions of where to go and where to turn. But, rather than being anxious, our Shepherd wants us to seek for the beautiful lily that is found only in the valley.

When we change our focus and seek for Him, we will find our Lord in a different light. We can appreciate the special beauty and fragrance of this unique flower as we learn to identify with and partake in the fellowship of the sufferings of Christ. We see Him in a new and very special way. He has been here before. In fact, the Shepherd passed through this valley before on his way to go to the "table set before me." The table is a high plateau that has a rich pasture.

The shepherd has to go through the valley to get to the table so he can prepare it by removing all the poisonous plants in it. Once they are removed and the table is prepared, he returns through the valley of the shadow to get his flock and lead them to these rich pastures. Even though going through the valley is new to us, we need not fear because our Shepherd has been here before and knew what to expect. We must labor to enter into His rest by trusting Him and not fear. The Lily of the Valley is my favorite of all flowers. It only blooms for a week or two at the most, so our journey in the Valley is only for a short time. Make the most of it while you're in it. Your Shepherd is leading you through it.

I'm praying you behold the beauty of the Lord and bask in His presence.

—Mr. N.

Risk Literacy and Savviness

The opposite of risk literacy is risk illiteracy (which is not being able to understand and deal with risk). Choosing to say that cross-cultural work is not really a risk leads one to not evaluate or assess risk. Risk literacy is defined as the basic knowledge required to deal with modern technological society and the ability to understand risk in situations where not all risks are known and calculable. Risk literacy includes the courage to face the risks.[150]

Risk savvy includes risk literacy, but is the ability to handle situations "where not all risks are known and calculable." Risk savvy is being acute, astute, and wise,[151] which is differentiated from risk aversion. Being risk savvy includes being well-informed, but it also "requires courage to face an uncertain future as well as to stand up to authority and ask critical questions." I like how Gerd Gingerenzer describes our response: "We can take the remote control for our emotions back into our hands. Using one's mind without another's guidance entails an inner psychological revolution. Such a revolt makes life more enlightening and less anxiety-ridden."[152]

For cross-cultural risk purposes, risk literacy could include the basic knowledge of Scriptures and the host culture to be able to recognize and respond to the risks in that culture and/or situation. Risk savvy includes the faith development able to give a mature emotional and reasoned response in light of the Holy Spirit's guidance.

Risk-savvy Christian workers are indispensable pillars of the body of Christ, but they require a "basic knowledge of our intuitive psychology as well as an understanding of statistical information,"[153] which includes the guidance of the Holy Spirit. Coming from risk-averse cultures and safety conscious organizations, the illusion of control and certainty greatly hampers risk judgments. Because risks and uncertainties are mathematically different (risks can be calculated while uncertainties cannot), "good rules of thumb and intuition are required."[154]

Cross-Cultural Risk and Uncertainty

Even King Saul wanted certainty (1 Samuel 28). He used divination to try to figure out what he should do, which got him into trouble. We live in a world of uncertainty but increasingly high probabilities of predicted outcomes for Christ-followers. Earlier I discussed the increasing intensity of persecution outlined by Jesus in Matthew 10. We can know with reasonable certainty that we will experience loss when we risk for him and his cause. Again, I am speaking of the short-term uncertainty in cross-cultural risk. Will the thing we fear the most happen? These fears must be dealt with, both practically and spiritually.

Somehow, this always seems to take us by surprise. We seem to think with certainty that God will protect us, and that if we live responsibly that we won't be betrayed to the police, for example. Biblically and practically, however, we have a reasonable amount of certainty of what will happen to us when we go out as sheep among wolves.

When we do the statistical analysis of risk events in our area, we can more easily identify with certainty the ones we are more likely to experience. There are three categories we need to know: We need to have the discernment to know the known risks for our situations, to know what we cannot know, and to realize when we have false certainty.[155]

Uncertainty is scary. Let's face it: going into a high-risk situation for the reasons we do *looks* irresponsible and irrational from a secular risk analysis standpoint. It doesn't meet the normal risk analysis standards described by the top scholarly books on risk out there today.[156]

Risk Assessment Theory

This is just a fancy way risk experts describe the components of risk identification, analysis, and decision-making. There doesn't seem to be one defined "theory" out there, except that risk must be both assessed and managed. Risk management includes risk mitigation (loss aversion) and decision-making. The "bow-tie model" is a well-known model of risk analysis, answering three key questions:[157]

1. What can go wrong? (Danger Identification)

2. What is the likelihood of that happening? (Frequency Analysis)

3. What are the consequences? (Consequence Analysis)

For our purposes here, we've adapted the bow-tie model to cross-cultural risk. The bow-tie model has been used in many other types of risk analysis (business, insurance, etc.), which demonstrates that risk assessment will include looking at all aspects of each risk event. We use this to label and assess each risk, including all possible causes of a potential situation, but also all possible consequences, including the good and damaging ones. This is one of the first steps to risk assessment of the likelihood of a particular risk occurring.

Risk assessment is both qualitative and quantitative. It is proactive, occurring *before* the risk event, not reactive, which is when crisis response teams engage and accident investigation takes place.[158]

Risk Aversion

Some risk theorists say that people can be divided into two groups when it comes to risk: risk tolerant and risk averse.[159] Other researchers on the psychology of risk say people are not consistently predictable, however. What is more often true is that people will fear what society or their peers fear. In the case of risk, we fear what our teammates fear, what the locals fear, and what the media says we should fear. Therefore, we need to clearly address these fears, including the likelihood of probable outcomes in risk with our teams, and hopefully be unified on which risks we will take and which ones we will avoid.

Each team, project, and organization must determine their level of risk tolerance. "How much risk is acceptable for a given return is a critical part of risk analysis."[160] Risk taking and risk aversion change for people as they enter different life stages.[161] From a secular statistical approach, risk averse individuals will be statistically much less likely to engage in the "pour it all out" approach to risk. If the perceived outcome has a high value for the cross-cultural worker and the people he or she works among, then a person is much more likely to take higher levels of risk to reach those outcomes (i.e., "eternal fruit").

In summary, risk aversion and risk tolerance changes over time and over the perceived value of outcome and return on "investment" of risks. Regarding cross-cultural risk, people may engage in an unpredictably risky behavior because of long-term, eternal benefits. This may not fit the current research models of behavior in uncertain high-risk situations.

Risk and Decision-Making

There is extensive research on how people make decisions in situations of uncertainty.[162] How decisions are made and the speed with which they are made is a crucial skill needed by both leaders and those living in risk. What are the processes by which people make decisions about known risks and uncertainties? How do we make decisions, and is there a rational way to make those decisions?

Researchers of secular risk have found that humans generally fail at rational decision-making.[163] We usually think we engage in less risky behavior than other folks, and we engage in "hindsight bias." This term means we look back at the risk event and think we predicted it or could have predicted it. While the secular research is complex and overwhelming, let's take a simple and humble approach.

In Chapter 4 I discussed listening to locals and to leadership in hearing the Holy Spirit's voice to aid our decision-making in risk. Another tool is to keep in mind the following question when it comes time to make decisions: "What does humility in risk-taking decisions look like in the face of extreme intensity and uncertainty?" What influences decision-making in uncertainty or the face of known risks is not as much "formal rational judgmental procedures as preexisting beliefs"[164] about life. How we frame our beliefs regarding the hazard will impact our decision-making.

For example, Neal and I met with a couple who shared that they had been successful according to their project goals and had been met with success in the culture. But they revealed through tears that they were losing their faith in God. They proceeded to share how so many of the locals they had worked with and befriended had betrayed them, slandered them, walked away from following God, and had left them. They were deciding to leave their risk situation, abandon the project, and leave God.

We were some of the last folks they talked to before slamming the door on God. Their beliefs needed reframing so they could make a different (better) decision. They had forgotten the words of Jesus in Matthew:

> If anyone will not receive you or listen to your words, shake off the dust from your feet when you leave that house or town. ... I am sending you out as sheep in the midst of wolves, so be wise as serpents and innocent as doves. ... Brother will deliver brother to death, the father his child, and children will rise against parents and have them put to death, and you will be hated by all for my name's sake (Matthew 10:14, 16, 21–22 ESV).

> At that time, many will fall away and betray one another and hate one another. Because lawlessness is increased, most people's love will grow cold. But the one who endures to the end, he will be saved (Matthew 24:10–13).

In summary, decision-making in cross-cultural risk requires accepting that some level of uncertainty will always be present. It is important to incorporate quantitative measurements when at all possible in decision-making in the cross-cultural risk event. Perfect certainty is not realistic.[165]

Application

1. What are your highest values for entering the high-risk situation? What motivates you the most?

2. Take time to record stories of your own or others' faithfulness in the high-risk situation. What other stories of eternal transformation have you heard? Record these so that you can remember them to strengthen your spirit in the future.

Chapter 8 Summary

1. Cross-cultural risk: Risk taking is depending on Christ's resurrection power and choosing to go or remain in a situation where one is willingly exposing oneself to persecution or suffering, or laying one's life down for the advancement of God's kingdom because of what Christ did on the cross to break the power of death and redeem us from the enemy's kingdom.

2. Risk as event: Evaluate your thinking about risk. Do you tend to think and speak conceptually or situationally?

3. Risk literacy is defined as the basic knowledge required to deal with modern technological society and also the ability to understand risk in situations where not all risks are known and calculable.

4. Risk savvy includes risk literacy; it also includes the basic knowledge of the Scriptures and the host culture to be able to recognize and respond to the risks in that culture and/or situation. It includes the faith development able to give a mature emotional and reasoned response in light of the Holy Spirit's guidance.

5. Risk and uncertainty: There are three categories we need to know. We need to have the discernment to know the known risks for our situation, to know what we cannot know, and to realize when we have false certainty.

6. Risk assessment theory: Five general steps to risk analysis (assessment and management):

   • Learn the environment: study the history and total context of the situation.

   • Identify the risks: what are the internal and external threats?

   • Analyze the risks: what are the frequencies, intensities, and the proximities of the threats?

   • Evaluate and prioritize the risks: arrange the risks by increasing threat levels.

   • Make a decision for next steps toward risk mitigation if remaining or loss aversion if leaving.

7. Risk aversion and loss aversion: Risk aversion and risk tolerance changes over time and perceived value of outcome and return on "investment" of risk. Regarding cross-cultural risk, people may engage in an unpredictably risky behavior because of long-term, eternal benefits.

8. Risk and decision-making: decision-making in cross-cultural risk requires accepting that some level of uncertainty will always be present.

chapter 9

Twelve Common Cross-Cultural Risk Myths

There are many statements made about risk to people in high-risk situations. Oftentimes these statements are made in an attempt to help comfort—either myself or the person speaking. Because there were so many statements repeatedly made about risk, I began to pay attention to the feelings and thoughts arising inside when I heard such statements. Why were these statements so often not comforting? Why did they not "ring true" with my life experience? What misunderstandings did I have about risk and safety? What didn't I understand about God's heart?

I turned to the Bible to research and try to find answers. Below are twelve risk myths, most of which I've personally had spoken to me. As I've interacted with believers from God's global body, I've heard slightly different versions of these, but the ones below touch on the various misunderstandings about risk and God's leading in risk.

Risk Myth #1: You Are Never Safer Than When You Are at the Center of God's Will.

This one was told to us often! In this myth, safety seems to imply freedom from hardship and danger of every kind. It seemed to help the people who said it, perhaps because by saying this myth enough times loudly enough it would make it seem true, and so they wouldn't worry about us. But it wasn't a comfort to me when we were returning to a war zone.

I remember the kind lady at a church we were visiting some years ago asking, "You're safe there, right dear?" I responded, "No ma'am, we're not safe." It was clear when her eyebrows went up that she was expecting a polite yes. I continued,

"It's not safe in Afghanistan. We are under daily threats and friends of ours have been kidnapped, some even killed."

In a world filled with safety standards and insurance coverage, safety regarding risk needs to be defined. The Bible is full of stories of men and women who died horrible deaths, although they were in the center of God's will (Hebrews 11:35–40). Plenty of God's people were killed. Were they not in God's will?

What is the biblical truth about safety? What is a consistent approach to understanding safety in the Bible? If safety means safe from eternal hell, then it can be argued one is safe and in God's will once one has chosen to follow Christ as Lord (John 17:3). However, I don't think that is what is meant when this myth is repeated as encouragement. I think most people mean, "If I am in God's will, then nothing bad will happen to me." The implication seems to be God's will is a place on earth where we are free from normal human tragedies.

It also leads Christ-followers to a dangerous self-understanding when something bad does happen, like a robbery, rape, or kidnapping. They may think they weren't in God's will. If the standard of measuring "success" in following God's will is defined by standards of being safe from all harm, then following Christ into high-risk situations is not only unwise but irresponsible. Very often the West is characterized as a risk-adverse litigious society.

God's will, by definition, means that there is something God is asking of us and from us. He needs us to accomplish his kingdom purposes on the earth, which he primarily does through our obedience. As we obey him, his rule is extended in the earth. Micah 6:8 makes it clear that God is in search of humans,[166] making clear his demands on us: "He has told you, O man, what is good; and what does the LORD require of you but to do justice, to love kindness, and to walk humbly with your God?"

The question now is, how do we live out Micah 6:8 in the risk moment? Even if using the suggested guide in this book, no process or method contains the complete answer. As his witnesses (Isaiah 43:12), we don't enter the cosmic war with evil without getting in harm's way and getting "shot at" ourselves. This myth simply doesn't hold up under fire in cross-cultural service.

Myth corrected: When called by God to unsafe places, we don't let fear paralyze us because God is always with us (Joshua 1:9; Psalm 91; Isaiah 43).

Risk Myth #2: The Blood of the Martyrs Is the Seed of the Church.[167]

This phrase has been repeated throughout the history of the church. "In the minds of some, it is paramount to challenging the very words of Scripture," writes Glenn Penner.[168] Statements like, "Persecution always causes church growth," and "Persecution typically causes the church to be purified and believers to walk more closely with God," are not always historically true (Albania being a modern example).

There is the truth that persecution benefits the church. Church father Tertullian wrote in his book *The Apology* in AD 197 to the Roman governor of his area: "Nor does your cruelty, however exquisite, avail you; it is rather a temptation to us. The oftener we are mown down by you, the more in number we grow; the blood of Christians is seed."[169] According to Glenn Penner, Romans 8:28 and 2 Timothy 3:12 are more accurate reflections of what the Bible has to say about persecution. God works all things together for good, and Paul teaches Timothy that all soldiers may expect persecution. While Penner doesn't deny Tertullian's quote, he suggests instead using a scriptural-based approach to discussing the reasons for and results of church growth. All the New Testament writers discuss the suffering of believers in the context of following Christ.

It's common to see John 12:24 used to demonstrate the fruit resulting from martyrdom. However, what Jesus was teaching here using the idea of a grain of wheat falling to the ground and dying was about his impending death. He had to die to defeat death and Satan and redeem us from the kingdom of darkness. This wasn't a prescriptive requirement for the growth of the church; it was a prescriptive requirement for our salvation. Otherwise, the danger is not to care about persecuted believers if it is believed to be inherently good for the body of Christ and the kingdom of heaven. And that is anathema to our calling as his disciples.

Myth corrected: The blood of Christ is the seed of the church (2 Samuel 4:11; Psalm 72:14; 79:3, 10; Isaiah 26:21; Joel 3:21; Revelation 6:10; 17:6; 18:24).

Risk Myth #3: Escape or Deliverance Is the Priority.

Organizations and individuals who maintain this perspective are characterized as highly risk adverse. This view emphasizing the priority of escape or deliverance is simply not biblical. Escape or deliverance is *not* the priority when facing extreme persecution or martyrdom—faithfulness is (Micah 6:8; Hebrews 11:35–38; Revelation 2:10).

The logical endpoint of those who maintain this perspective is either a crisis of faith or a feeling of failure if escape is not possible or deliverance doesn't happen. Escape or deliverance places emphasis on either our own efforts or a god we try to control. This perspective is really a spiritualized version of Satan's third temptation presented to Jesus:

> And [Satan] took [Jesus] to Jerusalem and set him on the
> pinnacle of the temple and said to him, "If you are the Son of
> God, throw yourself down from here, for it is written
>> 'He will command his angels concerning you, to
>> guard you,' and
>> 'On their hands they will bear you up,
>> lest you strike your foot against a stone.'"
> And Jesus answered him, "It is said, 'You shall not put the
> Lord your God to the test'" (Luke 4:9–12 ESV).

Why should we not put God to the test? Does he not promise throughout Scripture (like in Psalm 91) to deliver us? However, unlike Greek thought, which attempts to find only one "correct" answer, Hebraic thought often holds two opposing spiritual realities in tension: sometimes God delivers us out of evil or danger and sometimes he does not (Hebrews 11:1–39).

Like Job, we learn to say, "Though he slay me, I will hope in him" (Job 13:15 ESV). God is not a genie in a bottle or a puppet we pull with strings. He chooses to rain on the righteous and on the wicked, to deliver us out of or give us the courage to remain under. What is more important than escape or deliverance or remaining is discerning his will, and each risk situation must be considered and prayed through uniquely.

The Bible demonstrates the tension of risk. Proverbs 27:12 (ESV) states, "The prudent sees danger and hides himself, but the simple go on and suffer for it." There are times when we discern and assess danger, and then hide from it. Sometimes escape should be the priority, but it should not characterize our approach to risk.

Myth corrected: The Lord's eyes are on us; he will instruct us in the way we should go (Job 34:21; Psalm 32:8; Proverbs 27:10; Hebrews 11:1–39).

> What is more important than escape or deliverance or remaining is discerning his will, and each risk situation must be considered and prayed through uniquely.

Risk Myth #4: You Must Be Building Up All Kinds of Rewards because of the Risks You Are Taking.

When one is immersed in an atmosphere of martyrdom, areas where the "smell" of trauma and death is a constant companion, or in places of extreme poverty or spiritual darkness, this statement always grates. Yes, there will be rewards, but the whole focus of this statement is off. I am doubtful that many are encouraged in the short-term or find this helpful to increase risk resilience.

Why is this? It is because it does little to help process and refocus the emotions, to help in risk analysis, or assuage the real fear of suffering and potential death here on earth. It's hard to picture rewards in the "heat" of the risk moment. Remaining faithful in the risk moment is the path to eternal reward (Revelation 2–3), but at those moments of walking in faithfulness, the concept of reward somehow seems to be the lowest priority of the numerous confusing cross-cultural risk issues we need to be facing and working through, often in a short time and under great duress. This risk myth requires careful biblical study for clear understanding of eternal reward based on earthly behavior and its application to risk and suffering.

We look forward to the Father's justice and acknowledgment of what we have done in his name. However, when someone says this myth risk statement, the focus is usually on what I will receive, *not* on living faithfully and glorifying the Lord. It smacks of what is described as "quid pro quo" theology.[170] This is the Ancient Near East pagan religious philosophy that means when I give the right thing and the right amount to the idol, I can expect a certain amount in return. In reality, this is an ancient prosperity gospel. I put in a certain amount and can expect certain payment back (we still ask for fertility, money, rain, and food, don't we?).

The motivation to risk is out of balance because the focus is on the reward. People who pursue risk and/or suffering for its own sake (they think, "I need to do the hardest or most dangerous mission activity because that makes me special to God."), are really making risk an idol. This is clear when we see that one antonym to *hypotithemi* (risk) used by Paul in Romans 16:4 is a Greek word meaning to forget or neglect what is important.[171]

In contrast, the important thing is to focus on whatever God wants him or her to do (even if it is to move to safety). Furthermore, whenever the Bible speaks of the reward of the believer, it is always in the context of what the life of the believer looks like, both inside (the heart) and outside (the actions of faith). Jesus makes it clear that we are to lay up treasures in heaven, "for where your treasure is, there your heart will be also" (Matthew 6:21 ESV).

Joseph Ton wrote one of the few books connecting suffering, martyrdom, and reward, and he points out the gravity of Jesus's words, "Behold, I am coming quickly, and My reward is with Me, to render to every man according to what he has done" (Revelation 22:12).[172] The order of these words in the Greek places the emphasis on the suddenness of Christ's appearing, *not* on the reward.

Since Jesus will come in a quick, unexpected way, the time of the coming is always potentially "near."[173] The Hebraic worldview in these verses is on God's *kairos* time, not earthly *chronos* time. It does not mean that he is coming soon (measured by days or years), but his coming will seem sudden. Therefore, there is work to be done, and it is to be done faithfully and urgently—work and faithfulness are always intertwined.

Taking unassessed or ill-advised risks in the name of Christ does not automatically imply that Christ will reward a Christian worker in heaven. Going against the advice of veteran workers and sharing blatant materials and then getting thrown in jail does not automatically make one spiritual, a hero, or a spiritual hero. Sometimes being a hero is measured and seen only by God—and it means stepping down and stepping away in humility out of the risk situation. The measure of "success" on the field is awareness of God's presence, listening to and recognizing his voice (which may come through leadership or the community), and being faithful to obey with joy and no complaining, leaving the results up to God.

> According to the Holy fathers, one who performs saving works simply from fear of hell follows the way of bondage, and he who does the same just to be rewarded with the kingdom of heaven follows the same path of a bargainer with God. The one they call a slave, the other a hireling. But God wants us to come to Him as sons and daughters to their Father; He wants us to behave ourselves honorably from love for Him and zeal for His service; He wants us to find our happiness in uniting ourselves with Him in a saving union of mind and heart.[174]

Myth corrected: We will be rewarded for our faithful, joy-filled obedient endurance to our last breath (Hebrews 10:35).

Risk Myth #5: Just Keep a Positive Mental Attitude and Everything Will Be Okay.

This is based on a worldview known as "positivism." Positivism has been incredibly destructive to the vitality of Christ's body. It is the idea that problems and trials in one's life are the results of a lack of faith. Positivism also results in a lack of planning and attention to Spirit-led stewardship of kingdom resources. It is a passive response in the heat of a battle requiring preparation for spiritual combat. In the risk moment, it is common for "emotion to destroy the self-control that is essential to rational decision-making."[175]

In the case of a high-risk situation, especially those that are prolonged, there are often numerous factors outside of one's control. The reality is that often, despite one's attitude—no matter what it is—everything will not be okay ... depending upon one's definition of "okay." This is close to myth #1.

I often hear Psalm 91 cited as biblical data to "prove" that this is how God will act. This chapter was my grandmother's favorite. Indeed, my own grandparents, father, and aunt were protected from Stalin's Siberian death camps. I love how my father's family personally experienced the reality of this chapter. But how was I to respond in my lifetime when I saw friends and coworkers who were following God with their whole hearts killed in cold blood simply for trying to help people? My friends experienced "evil befalling them." I knew at any time it could happen to me, my children, or my husband. At what point does Psalm 91 apply or not apply to us?

So what is the answer to this myth? What is a more holistic biblical way of responding? It is to realize that positivism is grounded in sand. Hope in the Lord is grounded in the rock-solid reality of a God who sees all, knows all (he is outside of time), and controls all circumstances in my life, no matter what happens. This is why Job could say, "Though he slay me, I will hope in him; yet I will argue my ways to his face" (Job 13:15 ESV), and the psalmist could declare with confidence, "Behold, the eye of the LORD is on those who fear Him, on those who *hope* for His lovingkindness" (Psalm 33:18). Our faith is grounded in a personal God for whom we patiently and expectantly wait to act, and who walks with us through our troubles.

Myth corrected: We can always have hope because our hope is in God, not in our circumstances (Isaiah 52:12; Hosea 2:14–15; Hebrews 6:19–20).

Risk Myth #6: We're Aren't Really Risking.

The idea implied behind this statement is that we don't risk our lives because we have a sure confidence that if we are killed for the cause of Christ, in the end we gain eternity in heaven. The logic is that since what we gain is so much better, then losing a limb or life here on earth is irrelevant and will seem like no risk at all when we are in heaven; therefore, we don't actually risk.

Often cited as a classic text on risk is Jesus's words in Matthew 16:25 (ESV): "For whoever would save his life will lose it, but whoever loses his life for my sake will find it." Jesus was teaching on salvation, although the Greek words here are also used in trials in other New Testament writings. We know that when we follow Christ, we are giving up our choice to live life for the purpose of our own selfish hedonistic pleasure. At the point of salvation, we choose to "lose our life" for his sake. Additionally, at the moment we go into full-time work cross-culturally, especially in high-risk environments, we choose to "loose our life for his sake." It is a general spiritual principle that is true for all believers at all points in life. Why, as a mom in a high-risk environment, was this verse not a comfort to me?

When this verse is used as a prescription for risk and does not seem to account for a thoughtful "counting the cost again" in terms of what I am risking in each moment, it assumes that risk implies that I should "pour it all out" as a principle of risk, and this is not always in line with God's calling in the moment. To say that this is a risk verse and should be applied runs the danger of being out of balance with stewardship and the Jewish and biblical value of the reverence for life.

Jesus emphasized in this passage that our priorities, to "lose our life for his sake," is to ask what Christ wants from us. He is asking us to value what he values, for his sake, and when we feel "loss" he rewards us with the experience of a different type of life than we ever anticipated. The life I found as I persevered through severe risk was peace and joy and greater trust in my gentle heavenly Father. The spiritual principle of "finding life" from Matthew 16:25 is true, and we learned that by experience as we were called to endure risk.

The emphasis on "not really risking" is also contrary to the Jewish value called *Pikuach nefesh*—valuing life is an important biblical principle as well. The idea that physically sacrificing ourselves as a value in risk is completely outside of the viewpoint of the Bible and the rabbinic Judaism of Jesus's day. *Pikuach nefesh* is derived from, "Neither shall you stand by the blood of your neighbor" (Leviticus 19:16).[176] This principle means "saving a life," and it describes the belief that the preservation of human life overrides virtually any other religious consideration. When the life of a person is in danger, almost any negative commandment from the Bible becomes inapplicable.[177]

Jesus's healing on the Sabbath was an example of this. He "saved a life" while at the same time breaking a Sabbath law of "doing work." However, there are three limitations that one cannot violate, even when life is in danger. In these cases, one can only become a martyr if the option is between death and performing acts of idolatry, illegitimate sexual intercourse, or murder.[178]

Biblical risk includes thoughtful stewardship of our time, energies, resources, and very lives. It includes corporate discernment from leadership, those on the "ground," as well as the will of the Holy Spirit in each risk moment. A theology of action and a theology of waiting are always in tension, and the appropriate response is discerned through hearing God's voice. This myth is categorized as a "no-risk" risk perception that is based on faulty overspiritualized thinking. The danger of this view is that it will not lead to holistic risk assessment based on biblical stewardship principles.

What is the logical endpoint of this thinking as followers of Christ who are stewarding kingdom resources in high-risk environments? Choosing to say that cross-cultural work is not a risk leads one not to evaluate or assess risk at all. This is termed "risk illiteracy" (not being able to understand and deal with risk) and is the opposite of risk savvy (being acute, astute, and wise).[179] Ignoring or denying risk altogether is simply not good stewardship.

Myth corrected: In risk we experience short-term losses. Risk is real and to be expected. Biblical values call for it to be evaluated and often mitigated (Proverbs 27:12; Matthew 10; 24).

Risk Myth #7: We've Already Counted the Cost.

An aid worker was shot and killed two blocks from a team leader's home. The excuse the warlord used for killing her was that she was proselytizing local children. The murder caused a long chain of events, not least of which was a major downsizing of the expatriate community in the region.

As part of the risk assessment, the team leader couple met with each unit on the field to assess how staff were doing during the ongoing crisis. They needed to find out who required leaving sooner rather than later. One couple who had no children in the city, when asked how they were doing, responded, "We've already counted the cost." There are several problems with this statement that make it a risk myth.

First, it assumes that counting the cost is a one-time event, which it is not. Second, the addition of this one adverb—"We've *already* counted the cost"— mixed with the tone used made it obvious this couple was not paying attention to the changing security environment and engaging in real-time risk analysis. They were also not demonstrating empathy for their teammates, some of whom were struggling and had children who were also being threatened with kidnapping and murder by the dangerous elements.

Third, the tone used said it all: made with a prideful tone, dripping with sarcasm, and accompanied with a shoulder shrug and eye roll. The lack of humility and a merciful attitude toward struggling teammates meant this couple had sidelined themselves from being of real service to the leader couple and the team when mature courage was most needed. Not only that, but it also implies that everyone defines "counting the cost" in the same way. Many jump right to "dying for Christ" as the "cost." But living for Christ in a high-risk situation is also part of the full definition and requires a great deal of stamina, endurance, and joy.

And last, the statement can be used to imply that risk intervention and loss aversion strategies are not needed. It implies that if we've already counted the cost, then let the chips fall where they may. This attitude and thought pattern is a dangerous, reckless, and irresponsible stewardship analysis. It assumes that everyone is called to steward his or her life in the same way. But not everyone is called to the same level of risk tolerance.

Unfortunately, what this myth statement communicated to us was that they thought the leader couple (who had three young children) and all the other families (over one hundred people) had obviously not counted the cost. Counting the cost is *not* a one-time event. This is because life does not stay stagnant. We are always moving from one stage of life to another. At each stage of life, one has more relationships, physical possessions, and desires to give up for the cause of Christ. These changes require continual reassessment of what—and who—is being risked in the changing risk situations on the field.

The spiritual principle involved here is the constant dying to self. Paul wrote in 2 Corinthians 4:11 (ESV), "For we who live are always being given over to death for Jesus' sake, so that the life of Jesus also may be manifested in our mortal flesh. So death is at work in us, but life in you." And Jesus tells us that "we gain our lives by enduring" (Luke 21:19). Endurance means that we have the ability to persevere in an unpleasant or difficult process or situation without giving way. It implies a constant loss of something to self. Synonyms include toleration, bearing, sufferance, fortitude, forbearance, patience, and resignation.[180]

Jesus taught the need for endurance in the context of increasing threats to our safety and security. In Matthew 10 he taught his followers opposition increases in six stages: "prevented (vs. 14), rejected (vs. 14), detained (vs. 17–19), abused (vs. 17), pursued (vs. 23), and killed (vs. 28)."[181] When the "already" was added to this statement, it revealed a natural lack of motivation to be concerned about the risk because they were much less personally impacted (their children were not in the same danger level). They did not feel the same need for intervention as the numerous young families on the project. Their lack of empathy for others demonstrated they did not have real appreciation for risk analysis from an organizational, macro level. Ongoing (chronic), long-term high risk requires different levels of intervention,[182] and counting the cost is one of the first steps to risk analysis to assess how staff are doing.

Myth corrected: We know ministry will be costly, and so we will continue to count the cost in each stage of life and situation and follow Jesus with joy.

Risk Myth #8: Faith Is Proportional to the Amount of Risk.

In other words, when we risk a lot, that *must* mean we have a lot of faith. When we risk little, then there is little danger to us or our property, and we don't have a lot of faith. The danger of this myth is describing our faith in terms of how much risk we take. This isn't the way Scripture characterizes faithful people.

In risk, there are faithful people, foolish people, and cowardly people. We're all probably some combination of all of those at various times in our lives. To judge someone, and call them fools, cowards, or faithful, presumes that we can see into their hearts. Only God can see into our hearts and judge, but Neal and I have spent a great deal of time discussing the differences between these types of people—what they look like from the perspectives of looking at cross-cultural risk from the outside from the past fifty years of cross-cultural risk.

We want to be wise in assessing our motivations for why we continue to live and travel into high-risk situations with our children. What and who are we being motivated by? Do we still have a clear calling from the Lord? Are we addicted to what people say about us back home? Are we still hearing God's voice and being faithful to follow him?

Some people may risk a lot, foolishly risking and foolishly remaining, with a wrong perspective of what God will do, wrongly quoting Psalm 91 like Satan did to Jesus in the wilderness temptations. What do foolish risk and foolish remaining look like?

Foolish cross-cultural workers take a disproportional risk for the amount of spiritual fruit resulting from using those techniques. These people are driven by adventure, adrenaline, and getting the glory. They are like the stereotype of American cowboys. We've also seen those who are naively foolish yet courageously sharing the good news. Foolishly remaining means you are remaining not to avoid something but to gain something like adventure, acclaim, pats on the back, or the glory that comes from remaining in a high-risk situation.

What about those who cowardly remain? Cowardly remaining is staying in the dangerous situation because you have a greater fear of people criticizing your inability to stay. The negative impact of staying in a dangerous situation is less than the hit your ego will take if you leave. You are staying to avoid the fear and shame you feel if you leave. You are not staying out of boldness, resiliency, endurance, or from a calling from the Lord, but for fear of what others will say about you.

These foolish and cowardly ones do damage to locals, expatriates, themselves, and, far worse, to the honor of our heavenly Father. Because they are remaining based on their own ego and false bravado rather than a clear calling, they will not remain well because they are not utilizing the spiritual resources at our disposal as Christ-followers.

Courageously remaining means you care for your people well; you handle the challenges that God is leading you into in a godly and righteous way. You fight for a spirit of joy rather than a spirit of fear while remaining in the high-risk situation. You realize that being given the opportunity to stay in a high-risk situation is a high calling indeed, a privilege to steward, an honor to be able to identify with our Lord Jesus Christ. Because of this, you are to be commended by our heavenly Father (Romans 16:4; Revelation 2–4).

What about the small remnant who risk little but are incredibly faithful? Some people physically risk little but they have a depth of faith only seen in the spiritual realm. They are prayer warriors of the elite special-forces type, often warriors disguised as little old ladies and frail old men who are faithfully lifting up the saints before the throne, pleading with the Father for mercy and strength, and asking for the saints to endure with joy. These warriors are not praying for God to remove the dangers and the risks, but they are praying for endurance and for God to get the glory through the lives of the saints and future martyrs. To you unnamed prayer warriors, our heavenly Father also says, "Well done. Persevere in prayer. Don't stop until you draw your last breath. Your prayers make a difference" (Daniel 10:13; Ephesians 1:18).

Faith and faithfulness are mentioned in the NASB over four hundred times, and it is almost always in the context of righteous living and holding to the mysteries of faith in Jesus Christ (1 Timothy 3:9). It is a matter of enduring persistence in obedience to the calling of God. The moment of risk is, in essence, a moment of willingness to lay down our lives for the sake of the gospel out of our obedience to what the Holy Spirit is directing you or me to do. Persistence in obeying the commands of Christ in ruthlessly doing righteousness in my heart and actions over many years when the risk is low leads to deep faith.

Theologian Skip Moen discusses one parable Jesus used to describe faith (Luke 11:5–8):

> In this passage, the Greek word translated "persistence" is *anaideia*. "Probably the Hebrew word that best translates the Greek term *anaideia* is a form of the word *chutzpah*. ... In current English, perhaps 'raw nerve' would be a better definition. 'Chutzpah' means 'brazen tenacity' or 'bold perseverance.' 'Relentless diligence' or even 'impudence' is very near the meaning. ... The conclusion is almost inescapable. Does Jesus define faith as determined nerve?" Young is right. Our view of faith is anemic, cognitive, antiseptic verbal vomit. Yeshua's view of faith is dogged persistence and unrelenting determination.[183]

How doggedly persistent and unrelentingly determined are we to pursue God's glory by consistently (and faithfully) acting in righteousness in all that we do, whether risky or not?

Myth corrected: Faith is persistently obeying Christ, whatever the risk.

Risk Myth #9: If Something Bad Happens, It's because I Didn't Pray, Work, and Prepare Enough. It's My Responsibility to Be Faithful and Engage with God.

This myth states that when something bad happens, it is a consequence of my own actions or lack of actions. It's the idea that if you were walking down the street and got mugged, you weren't aware enough to see the mugger coming.

Some years ago in a corner of Asia, an international church service was in the middle of their Sunday morning meeting when extremists attacked with hand grenades. Five were killed and many were injured. Hard to believe, but a veteran worker of over thirty years responded by telling Neal and me, "Well, we weren't praying enough."

Our older colleague believed that risk was mitigated through prayer. God didn't say, "Pray for the garden." He "took the man and put him in the garden of Eden to work it and keep it" (Genesis 2:19 ESV). Work was required before bad things happened on earth, and work is still required after sin entered the cosmos (Genesis 3:16–19). Work leads us back to how we were intended to live in the garden of Eden.

The problem with this myth is that it avoids a theology of work. Sometimes prayer is more than a conversation. In a relationship with God, we do things *with* him, not just talking at him or asking him for things like safety. We do work with him just as we would with another friend.

In terms of risk, which is an event we are to steward, we are to do the work of responsible stewardship that includes prayer, but does not primarily constitute prayer. Risk mitigation takes time and energy and is right and responsible stewardship. This myth also betrays an unbiblical view of evil. What is needed is to recognize that evil is allowed to happen until it is finally vanquished.

Myth corrected: I pray and I work. Even when bad things happen, I live with the unbreakable conviction that Christ will bring justice with his imminent return.

Risk Myth #10: Freedom Means Security.

This one stems out of my own American cultural experience. When we lived in Afghanistan under the Taliban, we did not feel "free"; therefore, we did not feel secure. In actuality, however, we were protected by the Taliban government. Once Kabul was liberated from the Taliban, we felt free and therefore safe, but we were in the most personal danger we'd ever been in our lives and didn't know it.

If security is a myth in general, then what is the basis of our security? The honest truth about security from a biblical perspective is that when we go out as lambs among wolves, we can be fairly certain that there is a high probability that we will be in unsafe situations and experience loss. But are we to live in fear, not trusting anyone? That is not a helpful reaction. It's helpful to realize that in risk situations, security is not a feeling. We are called to be wise as serpents and as peaceful as doves, living each day in step with God's Spirit (Matthew 10:16).

What may be the most helpful to address this myth is a look through key prayers recorded in Scripture by God's saints when they were in the middle of or just surviving dangerous situations. Take a look at Hannah's prayer, Deborah's prayer, the song of Miriam, the prayer by Elizabeth, Mary, Daniel, Nebuchadnezzar, Stephen's last sermon, or Jesus's last prayer in John 17, and see what they based their security on. This will lead to true freedom, even when we are risking our lives in dangerous places.

Myth corrected: Security is not a feeling; my security is rooted in Hebrews 11–12.

Risk Myth #11: Risking Is Spiritual Service; All This Practical Talk and Assessment Is Unnecessary.

In other words, this myth says practical isn't spiritual. Some parts of the global church *do* have an acute awareness of spiritual warfare; they have a worldview that recognizes the spiritual world much more than our Western worldview does. By contrast, Christ-followers from a rationalistic Western worldview often overemphasize the practical aspects of risk assessment and management while ignoring the spiritual aspects. We Westerners like to categorize and separate. When the global church integrates the practical *and* spiritual aspects of risk, it greater glorifies God and is more reflective of God's design.

I've struggled to write this one. As a child of Western empirical thinking, I've been taught that solutions are arrived at through sequential, deductive thought.

It's common to view this issue as an either-or, meaning that either one way is right or the other way is right, but they can't both be right. Either spiritual is right or practical is right. The truth is that we like to know what's "right" and not have to live in tension. But this is nothing other than spiritual laziness and short-sighted thinking.

The issue of how we live and view the world is really a both-and. In other words, integrated living sees even our personal daily habits as spiritual acts glorifying God, especially in risk. It means that we work out the tension between the two every day. Why is this? When we choose to do the right thing in risk, even if it means getting enough sleep instead of tossing and turning in anxiety or disciplining ourselves to eat food despite the fear in our stomachs, we glorify God.

How do we develop a balanced approach to the practical *and* spiritual aspects of a theology of risk? Practical coping mechanisms are necessary. Remember, God had Elijah sleep and eat when he was exhausted and worried about his life—the birds brought him food by the brook. So many times as an exhausted young mom in Afghanistan having to cook everything from scratch, I wished for those birds.

Sleeping is sometimes one of the most spiritually practical things we can do in high-risk situations. Sometimes the best pastoral advice I can give people is to catch up on sleep. Remember, Jesus slept through the storm too. We'll see the world much more calmly if we get enough sleep, because high-risk situations are *exhausting*.

Taking a Sabbath day is also crucial. God made our body rhythms to need one day of rest a week. We learn in Genesis that God created the Sabbath and called it good. In Hebrews 4:1 (NIV), we learn that entering the Sabbath rest is still part of God's desire for us: "Therefore, since the promise of entering his rest still stands, let us be careful that none of you be found to have fallen short of it." It takes personal self-discipline to protect one day a week and say no to requests for ministry help, socialization, or hospitality, which are not restful on that day. Just like Jesus, we feel the pressure of the needs of the people all around us. But just like him, we need to regularly find periods of rest and solitude to renew our souls.

Keep a list of coping strategies to help you endure and persevere in risk. The list ideally will be *both* practical and spiritual. Living daily in risk for years on end,

I would regularly analyze what I needed in that moment. Do I need to eat, sleep, or have a cup of coffee with a girlfriend and process a difficult cultural day? Do I need to spend time worshiping the Lord and talking with him?

It has become commonplace for us to observe cross-cultural workers escape through entertainment while not successfully renewing their souls. For many, it has become a regular practice to equate escaping through movies and video games as renewing both the mind and the heart. Neal and I used to send young families on vacation, giving them an extra week away, but they'd come back and be exhausted within a few days of their return. They had escaped for a while but not renewed their souls.

Learn what it takes for you to be renewed in soul, for you to strengthen yourself in the Lord. Be cautious in the use of technology and the Internet as a coping mechanism. It may be a supportive means of help for short periods of time just to relax, but not the main tool of soul renewal.

Myth corrected: Even in the midst of the spiritual service and sacrifice of risk, Christ invites me to take practical steps to care for myself, my family, and my colleagues, and to enter into his rest.

Risk Myth #12: Suffering for Christ While Fulfilling My Cross-Cultural Calling Always Glorifies God.

Experiencing suffering or persecution because we are remaining in a risk situation surely looks good when viewed from outside the situation. We look heroic, courageous, and even godly to others. But God knows the reality of what is happening deep within our hearts. There are several key areas to examine closely.

You may say that you don't have this risk myth in mind when going into risk; however, this myth may be the one you fall back on in hindsight to rationalize the negative outcome. It is most commonly used as a platitude to reconcile suffering experienced in risk.

When I go into a risk situation, it would be a myth to go in with the intention to suffer. It would also be unrighteous to go in and think that because I'm risking I'm probably suffering and thus glorifying God, while at the same time my relationships are all suffering due to my sinful choices.

What's happening in my internal life? Am I filled with forgiveness toward my teammates? Am I critical of leadership? Do I assume the worst of others instead of the best (Philippians 2)? What's happening in my relational life? How am I treating my family or housemates? How am I responding to locals or the culture when I get angry? How do I handle my frustration toward a culture I don't really like sometimes? Does culture stress cause me to take my anger out on those closest to me?

How am I preparing for possible death? What does dying well even look like? While a martyr's death *is* the highest sacrifice (John 15:13), foolishly risking and dying because of ignoring God's voice or with broken relationships does *not* bring God the greatest glory. Dying well means we lived the last twenty-four hours internally and relationally as if they were our last. By living habitually in this way, we will be ready for death when it comes.

Myth corrected: Living faithfully for Christ in whatever situation I am in always glorifies God.

Application

1. Which myth do you recognize is part of your unspoken expectation of risk on the field?

2. What aspect of God's character does that unspoken expectation reveal you believe about him?

3. Which aspects of those you listed above are true of God and which are not?

Chapter 9 Summary

1. *Myth #1:* You are never safer than when you are at the center of God's will. Correction: When called by God to unsafe places, we don't let fear paralyze us because God is always with us (Deuteronomy 6:5; Joshua 1:9; Psalm 91; Isaiah 43; Luke 10:27; Matthew 22:37).

2. *Myth #2:* The blood of the martyrs is the seed of the church. Correction: The blood of Christ is the seed of the church (2 Samuel 4:11; Psalm 72:14; 79:3, 10; Isaiah 26:21; Joel 3:21; Revelation 6:10; 17:6; 18:24). The seed of the church is God's Spirit working through his people to bring others to him (Mark 1:8; John 1:33–34; Acts 1:4–5).

3. *Myth #3:* Escape or deliverance is the priority. Correction: The Lord's eyes are on us; he will instruct us in the way we should go (Job 34:21; Psalm 32:8; Proverbs 27:10; Hebrews 11:1–39).

4. *Myth #4:* You must be building up all kinds of reward because of the risks you are taking. Correction: We will be rewarded for our faithful, joy-filled obedient endurance to our last breath (Matthew 24:13; Hebrews 10:35).

5. *Myth #5:* Just keep a positive mental attitude and everything will be okay. Correction: We can always have hope because our hope is in God, not in our circumstances (Isaiah 52:12; Hosea 2:14–15; Hebrews 6:19–20).

6. *Myth #6:* We're not really risking. Correction: In risk we experience short-term losses. Risk is real and to be expected. Biblical values call for it to be evaluated and often mitigated (Proverbs 27:12; Matthew 10; 24).

7. *Myth #7:* We've already counted the cost. Correction: We know ministry will be costly, and so we will continue to count the cost in each stage of life and situation, following Jesus with joy.

8. *Myth #8:* Faith is proportional to the amount of risk. Correction: Faith is persistently obeying Christ, whatever the risk.

9. *Myth #9:* If something bad happens, it's because I didn't pray, work, or prepare enough. It's my responsibility to be faithful and engage with God. Correction: I will pray and I will work. Even when bad things happen, I live with the unbreakable conviction that Christ will bring justice with his imminent return.

10. *Myth #10:* Freedom means security. Correction: Security is not a feeling; my security is rooted in Hebrews 11–12.

11. *Myth #11:* Risking is spiritual service; all of this practical stuff is unnecessary. Correction: Even in the midst of the spiritual service and sacrifice of risk, Christ invites me to take practical steps to care for myself, my family, and my colleagues, and to enter into his rest.

12. *Myth #12:* Suffering for Christ while fulfilling my cross-cultural calling always glorifies God. Correction: Living faithfully for Christ in whatever situation I am in always glorifies God.

A free PDF download of Chapter 9 summary of risk myths and their corrections is available at http://better-than-gold-faith.blogspot.com.

chapter 10

Don't Forget Emotions

If you do not account for your emotions in risk, then your risk and danger assessment will be faulty. The last thirty-five years of research on emotions and risk consistently shows this to be true. Emotions *must* be paid attention to in risk. Glynis Breakwell wrote, "Risk analysis of the perceived threats and the resulting decision-making that fails to consider the emotion attached to a threat or the emotional state of the individual is inevitably flawed."[184] Increasingly, research says that holistic risk analysis must include two categories: the rational-logical danger analysis and the "experiential-emotional" analysis.

Both our minds and our emotions are intimately interrelated. The research also reveals that neither one stands alone; neither one operates without the other, even when we think we are being totally logical.[185] Researchers on risk will even argue that "intuitive emotional reactions are the predominant method by which human beings evaluate risk."[186] Why is this? Studies show that our emotions are attached either to the perceived hazard or to our reaction to the perceived hazard, and the emotions attached to both of these vary in intensity. Our emotions play a role, even when we don't realize it.[187]

We lower our risk resiliency when we ignore our emotions and the accompanying thought patterns. God uses our emotions to guide us. An integrated holistic person values emotions because God values emotions too. Those who say that our emotions are unimportant in evaluating risk are far less integrated when approaching risk and will not be aware of the emotional impact on their teams. Leaders who say, "I'm not an emotional person; I don't need them and don't speak in those terms," often don't pay attention to the "emotional temperature" of the people they are leading.

We've seen one team in a very high-risk situation totally implode over the leader's neglect of emotions. We've also seen another team in a medium-risk

> We lower our risk resiliency when we ignore our emotions and the accompanying thought patterns.

situation lose half of their staff. A significant factor in these two teams was the leader's neglect of staff and their lack of awareness of their emotional well-being. Losing a team for these reasons is poor stewardship.

Jesus taught, "The good man out of the good treasure of his heart brings forth what is good, and the evil man out of the evil treasure brings forth what is evil; for his mouth speaks from that which fills his heart" (Luke 6:45). What came out of my mouth during numerous high-risk situations we faced was not always pretty; I knew I wasn't handling the ongoing risk situations well when I yelled at my children. Some ugly sin or deep fear was influencing my soul, and life wasn't good for everyone in my path when I let sin govern my responses and speech.

Integration of Emotions, Spirituality, and Mind

We often experience strong emotions and reinforced thinking about certain convictions during risk. At the same time, there may be confusion about *what* to think and *what* to feel. In general, Neal and I experience cross-cultural workers often being quite confused and dismayed about what they think they "should" think and feel and what is their actual reality. Learning to integrate our thinking, emotions, and spirituality leads to mature faith. Curt Thompson writes, "Integrating our understanding of the mind and behavioral development, along with our spirituality, is now becoming a well-accepted, necessary paradigm for engaging our interpersonal and intercultural problems."[188]

How can we handle our emotions and become better aware of them when facing danger? How do our emotions impact our willingness to face risk and stay in risk? What is an appropriate proper attitude about emotions when facing danger? And how might the Holy Spirit be using our emotions to go into or remain in the risk situation? These are all questions we need to acknowledge and wrestle with, whether we are leading a team or not.

Integrating Emotions and Decision-Making

There are two main areas of emotions in risk that are of primary importance: The first is understanding how emotions impact our perceptions, responses, and decision-making in risk; the second has to do with discerning how God works through our emotions. The highlights here integrate both the secular findings on emotions and risk and also how God may be desiring to speak to us through our emotions, specifically in risk situations.

Determine the Sources of Our Emotions

When we are thinking about our emotions in the risk situation, it's important to differentiate between the emotion we feel attached to a perceived risk and emotions of our inner life because we are in a risk situation.[189] These are two different emotional "events" occurring at the same time, and there are two very different reasons for these emotions. It would be difficult to *not* be affected emotionally by the perceived risk and decisions we may need to make in the future.

Handling Our Emotions When Facing Danger

There are a couple of key steps to becoming of aware and handling our emotions in facing danger. The first is "Name It to Tame It."[190] What Curt Thompson means by this phrase is that when we identify the emotion, problem, or obstacle we are facing by naming it, somehow the power it has over us diminishes. As we correctly identify what is going on, we are empowered then to respond appropriately.

When we name something, a spiritual principle is enacted. We begin to see how small the emotion and behavior are before the throne of God, and so we don't have to passively let our emotions control our responses. When we name what we are feeling, we are "owning the feeling," and then we are more easily able to give it to Christ.[191]

Researchers have categorized hundreds of emotions into eight major categories.[192] I was surprised when I saw a chart that took the eight categories below and organized a couple more hundred "nuances" of these emotions by category. For people like me who need a lot more time to figure out what we are feeling, charts of emotions are truly a practical help. Here are the eight categories:

- Anger: fury, hostility, irritability, annoyance

- Sadness: grief, self-pity, despair, dejection, loneliness

- Fear: anxiety, edginess, nervousness, fright, terror, apprehension

- Enjoyment: joy, relief, contentment, delight, thrill, euphoria, ecstasy

- Love: acceptance, trust, devotion, adoration

- Surprise: shock, amazement, wonder

- Disgust: contempt, scorn, aversion, distaste, revulsion

- Shame: guilt, remorse, humiliation, embarrassment, chagrin

Emotions as Information

Our emotions give us information. We need to be able to acknowledge and identify the emotions we are feeling at any given time because they are indications of something going on under the surface. Some people come from families or backgrounds that don't talk about emotions and don't regularly think about them.[193] It may be that the idea that emotions are not only a gift from God but are part of what it means to be made in the image of God is something you haven't before considered. Not only does God feel, but as beings made in the image of God our feelings are reflective of his feelings, even though ours are tainted with sin.

Acknowledging emotion is an integral part of working through risk. We can grow in the skill of identifying and naming the emotions we feel in increasingly shorter time frames. What used to take me a couple of days to figure out what I was feeling now takes me much less time.

Disproportionate Response

It is not uncommon to experience a disproportionate response to some event or problem while in risk. A disproportionate response looks like going into rage over a small trifle, like dirty dishes in the sink; it tells us to pay attention to our inner life before we do more damage to others. "The increased stress can magnify emotional responses and make it more difficult to respond from values and beliefs, rather than primarily from those emotions."[194] Humility and an apology that acknowledges the other person's feelings goes a long way in healing the damage from our disproportional response.

Self-control and self-awareness help us to not act out disproportionately when our perception and judgment are skewed. Proportional responses are what spiritual vitality looks like.[195] To restate this positively, responding proportionately to risk events indicates emotional maturity, a healthy stress-balance management, and a daily habit of cultivating appropriate perspective (not overspiritualized perspective).

Normalize the Feeling

To normalize the feeling means to normalize an experience that makes most sufferers feel abnormal and unspiritual. There was one woman who wondered aloud to me what was wrong with her because she could not stop crying all of the time. I asked her how "normal" would it be for her to be stoic, considering how many friends had been murdered in the expatriate community recently. Her crying was indeed normal and needed to be affirmed as an expected human response. In fact, Jesus cried when his friend Lazarus died. He modeled a God who cries.

Sometimes in risk there are so many feelings that it's helpful to try to look at our situations from the perspective of someone back home. What would they most likely feel about what we are going through? Imagining the perspective from folks at home may be one way to guide us in figuring out normal emotional responses to some of the severe risks we face cross-culturally.

How Our Emotions Impact Our Decision-Making in Risk

Research shows that how we are affected in risk directly impacts our risk perceptions, judgments, and decision-making.[196] It also shows that "in a wide range of contexts the emotional reaction at the moment is more influential in determining choice than the rational evaluation of the options that may have been conducted beforehand."[197] When we pay attention to our emotional state, our judgments are influenced by them. Our focus is different. This gives more options—for we can choose which we will be more influenced by—to our cognitive or emotional response to the risk.[198]

Additionally, secular studies show that emotions influence decision-making in four different ways: emotions give information, they act as a spotlight, they act as a motivator, and they act as common currency.[199] That is to say that emotions give us information about our feelings about the perceived risk; emotions as a spotlight focus our attention on the relevant aspects of a decision needing to be made; emotions as a motivator enable us to make the decision under time pressure; and finally, emotions as common currency "generate commitment concerning morally and socially significant decisions."[200] This last one is experienced when we make decisions in risk and then explain our decision and experience of risk to others.

Let's use a story I've already shared to demonstrate this. In the Preface, I related a risk story Luke and I experienced in 2004. In this story, I relayed the fact that a mob had surrounded our van. Here are the four ways that emotions influenced my decision-making.

Emotion as Information

The emotion I have attached to mob behavior is a dread risk, meaning deep fear. This dread risk emotion is attached to a story my husband told me earlier in our marriage. When he was living in Albania as a single person, he saw a mob of people tear down a brick wall with their bare hands. His story instilled in me a deep fear of mobs.

In hindsight, I'm not sure the van was being mobbed. The rational-logical part of me remembers it was probably more like people pounding on the back right panel and probably a few other places, possibly with a wooden club, so it sounded loud and scary and all around me. There seemed to be people surrounding the van. I don't know how many people were around the van and if they were paying attention to my van or not. But at that moment, it felt and looked like a mob, and I could see there was no way to protect Luke from physical harm or kidnapping in the location I was in. This dramatically elevated my fear level to probably the most intense fear I've ever felt.

Emotion as a Spotlight

I next relayed in the story that the police officer began pulling my driver out of the van and punching him. The fear I had attached to this was that if the driver was gone, how was I to get out of the situation? I could see the only way out was to drive, and when it comes to the "flight or fight" response and my children are involved, I will always fight. The seat wall was high, and with my long skirt, *chapan*, and veil, how could I climb over it and get in the driver's seat? I wasn't about to open the van door.

Emotion as a Motivator

My fear and adrenaline pushed my decision-making to the next step: I needed to get the police to back down and have my driver start driving once again. So I let my veil fall so he could see my light skin and hair color, called my husband on my cell phone so there was a "listening witness," flashed my American passport, and started screaming in both Dari and English, hoping that being a Westerner would make a difference.

Emotion as Common Currency

This is the story as I recall experiencing it. I told it with my interpretation of the risk situation I found myself in from an emotional standpoint, and research reveals this is entirely valid and common.[201] It was extremely frightening. It ripped away a false belief and a core question I had of God that even now is too painful to relate. It took me ten years before I could publically tell this story without completely breaking down and sobbing. Even as I write, eleven years after I experienced this event, I can still feel the pit of fear in my stomach as I relive the experience. The common currency of the fear of being unable to protect our children is a common one that parents often feel.

Summary of the Steps

Despite what we think, our emotions affect risk. Decisions we think we are making logically are often made affected by our emotions. Accepting this reality will help us move to the next step.

It is important that we identify and acknowledge our emotions. How do we feel about the perceived risk and outcome? What is happening in our inner lives with God? Our emotions impact our decision-making, which helps us to recognize what is happening so we can see what our emotions are actually doing. We can see how God may be leading through our emotions, find constructive ways to handle strong emotions, understand how our emotions affect our decision-making in risk, and incorporate this into the risk analysis accordingly.

If we feel that we are continuing to depend upon God, giving him our fears on a minute-by-minute basis in the risk event, but we still lack peace, perhaps God is leading us to make a change in our direction. This lack of peace may also be described as a lack of energy when looking at the situation, and also an internal physical feeling of not being well. The emotions can be expressed through the physical, which could be a sign of God's leading to a different direction.

Another way God leads through emotions is that he leads us to something that we "know" is right. But this knowing, while also described as discernment from the Spirit of God, also feels like health in our flesh—a calmness, rightness. There is peace, even if it means staying in a risky, frightening situation. I also discussed using the guide of three key questions from 1 Corinthians 13: Are my feelings, thought patterns, and actions increasing my faith in God and people? Do I have greater hope in the Lord or greater doubt in his justice and mercy? Do I love myself, God, and others better in this situation?

And how about our core questions? These are often asked out of strong emotions. They feel destabilizing to us because they go against long-held beliefs and expectations. Emotionally, it is uncomfortable to ask these questions. Sometimes the core questions we are asking at the deepest levels are directly related to what God is asking us to do. For example, we ask, "Can I trust you?" At the same time, he is asking us, "Will you trust me?" He is asking us to trust him by making the step he is asking us to take, whether standing firm, moving forward, or retreating.

Learning to sort through our inner lives in the risk moment will be easier if we can talk with wise and mature Christ-followers who won't be shocked by what comes out of our mouths and the stress we are under in risk.

A Little Fear Won't Harm You

When we feel numb emotionally or mentally, we are in the gravest danger of burnout or making a poor decision in risk. Psychologists call this "psychic numbing."[202] Pastoral-care workers call it burnout; on the field, we called it compassion fatigue.

In relation to risk, this numbing happens when we have such strong emotional reactions for so long, so intensely and repeatedly, that we begin to feel that the problems and risks we face are too big to change, and so we begin to live in denial. It's almost as if we become unwilling to see or hear the growth of the hazard and its potential impact.[203] One idiom describing this phenomenon is like a frog in a kettle of water that is heated up. The frog doesn't feel the water slowly heating up because it gets used to the increasing heat. When the water nears the boiling point, it is too late for the frog to jump out ... it is already dead.

Numbness is a major warning signal. This is the time when we probably need to leave the risk situation, take a break, possibly get some debriefing or counseling, and have time for soul renewal. Feeling the emotion of fear lets us know that we are still alive, still feeling, and still aware of our surroundings and not overwhelmed by them. A little fear is not a bad thing in risk. In fact, it is a God-given emotion to warn us of impending danger or threat. Humans feel fear and anxiety emotionally and physically. In order to be more aware of our emotions, we need to set aside some time for reflection. It's too easy to stay busy and ignore our emotions.

Identify where you feel fear and stress in your body. Do you get headaches or back aches at specific times? How are your breathing and sleeping? We all physically feel fear and anxiety differently. How do your children demonstrate their fear? Do you know?

The Bible repeatedly teaches us not to walk in fear. How am I supposed to "not fear" when I feel fear? Very often, the "don't fear" phrases in the Bible are verbs, which means, "Don't turn into wax. Don't remain passively in fear."[204]

When I didn't let my fears overwhelm me, when I didn't ignore, deny, or repress my fear but entered into it, experienced it fully, and allowed my fears to drive me to God, I won the battle over fear ... for that minute. When I kept doing this, I was able to continually work through my fears. It didn't mean I didn't do risk mitigation and planning for the future, but I wasn't constantly worried about the future. I could actually live in the moment. Doing this repeatedly led to emotional and spiritual resiliency. There is no shortcut to lived experience in walking with God.

As Christ-followers, we are also not to be paralyzed by our fears. When we feel the powerlessness from overwhelming fear, we are unable to listen to God speaking to us. So we choose not to feed and be fed by fear. Sometimes, God calls us to do things that are genuinely frightening. In obedience to that calling, we keep giving our fears and anxieties to God, even when we need to do it minute by minute. Then we are enabled by his Spirit to act boldly, trusting in God.[205]

The Downside of Fear

It would seem that logically, when we feel fear, we act out of self-protective measures. But secular research reveals that fear "appears to dampen efforts at risk minimization."[206] Fearful people make pessimistic judgments about a hazard, whereas angry people make more optimistic judgments.[207] Why is this? Charlie Schaefer addressed this with me in personal correspondence:

> Anger is considered by psychologists to be a secondary emotion that is our body's way of responding to a vulnerable emotion (fear, hurt, shame, guilt). It revs up our engines to a higher speed (adrenaline is secreted, pupils dilate, breathe faster with more oxygen in the system, etc.) so that we are empowered to act in response to the threat. That's why we become more optimistic about a risk analysis—we're all charged up, feeling more powerful, and ready to act. However, our bodies don't do well if we sustain that anger for long. It is corrosive internally.[208]

Paying attention to the degree of fear experienced will be important in determining responses to hazards.[209] Fear causes us to think the risks are much higher; whereas anger causes us to perceive the risks are lower.[210]

What Does Acting in Fear Look Like?[211]

We are not objective when we are afraid. Instead, we think up foolish ideas, either overreacting or underreacting to the threat level. We draw incorrect conclusions of people's motives because we don't take the time to ask clarifying questions, and those decisions result in poor judgments. We don't take care of the daily tasks; we are too worried about the future. In fear, people feel more helpless and out of control, so they don't mitigate risk. Thus, assessing how intense our fear is will be helpful to try to work out a proper response to the threat level and thus act accordingly.

For leaders, it's important to note that when we are angry about a threat situation, we are actually statistically more likely to be optimistic about our risk analysis of the threats. This will impact our decision-making and can create a more dangerous situation than is actual reality.[212]

Even when we feel fear, what does it look like in risk to act out of our faith and hope? In the quietness of our hearts or with trusted, close friends with whom we can be open in conversation and prayer, we can discern what is causing our fears. What situations, thought patterns, or lies are causing us to spiral into overwhelming fear? We acknowledge the physical aspects to our fear situation: Am I hungry, angry, lonely, or tired (HALT)? Will I feel less fearful if I deal with the physical issues first?

The truth is that we name these situations, lies, or thought tendencies, and verbally acknowledge them and take them captive to Christ. Then we discern what action is appropriate to our situation at that time. Do we need to eat, talk with a friend, sleep, pray, or worship God? We sleep; we don't stay awake at night, worrying about threats outside of our control. Not only that, but we keep the uncertainty and confusion in perspective of our understanding of God's sovereignty—we are not in control, but God is.

We keep doing this as often as it takes to remain faithful and attune to the Spirit, *not* our fears. Then in risk, especially when we are in the long risk event for days, weeks, or months on end, we grow in courage, resiliency, and mature, courageous faith.

Worry: A Less Intense Form of Fear

Worry for our teams, families, and selves can be mitigated by equipping field-based workers to deal with potential outcomes of risks. For example, one of my biggest fears was being kidnapped and raped. After going through rigorous security training and being given the statistical probabilities of being raped based on the past twenty years of kidnapping expatriates in similar situations,[213] my fears were greatly relieved. I was equipped in how to behave in a way to minimize my risk of being raped, which increased my overall resiliency in the ongoing high-risk situation we were in. Potential rape was no longer on my radar (as much).

My worry was diminished when Neal and I planned for the worst-case scenarios. I had trust, knowing how he would be handling himself in a kidnapping, and he knew what I would do as well. Leaders will benefit from increased team unity and loyalty by knowing that the "degree to which emotions play a role is intimately connected to the availability of information in risk."[214] My worries diminished when leadership told our team their plan for dealing with crises. They revealed who they would be consulting with and what the intentions of their hearts were in caring for us in that situation. Knowing that planning never goes the way as anticipated before the crisis, hearing their general plan had a calming effect in my soul.

Fear and Dread Risks

What causes the greatest fear in you? Dread is an emotion—if we dread something, it will impact our risk perception.[215] We experience the reality of dread emotionally, spiritually, and physically. I referred to the spiritual tactic of our enemy to try to frighten us before anything bad has happened to us. Not only is this spiritual, but it's the reality of the intentions of terrorists. Gerd Gingerenzer wrote in *Risk Savvy*, "Al-Qaeda spent $500,000 on the 9/11 terrorist event. America, in the incident and aftermath, lost more than $500 billion, meaning that every dollar of Al-Qaeda defeated a million dollars."[216]

Gingerenzer goes on to write that terrorists exploit our brain psychology through what are called "dread risks." These are "low probability events in which many people are suddenly killed, triggering an unconscious psychological principle: If many people die at one point in time, react with fear and avoid that situation."[217] In high-risk situations, resisting terrorist manipulation results in greater resiliency and strategic opportunities often result. Let's decide right now, as faith-based cross-cultural workers, that we will not be manipulated by terrorists in the face of our calling from God.

There were some risks Neal and I never took personally, and to this day strong emotions arise when we think about threats we avoided. Some of our most intense and deepest fears resulted in us making decisions that may have seemed odd to others, even when they took those risks and we supported them in their choices. Some of this is related to the pain-bearing that leaders carry, but part of it is related to our emotional boundaries of what we felt we could endure long-term.

However, the decisions we made enabled us as a couple to handle other grave risks we faced as a family and as leaders responsible for a large team and project in a high-risk situation. Knowing these boundaries for ourselves, and being able to handle the occasional odd look, or even having others think we lacked courage, was okay with us. There were some risks we could not step into and still thrive in Afghanistan.

Acute Chronic Fear and Resilience

When living long-term in a high-risk situation like we did in Afghanistan, a number of consequences resulted. Living long-term at a heightened level of fear and concern for security impacted us physically, mentally, emotionally, and spiritually. Our physical health began to show signs of breaking down. There was the continual weight of chronic concern of safety for our family in a high-risk environment. Husbands have to take this into consideration when going into such places with their families. We bore the weight for years of the security of our teammates and the large number of children on our team and their safety.

Mentally, I knew I was most likely on the scale of mild clinical depression, and so were others in my community. My depression was normal situational depression due to the ongoing daily threats—it would lift when we left. High-risk situations are mentally tough places to be in. Clinical research has shown that depression often does result from long-term situations of distress, which in our case (as an international community) was the continual significant threats against all of us—locals and expatriates alike.[218]

We learned emotional resilience. We laughed together. We enjoyed unique humor to our situation (there were no Walmarts but we had a "Target" on every corner) and we had lots of fun times with friends. We appreciated so many little things in life: the smell of fresh bread or cookies baking; the laughter of our children; family dinners by candlelight (the electricity was often out); being alive; having enough food to eat; and electricity. The heightened chronic fear situation caused our senses to be alive.

Spiritually, it was a time like no other—I wouldn't trade it for the world. Really. We experienced the reality of God's presence. Our fears, well ... they were still there, but it was like the chorus of his peace and presence drowned out the sound of "lions roaring." We got front-row seats to what he was doing not only in our lives but in the lives of those around us: national friends had visions that were given by the Father, miraculous healings took place, water was supernaturally turned from salty to sweet, and we experienced the unity of the Spirit in our community.

A Pastoral Response

Since 1980, secular researchers have been studying emotions and risk. Additionally, Christian scholars such as Dr. Len Cerny and Dr. David Smith have examined cross-cultural adjustment and developed the following stress mapping scales on the CernySmith Assessment (CSA): well-being (emotional), focus (cognitive perceptual), and past stresses (present impact), along with a situational crisis (perceived safety) and spirituality (actualization of beliefs).[219] It would seem appropriate to integrate faith-based cross-cultural work and these scholarly findings on the psychology of risk with an awareness of the empowering of the Holy Spirit. It seems we are missing a great deal of relevant information to inform our thinking about resiliency in high-risk situations when we ignore the research.

The truth is that emotions connect our inner and outer lives. They are sometimes painful to feel, and we naturally want to avoid pain, so we avoid, repress, or ignore our feelings. But God gave us feelings to bring us back to him, to understand his heart forming in us. "Ignoring our emotions is turning our back on reality; listening to our emotions ushers us into reality. And reality is where we meet God."[220] Listen to your emotions in risk and learn to face what God is doing in you to put his heart in you (Jeremiah 24:7).

After Leaving Risk

After we leave the risk event or situation, it's not uncommon to spend all sorts of time harshly judging ourselves and second-guessing what and how we did. We think we should have done more even than is humanly possible. Very often, we are much harder on ourselves in the risk situation than the Lord. We speak more critically of ourselves and others than the Lord does when we are under the incredible pressure of the cross-cultural risk situation.

Who Is the Right One to Give Counsel?

I am not a doctor or a mental-health clinician. In our pastoral role to cross-cultural workers, there are many times when we refer people to receive medical and psychological attention. Clinical counseling can be helpful and for many situations necessary. I have appreciated the input into my life from biblical counselors, psychologists, and psychiatrists. Counseling from trusted, wise clinically licensed counselors is often extremely effective for personal resiliency and healing.

While biblical counseling and clinical counseling are not the same, both of them working in tandem are important and valuable. Please also note that some clinical counselors work at integrating their Christian spirituality with psychological counseling, which is a more holistic and integrated perspective than just a psychological approach.

Like other field-based workers, I've learned the hard way to be careful who I approach when I feel the need for counseling of any type. Just because someone has a professional license or calls him- or herself a counselor does not mean he or she is "safe" or understands the high-risk situation. The depth of a person's spirituality and one's personal awareness of and intimacy with Christ is the depth he or she can help you, no matter the credentials.

Pray about who God wants you to meet with. Is it a counselor? If so, which counselor? Meet a few and go through the introductory meeting and see how comfortable you feel with them. Get referrals and ask for reviews on counselors. Do you need to see someone trained in inner healing prayer instead? As in risk, the Holy Spirit's leading in recovering from the risk situation is essential. He knows what you need and who will help you best.

Gentle Grace

I am firmly convinced, even in risk, that the Lord gently leads us. I love the gentleness with which the Lord speaks to us in Isaiah 40. Particularly in verse 11, it says, "Like a shepherd He will tend His flock, in His arm He will gather the lambs and carry them in His bosom; He will gently lead the nursing ewes."

Take a clear drinking glass and a clear glass pitcher. Over your kitchen sink, fill the pitcher all the way to the top. And then fill the drinking glass all the way to the top. Gently set the glass inside the pitcher and observe the water flowing out. You are the glass, immersed in the pitcher of God's grace that never runs dry. In your mind, pour God's grace all over the situation you are facing and how you feel about yourself. You are immersed in his grace in the risk situation, no matter what you've done or how you are doing. Stop. Breathe deeply. Picture his grace flowing around you. This is reality.[221]

Risk resiliency is not learned from books, but from repeated experiences in risk. Sometimes we fail in responding with grace in risk. However, mature Christ-followers are characterized with perseverance. Don't give up. Resolve to not beat yourself up, but ask for God's help to face your reality and help you see clearly and keep going.

Application

1. From the discussion on our emotions attached to perceived risks, how will you think and analyze risk differently?

2. What will you do to be more aware of your emotions in decision-making?

3. What will you do to be more aware of your family's and your teammates' emotions in risk and decision-making?

4. What changes do you need to make to handle your fears?

Chapter 10 Summary

1. Integrating emotions and decision-making:

    *   Determining the source of our emotions. There are two main sources in risk—emotions attached to the perceived hazard and the emotional state of our inner life.

    *   Handling our emotions when facing danger. Name it to tame it—learn to identify our emotions and normalize our feelings.

    *   How our emotions impact decision-making and risk. Emotions influence decision-making in four ways: emotions give information, they act as a spotlight, they act as a motivator, and they act as common currency.

2. A little fear won't harm you. It lets us know we are not "numb" to the risks we are facing.

3. The downside of fear is that fear can minimize our perception of the level of risk we are facing. Fearful people make pessimistic judgments about hazards, whereas angry people make more optimistic judgments.[222] Paying attention to the degree of fear experienced will be important in determining responses to hazards.[223] Fear causes us to think the risks are much higher; whereas anger causes us to perceive the risks are lower.[224]

4. When we act in fear, we are not objective and think up foolish ideas and either overreact or underreact to the threat level. This causes us to draw incorrect conclusions of people's motives because we don't take the time to ask clarifying questions. We make decisions resulting in poor judgments. And we don't take care of the daily tasks because we are too worried about the future.

5. When we feel fear, what does it look like to act in faith? We discern what is causing our fears, what situations, thought patterns, or lies that cause us to spiral into overwhelming fear. We also acknowledge the physical aspects to our fear situations.

6. Worry: A less intense form of fear. Being given information decreases worry and often increases emotional resiliency.

7. Dread risk: What causes the greatest fear? Dread is an emotion and impacts our risk perception.

8. Acute chronic fear: Living in chronic high-risk situations will impact us physically, emotionally, mentally, and spiritually. How we respond on a daily basis will dictate whether we grow in mature courage and resiliency or end up in burnout.

9. A pastoral response: Risk resiliency is not learned from books but from repeated experiences in risk. Sometimes we fail in responding with grace, but mature Christ-followers are characterized with perseverance. Don't give up. Resolve to not beat yourself up, but ask for God's help to face your reality and help you see clearly and keep going.

chapter 11

Stewardship in Risk

I have already discussed the biblical aspects of stewardship and risk. The challenge next is to integrate "a rationalistic approach to risking" with a biblical foundation of risk, allowing for the Holy Spirit's leading to choose to potentially place a believer in a situation of laying down one's life and remaining there.[225] When we follow God's leading into dangerous environments, it is normal to experience a consistent tension between two extremes of risking and stewarding. Biblical stewardship implies responsibility, so earthly risk assessment must harmonize with biblical discernment. The tension must always be kept in perspective.

J. Oswald Sanders, in his book *Spiritual Leadership: A Commitment to Excellence*, writes, "The greatest achievements in the history of [cross-cultural service] have come from leaders close to God, who took courageous, calculated risks. A great deal more failure is the result of an excess of caution than of bold experimentation with new ideas."[226] However, we must remember that "the most important decisions we usually make occur under complex, confusing, indistinct, or frightening conditions."[227]

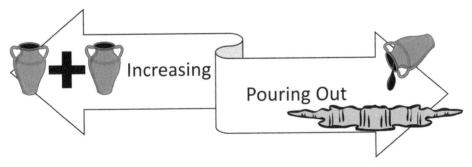

Now we begin to map out what it looks like in the middle of the dust of whatever yurt, hut, apartment, or house we live in. Comprehensive consideration of all the elements to be stewarded requires listing those elements and working through them systematically long *before* the risk event. Stewardship means we organize all the elements we can think of in our lives and have an idea of how we will manage them to the best of our abilities in the risk moment. We first ask, "What or whom has God given me to steward?"

Stewardship includes the physical and nonphysical components to be stewarded or risked. It also includes stewardship of self in terms of our relationship with God, our relationship with others, and stewardship of our inner life.

Stewarding Resources

First, stewardship of resources includes the physical and nonphysical (intangible) elements to be stewarded in risk. This includes all of the things and people I am responsible to steward external to myself.

Physical resources include:

- Office, the contents of the office, and office papers. (Do you need to shred security sensitive papers?)

- Machinery. (How do you steward machinery, either your organization's or your own?)

- Technology (computers, Internet hardware).

- Project or office car.

- Money (cash on hand, credit cards, money you may have in the local bank).

- Passports and personal papers (i.e., visas, birth certificates, wedding certificate, etc.).

- Home, irreplaceable items in the home, and the contents of the home.

- Expatriate staff for whom you are responsible.

- Children.

- Family back home and the impact on them.

- Personal vehicle.

- National staff impacted by your presence or absence.

- National believers impacted by you taking a risk.

- Unbelievers who will see God at work.

Nonphysical resources include:

- Potential opportunities to return (visa approvals, invitations).

- Goodwill of the national believers.

- Potential opportunities to stay.

- Potential opportunities to communicate the love of God.

- Permission, blessing, and approval by leadership.

- Blessing of partners back home.

- Personal health.

- Personal physical energy.

- Personal mental energy.

- Information. (How do you need to steward information going to your family, team, community, partners, and family back home? What goes on social media and national media? Who is your designated spokesperson?)

Stewarding Self

Ideally, as Paul Richardson relates, "Most want to be problem solvers, responding with words of wisdom to others while living joyful, courageous lives."[228] Stewarding self means paying attention to what is happening to your relationship with God, with others, and in your internal life.

Relationship with God: Your relationship with God includes awareness of where you are at on your spiritual journey and the elements leading to faith (Chapter 6), and the core questions you are asking of God (Chapter 7). Working through and listing the elements on one sheet of paper where it can all be seen will give a better picture of what God may be doing in you through the cross-cultural risk event or situation.

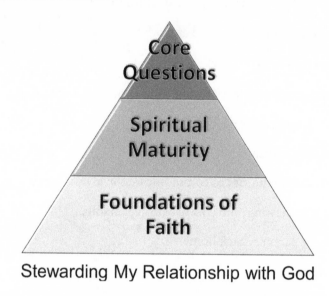

Stewarding My Relationship with God

Relationship with others: How are you responding to your family, teammates, and national colleagues? In consideration of your leaders and authorities, how are you responding to them?

Emotions and thought patterns: What risk myths have you been holding on to? What expectations of yourself have you not met or have met in risk so far? What mental or emotional patterns are increasingly revealed to you in the risk event or situation? When you consider your greatest fear in risk, what does that reveal not just about your core question of God but what you've been trying to hold on to yourself? How are you handling your fear or anxiety right now?

Physical body: This can be broken into two parts, your energy and your overall physical health. When it comes to your energy, what would be helpful for stewarding your mental and emotional energy so that you have "margin" for the emergencies and crises that arise in the risk situation?

Regarding your physical health, in crises it is common to need more sleep. Neal and I sometimes retired in the evenings after the children were in bed, as early as seven thirty some nights. I didn't always feel like eating, but a basic assessment of the calories needed to fuel my body led me, out of obedience and stewardship of my health, to eat foods required to keep me going. I counted it as spiritual service to God to care for my body so I could endure as well as possible.

Stewarding Children and Risk

For our young ones in the child-development phase, the stressors on the field, if not framed carefully by Mom and Dad, could potentially lead to emotional, mental, or spiritual problems. We continually monitored how much information was healthy for each child at each age in the risk situation. There is no one guide for this.

As a mom, it is my job to explain and "frame" the reality of what is happening for my children. It is important to not lie to the kids. When they ask what's happening, frame the gunfire or the explosion or the threat in a language they can understand. Younger kids have an especially simplistic view of the world: there are "good guys" and "bad guys."

We used to have "run to safety" drills in our home. After one practice, because there had been a mob going by our home that day, I was tucking our youngest, Danny, into his bed. He was about four or five years old at the time. He said, "Mommy, if the bad guys come, I'll protect you, see?" And he showed me he had tucked his Nerf gun right by his pillow. I was so impressed with the male instinct to protect! I affirmed his desire to protect us and covered his face in kisses that night. He needed to know who the bad guys and good guys were, and be encouraged in his desire to help.

Parenting our children in high-risk situations is a moment-by-moment unique-to-each-kid style best discerned by Mom and Dad in consultation with other parents who have had similar experiences. A child psychologist or someone else with expertise on how young people respond in crisis may be helpful here too, but be discerning about incorporating their input. Those who are unaware of the extraordinary resilience often developed in third culture children while growing up in dangerous environments may not be able to appropriately compensate for this unfamiliar reality.

We put together a guide for on-field lay-debriefing of children in high-risk situations. This guide isn't meant to replace a proper child-expert psychological debriefing, but parents can be trained to carefully draw out their children and help them process their feelings. The important thing is to ask open-ended questions without giving them the words to describe how they feel. Often some pliable object they like, such as playdough or crayons, a toy car, Legos, or other hands-on objects can help them explain their feelings.

Preparing for Risk: Developing Endurance Strategies

There are some incredibly strategic endurance strategies that enable one to be better prepared for running well through risk.

Physical Preparation

Although not all risk conditions are alike, there are frequently consistent procedures of preparing for crisis in precarious environments. Here are some we would recommend.

Keep organized: Keep your closets and junk drawers organized. It was stressful when I only had thirty-six hours to evacuate. I was dismayed by my lack of organization and the resulting added stress in an already high-risk situation. By keeping things organized, I could quickly photograph all the contents of my home to remember what I had and what I may lose. We organized our physical preparation into a five-minute, a two-hour, and a two-day window of time.

Keep it simple: Don't bring physical items into high-risk environments that you will regret losing. Live simply. We digitized our music and photos and kept our personal mementos to under two kilos (4.4 pounds). Make these decisions proportional to the level of risk you are in.

Keep appropriate reserves: Some environments may require a reserve of food. I kept a two-week supply of beans and rice on hand. I rotated the beans and rice by giving them away whenever a beggar came to the gate. This kept the supply fresh since our family couldn't eat it fast enough before going "buggy." You may need to prepare for other potential shortages too. An extra water supply kept in a clean barrel with a lid may lower stress in the high-risk situation. Rotate the water every few weeks, but keep it filled.

In times of chaos electricity is often cut, so it is wise to plan ahead and have what is needed to charge cell phones and have some light during the night. Keeping a store of kerosene for lanterns, batteries for flashlights, and a solar charger for cell phones is good preparation for possible chaotic times. Evaluate the potential that resources might be unavailable and what the consequences would be if you could not get them. Every situation is unique, so taking the time to evaluate the risk for potential scenarios is essential.

Keep a backup of communication systems: In high-tech countries, even when chaos happens, the cell phone systems often go down. If the Internet is still up, then communication via Skype and other Internet means will be helpful. For those living in the highest risk situations, a satellite phone is imperative. Do what you can to afford purchasing one of these and keep it charged up. That one phone call in an emergency situation will make the cost well worth it.

Keep cash on hand: Have enough hard cash on hand to purchase your family's transportation out of immediate danger.

Keep medevac options available: For health issues, have medical evacuation plans, if at all possible. Where will you be medevaced to, and how will you pay for it?

Keep a kidnapping response plan: Knowing what we would do in the event one of us should be kidnapped proved to be a major stress reducer in high-risk situations. For Neal and I, we agreed that if the other is kidnapped, we'd take the children and leave the country immediately. That way, the spouse in the kidnap situation will know that the family is safe and can better focus on surviving the kidnapping. It is also important to get to a safe place where the family is not a target of the kidnappers, and a place to get help with potential media issues.

Keep an untimely death response plan: Normally, when a cross-cultural worker dies on the field, the burial takes place there where the person died. We made it clear to our families back home that we did not wish what money we had to be used to bring our bodies back. We expected burial in the country of death.

Having clear written expectations with extended family back home on all of these issues will help lower their stress as well. Knowing your wishes in any of these high-risk scenarios will be a comfort to them as they navigate grief and loss from far away. This is a kindness we do for them. Both Neal and I keep our funeral wishes written out to minimize the stress the other will be under if losing a marriage partner. We prepare for death in the high-risk situations by cultivating daily habits that we want to characterize our last twenty-four hours on earth. We are ready for death at any moment.[229]

Relationally, are there any issues you need to take care of? Keeping a clear conscience between you and others and you and God will help you face death more calmly as well. Have you said "I love you" to friends and family members lately? Are there those you think highly of but haven't ever told what you appreciate about them?

Policy Preparation

The discussion on conceptual versus situational thinking in Chapter 8 referred to the complications from having policies that follow a one-size-fits-all approach. Don't have your people mitigate risks that aren't there for them. This is a waste of time and energy, which are two resources we need to steward on the field in high-risk situations.

However, for each risk situation, responsible stewardship of resources means there is some risk mitigation and planning that takes place for the assessed risks for that situation. This includes discussing with significant others (spouse, sending churches, partners, and organizations) so that appropriate people are in place to handle negotiations, risk communication (i.e., media), and all additional fallout for any of these events. There are agencies around the world that specialize in advising humanitarian agencies in this type of planning. Key risk events, if they are a risk in your area, should be planned for. Here are a few (this is not an exhaustive list).

- Payment of ransom, yielding to extortion: Do you permit payment for yourself or your loved one?

- Negotiation with kidnappers and hostage takers: Who will do this?

- Family relocation: How will children get taken to a safe place and who has legal permission to do this?

- Notification to governments in kidnapping and hostage taking: Who will talk with the governments?

- Contingency plans: Who can help you put this together?

- The crisis management team: Who will be on it?

- Information management: Who will be the spokesperson for you?

- Pastoral care: What pastor in your life understands your situation and can provide appropriate care to you and your children?

- Evacuation authority: Who decides when we leave?

- Evacuation criteria: What are the parameters for when we need to leave?

Evacuation Plan[230]

One key way to lower stressors and increase personal resilience is always to keep the list of items to take in an evacuation and the list of "to-dos" to take care of if you have to leave the home or office in a hurry. The evacuation list is organized by time: What would you take if there are only five minutes to gather the items and the limit is two kilos (4.4 pounds), or eight kilos (17.6 pounds)? What if there are thirty minutes to prepare? Is there time to take or shred certain papers? What if you have twenty-four to thirty-six hours to leave the country and can take a suitcase?

Having this list organized and ready helps your mind be at ease, knowing there is a plan and you don't have to rely on your memory when under duress. Keep the list of items to take and things to do in a safe place where it can be easily and quickly found in an emergency. Prioritize the list, and work through it systematically when the emergency arises. The list may include your child's special toy and perhaps a precious memento. Take a picture occasionally of your children's toys so they have a memory of what was precious to them at the time. And make a note next to each item on the list of where it is located in the home so it can be found and gathered quickly.

Process papers that need to be shredded or burned—don't let them pile up too much. It helps to keep printed papers to a minimum (those you wouldn't want to fall into the wrong hands). As already mentioned, keep closets and junk drawers organized because it's a major stressor to have to search in five minutes to find certain items. Consider taking digital pictures of all areas of your home a couple times a year—it will be helpful to have these if you have to evacuate in a hurry. Have you brought too many "keepsakes"? Consider taking some of those items back to your passport country next time you have an opportunity. Living unencumbered by "things" helps us focus on what is truly eternally significant.

Evacuation Criteria

Risk analysis includes discussing what criteria guide us in determining when to pull out of the risk situation. And we also want a guide to know when to pull out the whole team. In other words, we need to ask, "When is the community no longer sustainable if certain companies pull out?" For example, where we were located, if one specific organization left, there would not have been enough teachers available for the international school and thus other companies and organizations would not have the ability to stay.

For individuals, the evacuation criteria also need to be determined. Who determines these criteria? Evacuation criteria will look different for each person or family. Ideally this is a decision made in dialogue with others who understand the risk situation.

Evacuation criteria are ideally set before entering risk, and then they are continually reassessed. It is important to define and describe evacuation criteria to protect oneself from becoming desensitized to and unaware of increasing violence and danger levels. Rational risk assessment helps discern when previously set evacuation criteria are reached. Then a prayerful decision can be made, in dialogue with others, on whether the Lord is calling one to stay or go in that risk situation.

Endurance Methods

Developing healthy team and individual endurance (coping) mechanisms in high-risk and high-stress situations are crucial for endurance, especially in long-term risk situations like the eight-month "lockdown" I mentioned earlier. As a team, pastoral-care person, or an individual, it is crucial to evaluate and incorporate endurance mechanisms so they lead to resiliency and even thriving in risk.

I found it helpful in risk to "systematize" my endurance mechanisms into separate categories. The reason for this is that long-term risk is such an exhausting endeavor that systematically evaluating myself helped to account for all aspects of my life. It helped me to pay attention to my body, mind, emotions, and faith walk. Obviously, it will look somewhat different for men versus women, and for children as well. But here is how I self-evaluated as a young mom in long-term risk.

Physical Coping Tools

Do I need food, sleep, time off from house chores or work? Do I just need a "sweet" or comfort food? While not advocating overeating, sometimes a home-cooked meal is restorative. I kept a special cupboard of sweets like chocolate for me to dip into on occasion. What is helpful for you to take a moment of calmness and peace?

I think of an older woman who called the day after the major robbery we experienced in our home. She announced, "I'm coming over Thursday, and I'm going to cook for you all day. I will make you pizza, Stromboli, cinnamon rolls, and bread, using one recipe that I'll leave with you." What she did that day was significant. She filled our recently-invaded home with the smells of food, fed us, and gave me a tool (the recipe) to repeat later on. It's the one recipe I have used for all of these years while raising my family. Needless to say, we felt loved that day with all the good "comfort" food in our home. (I've included B's Robbery Recovery Recipe in Appendix D.)

Mental and Emotional Tools

Do I just need a good cry? Do I need to escape through a good book or entertainment? What physical activities will bring calmness to my mind and soul? For me, I learned I needed an hour every day, outside of my quiet times, to study and read a spiritual or theology book. My soul was renewed when my husband could help take care of the children and give me that hour.

Neal and I rarely have been able to have an evening date, and less so when the children were young. This was because it was often too dangerous to go to town at nighttime, and after the robbery we minimized leaving our kids at night. So we used to have "date night" by preparing a special evening coffee and sitting on our veranda together in the peace of the night. We'd read a chapter of a book together and discuss it. It provided mental stimulation on a topic unrelated to work, and emotionally we could connect outside of the stress of the high-risk situation we lived in for so many years.

Spiritual Coping Tools

Do I just need to spend time worshiping? How can I disassociate from the stress of the day and give it over to the Lord? We budgeted money to purchase worship videos, and through these we could "attend" concerts of some of our favorite Christian music artists. When we didn't feel like we had the energy to worship, these videos helped us immensely. There was a period of time when Neal came home from work every day and listened to the same worship song before he could let go of the challenges of the day.

There was one sermon by a particular preacher that we listened to almost half a dozen times. That was about the only sermon we ever listened to that much. But it helped reframe our perspective on risk and strengthened our faith when we were spiritually weary. What preacher or sermons have been encouraging to you?

Social-Relational Tools

Do we need to have a coffee with a friend? Do we need to have a party and just relax? We used to throw huge parties once a month and invite friends over and eat pizza together. It was amazing how people would relax over great pizza and share their lives. Laughing together, even "dark humor," helped us endure together.

During that time, we'd purposefully draw out our friends to hear stories of eternal transformation happening through their work projects. This always was a major key to our resilience, when we could see the combined significance of our work as a community. We repeated these stories to our children, and eventually to partners back home, so that Christ's body would be encouraged. God was working through all of us, and we took encouragement from that to continue to endure.

Culture and Security Stress Tools

In high-risk situations, usually the culture stress and resulting security issues impact resiliency. What are some ways you have found helpful to cope with culture stress? Humor is a significant factor in mental health in these high-risk situations. Being with friends in social situations helps the humor flow and lightens up the focus on the threat of death for a while. We need these "breaks" together as a community in high-stress situations.

I never forgot a fun party my good friend hosted during the days Kabul was controlled by the Taliban. She informed the community of expatriates that she was having a *Sound of Music* party and everyone was to come dressed as a character from the movie. All evening she had the movie playing on the television, and she had everyone stand on the stairs and sing the "So Long, Farewell" song from the movie at the end of the evening. It was a crazy fun party. This relieved stress for an evening and built the unity of the Spirit in the community!

Application

1. Looking at the list of items to steward, what needs to be added to *your* list to steward?

2. How can you minimize the number of items you need to steward and lower the stress in risk situations?

3. What is keeping you from taking the time to assess and analyze what you are called to steward?

Chapter 11 Summary

1. Stewardship of resources: Stewardship includes the physical and non-physical components to be stewarded or risked. It also includes stewardship of self in terms of our relationship with God, our relationship with others, and stewardship of our inner life.

2. Children and risk: For our young ones in the child-development phase, the stressors on the field, if not framed carefully by us, could potentially lead to emotional, mental, or spiritual problems. We continually monitored how much information was healthy for each child at each age in the risk situation.

3. Preparing for risk: There are some incredibly strategic endurance strategies that enable one to be better prepared for running well through risk, which include staying organized, keeping it simple, having a two-week food and water supply on hand, backup communications resources, cash, medivac plans, and preparation for kidnapping and what to do if we died.

4. Evacuation plan: One way to lower stressors and increase personal resilience is always to keep a list of items to take in an evacuation and a list of "to-dos" to take care of if you have to leave the home or office in a hurry.

5. Evacuation criteria: Risk analysis includes discussing what criteria guide us in determining when to pull out of the risk situation, and when to know when to pull out the whole team.

6. Endurance methods: Developing healthy team and individual endurance (coping) mechanisms in high-risk and high-stress situations are crucial for endurance, especially in long-term risk situations.

   - Physical tools: Do I need food, sleep, time off from house chores or work? Do I just need a comfort food? While not advocating overeating, sometimes a home-cooked meal is restorative.

   - Mental-emotional tools: Do I just need a good cry? Do I need to escape through a good book or entertainment? What physical activities will bring calmness to my mind and soul?

   - Spiritual tools: Neal and I budgeted money to purchase worship videos, and through these we could "attend" concerts of some of our favorite Christian music artists.

   - Social-relational tools: We used to throw huge parties once a month and invite friends over and eat pizza together. It was amazing how people would relax over great pizza and share their lives.

   - Culture-security stress tools: What are some ways you have found helpful to cope with culture stress?

chapter 12

Danger Risk Management

Knowledge without courage is useless. ... Courage without knowledge leads us into the most abominable messes.[231]

Danger risk management includes both risk assessment and risk management (mitigation). There must be a balance between rational risk analysis and effective risk analysis in order to discover what true courage is required for that particular situation. The balance will look different in each situation and with each person, leading to several questions: What is the difference between these two types of analyses? How do I know I've achieved a good balance in analyses? And if there *must* be a balance, then what is the risk if I am out of balance? I'll attempt to answer these three questions in this chapter.

Risk information needs to be specific and clear in order to best minimize the dangers and losses of risk. In this chapter, I explain a systematic, rational way to analyze the specific dangers in any cross-cultural risk situation. Each step will build on the next. The safest place for an aircraft is parked in the shelter of its hangar; but an aircraft was not created to remain in a hangar. Prior to deploying an aircraft to do what it was created to do, resources are first used to assess the conditions of the flight environment, aircraft, and its crew.

Safety and security of people and resources are important. The chapter on stewardship discussed discernment in knowing what kind of stewardship of God's resources, including people, needs to happen in each risk situation. But safety can be made into an idol too. Some organizations and teams obsess over safety and security and thereby do not move forward into the heat of the battle. "The wife of Archbishop Mowll said, 'The frontiers of the kingdom of God never advanced by men and women of caution.'"[232] Safety is not the ultimate guide in pursuing kingdom purposes.

We must do rational risk analysis as part of making an informed decision. The task is to take the time to examine as many solid facts as possible and take the time to think them through rationally. That can be a difficult thing to do when we are facing dangerous situations. Confronting risk at first may cause anxiety, which interferes with our abilities to perceive reality clearly. We may find ourselves placing too much importance on immaterial facts and completely overlooking noteworthy specifics.

Utilizing a dispassionate, rational-risk analysis tool is an effective way to protect against the tendency to make impulsive, unreasonable decisions when responding to risk. A good tool will give easy-to-understand impact and probability data and deliver it in a consistent manner so that risks can be assessed and prioritized in relation to one another. It must also be dynamic enough to endure alteration as the environment changes. As we examine the facts, oftentimes our anxiety will decrease as we recognize that actual reality (based on the current facts) is different from perceived reality (the confusing "whirl" in our head before we document and graph the risks on paper).

A Basic Assessment Tool

A good starting point for assessment (especially in environments with relatively low risk) is simply plotting potential risk events on a graph with two axes, one reflecting the severity of consequences and the other reflecting the likelihood of the risk event taking place. The result is an instrument that visually portrays the two foundational risk assessment questions: "What could happen?" and "How bad would it be?" while adding assessment query, "How likely is it to happen?"

Let's put it into practice by addressing some risks in a fictional setting. We'll start by addressing the question, "What could happen?" Let's say that car accidents, theft, losing one's visa, and murder are all possible risk events in our imaginary environment. We now have defined the events that we would like plotted on our graph, and so we must now continue with the other evaluation questions.

How bad would it be if these risk events happened? While answering that question, it is important to keep in mind that there may be quite a bit of variation in the answer. How bad would a car accident be if it happened? It *could* be very bad. Suffering significant losses of life and materials are both possibilities. However, it

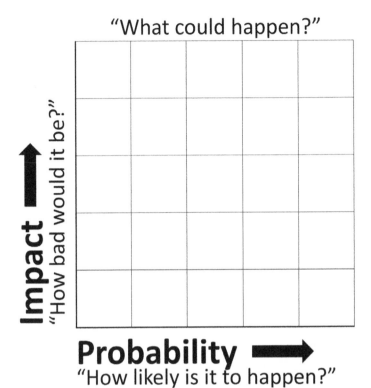

"What could happen?"

Impact "How bad would it be?"

Probability ➡
"How likely is it to happen?"

could also have only an inconsequential impact if it is merely a minor mishap. In these situations, it is important to maintain a probability perspective in forming an assessment. It may be helpful to modify the question slightly: "How bad is it likely to be if it happened?" In our made-up environment, car accidents happen often, but they also tend to result in relatively minor damage to the vehicle, and repairs are available and inexpensive.

The murder of a team member would have a serious impact, however, causing widespread damage to our abilities to accomplish our callings. It would also be far-reaching, impacting a wide community in many different countries.

We have determined that thefts are likely to be petty in nature and would most often occur during moments of opportunity without others around. It is useful to begin evaluating impact theft in relation to the other risk events that we are assessing. We may say that theft is likely to impact us more seriously than the car accident, but only slightly. Finally, we will look at the possibility of losing one's visa. Perhaps we determine that this would have significant negative consequences.

Now we must move to the final question and address probability: How likely is it that these risk events might occur? We determine that it is unlikely that someone on our team will experience murder but that it is likely for us to experience a car accident or theft. We also may determine that it is likely that someone on our team loses a visa. We now can plot our risk events on the graph.

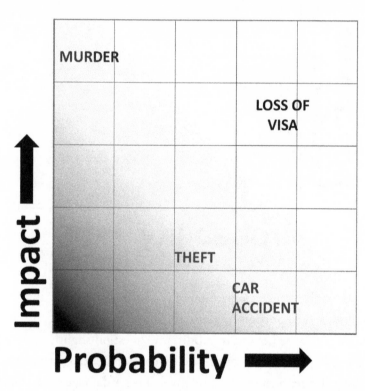

During this process, it is common for the original assessment rating to change significantly. As the evaluation becomes more thorough, it can reveal greater awareness of the risks, which may prompt a sense of urgency to address the vulnerability. It may also cause us to realize we have been feeling more anxiety for a potential risk that is in actuality relatively lower than others.

Handling Information

One of the most difficult aspects of rational risk assessment is deciding how much information needs to be obtained to make a solid decision and how much is too little before making the decision. At some point, having weighed all of the factors, a decision must be made. Psychologists have studied decision-making in risk and that moment in time when people "feel" they have enough information to make a decision in a risk situation. How can we become more aware of a psychological versus a Spirit-led response, or when the two types of responses are working in tandem?

Here are a few questions and thoughts to consider in regards to this question:

- How much information is the right amount? It is challenging to recognize how much is enough in risk when people's lives are at stake.

- More anxious individuals may "pay excessive attention to low-probability events and overlook events that regularly happen."[233]

- People treat costs of risking and uncompensated losses differently, even though their impact on resources are identical.

- People have more clarity and courage on the path forward when knowing the potential risks, rewards, and losses. Calculating risk requires us to name all aspects that must be weighed before making the decision.

- What additional strategies would be helpful to make a more rational rather than an anxiety-based decision? It could include something as simple as deep breathing and relaxation, getting a good night's sleep, or even delegating a decision to experienced leaders.

List Potential Dangers and Traumas

Danger assessment must list all of the known dangers specific to that risk environment. (See Appendix C for a list of dangers, although this list is not exhaustive in nature.) A question we will often ask people when we are working with teams is about the dangers unique to their situation and what risks they are facing. What risks have been faced in the recent past? It is helpful for individuals and teams to work through this question for their unique environments, and then be guided through the assessment and mitigation steps on the following pages.

One Major Caution: Data Sets Used for Comparison Must Be Similar

It has not been uncommon for Neal and me to hear risk analysis like, "The risk of another bombing attack is much lower than the risk of being in a car accident." The logical conclusion made by several leaders was to deduce that therefore the likelihood of an attack was very low.

This is a major error in calculating risk because the two data sets are not at all in the same risk categories. Traffic accidents are just that—accidents. They happen more frequently where the population engages in risky behavior like drinking while driving and texting while driving. Traffic accidents do not target a specific population. The threat of a bombing attack made by real terrorists against a foreign population living in a host city is much different. If there are three hundred Christians in one Muslim city, and the terrorists have made real threats against that population, then the risk of experiencing a bombing attack is extremely high for that Christian demographic.

Components to Calculating Cross-Cultural Risk

There are four key areas to comprehensively calculate cross-cultural risk. First, there is the spiritual and emotional risk assessment. This means looking at what is happening in my relationship with God. If you are a team leader, ask open-ended questions of your team to find out how they are doing. Doing a spiritual and risk assessment includes looking at where one describes his or her present spiritual journey, what foundations of faith one is cultivating, and what core questions one may be asking of God. It also includes assessing one's mental and emotional health, and what spiritual authorities may be saying.

Second, there is the danger risk assessment. This is security analysis of what is going on: listing, assessing, and evaluating the external dangers in a systematic and fact-based way. Third, there is stewardship analysis: What and who needs to be stewarded? What losses may be incurred and what are the limits of loss that will be considered wise versus unwise stewardship? What is the impact of the perceptions of the specific risks, as well as the impact of the actual event on me, my family, and my staff? In *The Psychology of Risk*, Glynis

Breakwell writes:

> Impact is a difficult dimension to rate. For many risks, impact will actually be functionally dependent upon whether leadership takes appropriate action quickly enough. Leaders need to try to find out what their staff's unspoken expectations from leadership are in the risk event.[234]

Fourth, there is spiritual discernment. What is the Holy Spirit saying and where does God seem to be at work? Chapter 5 provided more helpful details about how we can discern the guidance of the Holy Spirit in risk; he often speaks through some combination of sources. However, since leaders are entrusted with discerning the Holy Spirit's leading, and if they discern that leaving is best, then workers need to be willing to respect that discernment and submit to their chosen authorities.

An Advanced Tool for Measuring and Comparing Risk[235]

While helpful, we found the basic tool described earlier in this chapter to be inadequate in managing the complex risk environment we experienced. When leading a large team, Neal created a tool for measuring the threats of danger. Using simple graphing and an Excel spreadsheet, it listed the four key areas of danger analysis: frequency, geographic proximity, demographic proximity, and intensity. These can be graphed for easier risk assessment.

Objective: To blend the subjective evaluation of risk levels with an objective tool that can be used to measure and compare risk levels in applicable categories.

Step One: Determine applicable categories. Just as a finance manager would create a customized chart of accounts that would apply to her company's situation, a team leader creates risk categories that apply to the risks associated with the team's operating environment. Take care to choose categories general enough to measure risks but detailed enough to provide thorough information. An example of a list of risk categories might be:

- assault (includes physical assault, robberies, bombings, etc.),

- kidnapping (includes abductions, hostage taking, etc.),

- political unrest (includes riots, coups, election instability, etc.), and

- health (includes outbreaks, lack of medical care, etc.).

Step Two: Create a graph to evaluate and measure all four factors associated with each risk event within the danger categories. Each axis of the graph will be used to plot one of the four factors. These factors are

- severity (the weight of the impact on individuals and team),

- frequency (the rate at which the events occur),

- geographic proximity (the closeness of events), and

- demographic proximity (a measurement of similarities the team shares with the targets of the events).

The graph serves a function of probability assessment for each axis rather than only having one probability axis as the earlier graph had. Each axis of Neal's assessment grid asks the question of likelihood:

- How *likely* is it that the risk event will be severe? (Severity)

- How *likely* is it that the risk event occurs often? (Frequency)

- How *likely* is it that the risk event would occur close by? (Geographic proximity)

- How *likely* is it that the risk event happens to people like me? (Demographic proximity)

Please see the following page for the assessment graph Neal created:

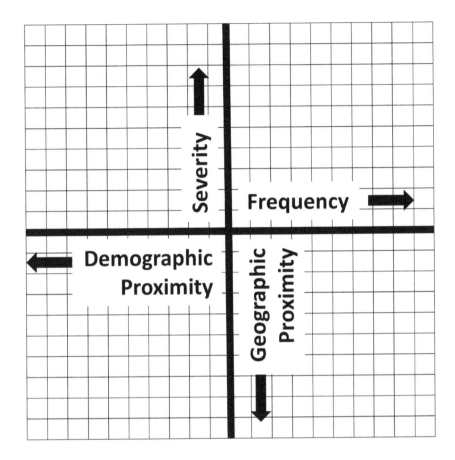

Step Three: Define the suitable scale for measuring risks by estimating based on security inputs (i.e., security consultant information, government and NGO security reports, information from leaders and locals, local news reports, etc.). For example, a 0–10 scale can be used to plot the evaluated levels of factors in each risk category. Providing corresponding descriptive words is helpful for adding continuity when multiple people will be assessing the risk.

For example:

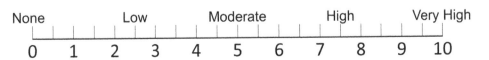

Step Four: Create a table to record the assessed levels.

	Severity	Frequency	Geographic Proximity	Demographic Proximity
Assault	2	8	9	1
Kidnapping	7	4	9	8
Political Unrest	2	6	10	1
Health	8	4	9	3

Step Five: Plot the results of the table on the graph and connect the four points to create a visual image of the risk level for each category. Using the previous example, the visual aid for the assessed risk in the category of assault would look like this:

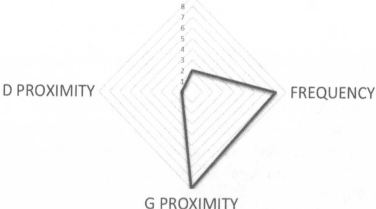

ASSAULT

The visual image shows low risk of assault in the areas of severity and demographic proximity, but high risk of assault in frequency and geographic proximity. Plotting all of the results would look like this:

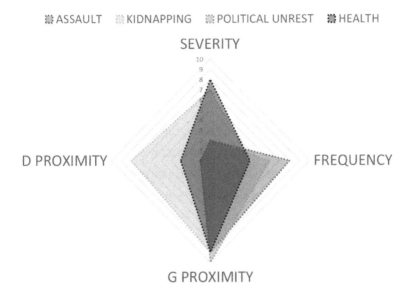

ASSAULT   KIDNAPPING   POLITICAL UNREST   HEALTH

This shows all categories of danger and helps in developing a risk reduction strategy so the risks can be assessed and mitigated in order of perceived priority.

Now What Do We Do?

After having done all this assessment and analysis, how do we respond to and manage the risk? It is not the intent of this book to describe in detail some of the well-designed risk mitigation tactics that could be employed for some of the common threats to cross-cultural service. However, there are four general categories that can help guide us as we consider risk management for each assessed risk.

The risk could be *avoided*. We can choose to not place ourselves in a situation where we are vulnerable to the risks that we have assessed. Avoiding the risk altogether would likely involve withdrawing from a hazardous environment or opting to not attempt to accomplish a high-risk activity. We may also choose to *accept* the risk as it exists. We would do this with a clearer focus for what resources are vulnerable by accepting the risk. Accepting the risk means moving into the precarious situation or choosing to engage in an activity while understanding and tolerating the dangers as they are.

However, there are also two additional methods of managing risk. We have the option of *transferring* the risk to another entity. For example, if we needed to transport important material via a hazardous roadway, we could hire a company to accomplish the transportation portion of the task. Transference can help us accomplish our goals while offloading hazardous duties on other (perhaps more appropriate) entities.

The most common technique for managing risk is by *limiting* it. Using this approach, we would incorporate the information discovered in our assessment effort into a limitation strategy. Effort is made to reduce the amount of vulnerability by reducing the extent of exposure we have while accomplishing our goals.

We see in the parable of the talents that multiplying resources was affirmed by Christ. We also see that the woman who poured out resources as an offering was commended by our Savior. Rather than viewing these approaches as incompatible, I simply accept them as different Holy Spirit–led perceptions. If we integrate these different perspectives into the four general categories for managing risk, it might look like this:

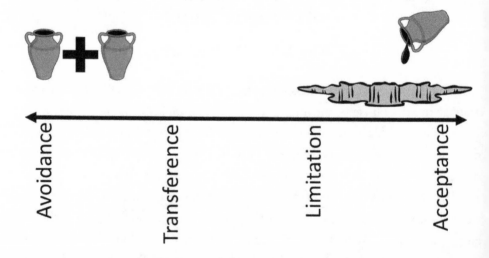

There were times when Paul escaped or avoided risk altogether; sometimes he transferred it to those who stayed in the situation. He limited risk at times by not entering a more dangerous situation, and he accepted it when he purposefully headed into known danger.

It is paramount to manage risk by mitigating the causes that might factor in to the likelihood of a risk event occurring while also preparing for the expected consequences if the event occurs. What does this mean? For example, if accomplishing one's calling means operating in a location where kidnappings are common, procedures that prevent being abducted are necessary. Engage in things like surveillance detection methods, randomized schedules, and curfews. It would also be important to mitigate the severity of the consequences by similarly engaging in developing supportive reactive resources (i.e., hostage response training, developing consultation resources, defining contingency team roles, etc.)

What else can help you in your response to managing risk? Chapter 5 described ways to obtain additional information on managing risk and learning how to respond. Additionally, there are common sense ways to minimize risks too. For example, I taught my children some of those techniques to avoid being kidnapped. I learned from security experts how to survive kidnapping and increase the possibility of being able to avoid being raped. When possible, seek the counsel of security experts if they visit your community.

Conclusion

Why go through all of these steps? At the beginning of this chapter, I mentioned rational risk analysis and effective risk analysis. There were three key questions guiding our understanding of these two types of analyses: What is the difference between these two types of analyses? What does a good balance look like? And if there *must* be balance, then what is the risk if I am out of balance?

Rational risk analysis is a term used to describe all objective aspects of risk that can be reasonably quantified and qualified as described in the tools above. It is fact-based, concrete, and accounts for the totality of risk—the causes of the potential risk, the risk event itself, and the combination of consequences that can be the most likely outcomes. Effective risk analysis, however, takes into account the Holy Spirit, the discernment of individuals, and what God is doing in the larger picture of the team, the community, and the nation. Only incorporating a rational approach to risk analysis, even when based on the best understanding of human emotions and psychology, will not be complete without discerning God's activity in the situation and being able to be flexible throughout the risk event.

If organizational risk policies drive people's responses to risk analysis and mitigation, if there is dogmatic doctrinal and conceptual thinking, then there will not be effective risk analysis. Risk is often a fluid situation requiring flexibility, adaptation, and unique endurance patterns. Balance between these two means *both* have been done. It does take time in risk to systematically think through all the reasonable potential risks—all of their causes and resulting consequences. It would be easy to skip this and simply spiritualize that God is working and will work, no matter what happens. But this would be a major mistake.

Endurance happens more effectively and more easily when real rational risks have been acknowledged, analyzed, and understood in totality. Simply, the risk has been faced. When I knew my husband had done all this work of risk analysis using the tools described above, when he took time to explain them to me as well as to the team we were leading, greater endurance resulted. We knew as much as we could while going into graver risks, and we were ready to deal with whatever happened.

Not only was it crucial for our endurance on the field to have comprehensive risk analysis, but effective risk analysis means we also carefully examined what God seemed to be doing in the larger picture. We had a larger perspective that effective risk analysis revealed to us as we moved into more serious risk situations. This was a major factor in our endurance and resiliency as we continued to experience dangerous events. Knowing that we had done our best to minimize the consequences of risk, and knowing we had leaders who had wise security and risk advisors, increased our trust of our leadership and actually increased our endurance on the field.

Not doing both of these types of risk analysis—rational risk analysis and effective risk analysis—results in less ability for field staff to endure in challenging risk situations. It is as simple as that. Taking the time to do rational and effective risk analysis is actually good stewardship of the resources needed to navigate complex and dangerous risk situations.

Application

1. Which aspect or tool of danger assessment is most helpful for you?

2. Which part of danger assessment may need to be added to your current risk assessment strategy?

Chapter 12 Summary

1. Danger risk management includes both risk assessment and risk management (mitigation). There must be a balance between rational risk analysis and effective risk analysis in order to discover what true courage is required for that particular situation.

2. A basic assessment tool: A good starting point for assessment (especially in environments with relatively low risk) is simply plotting potential risk events on a graph with two axes, one reflecting the severity of consequences and the other reflecting the likelihood of the risk event taking place.

3. Handling information: One of the most difficult aspects of rational risk assessment is deciding how much information needs to be obtained in order to make a solid decision and how much is too little before making the decision. At some point, having weighed all of the factors, a decision must be made.

4. Danger assessment must list all of the known dangers specific to that risk environment.

5. Policy preparation: It has not been uncommon for us to hear risk analysis like, "The risk of another bombing attack is much lower than the risk of being in a car accident." The logical conclusion made by several leaders was to deduce that therefore the likelihood of an attack was low. This is a major error in calculating risk because the two data sets are not at all in the same risk categories.

6. Components to calculating cross-cultural risk: There are four key areas

to comprehensively calculate cross-cultural risk: There is the spiritual and emotional risk assessment, there is the danger risk assessment, there is stewardship analysis, and there is spiritual discernment.

7. A tool for measuring and comparing risk: Using simple graphing, it listed the four key areas of danger analysis: frequency, geographic proximity, demographic proximity, and intensity. These can be graphed for easier risk assessment.

chapter 13

Under-Shepherds & Risk

I marveled at the way Heinrich led the meeting. Heinrich, I thought, was a brilliant leader. He had served on our team for a long time and had been asked to take the leadership role around five years prior. I had observed him demonstrate courage, fairness, empathy, and, most importantly, discernment during my years of serving under him.

I say that his strength of discernment was most important because we were especially in need of his wisdom during that time. The government had just issued an edict that threatened deportation or imprisonment for any foreigner discussing an alternative faith with a local person. It was worse for our national friends. Any citizen caught conversing about a belief other than the local religion would be put to death. What did this mean for us? Were we safe? What about our local friends? The path forward seemed confusing and hazardous.

Heinrich took time to describe the changes in the situation, and explained the government's new law in detail. He shared openly about his own assessment and about how he had come to those conclusions, even quoting from some of the consultative resources he had drawn upon. He let us know that he had made it a matter of prayer and yet avoided describing his opinions as "divinely inspired." "Prayerfully and soberly discussed" would have been a better description for how he and the leadership team had arrived at the organizational response he described to us.

The changes to our team's security guidelines were hard to receive. There were limitations on literature distribution, mobility restrictions, and mandated curfews to be followed. Most difficult for us were the changes in the way we were permitted to interact with those in the local culture who had become dear to us.

After Heinrich described the policy changes, he opened it up to the team. Heinrich was a consensus-building leader. It was common for him to solicit input from team members. He often would incorporate good ideas from the team on-the-spot and it was encouraging to feel a part of team decisions. He empathized. He validated the feelings of loss. In a tangible way, Heinrich even grieved with us as the weight of the new forbidding season settled upon us. However, something about the way Heinrich responded to my teammates' reactions was unlike other times.

"I am grateful for your input," he said. "It helps me to know that you care deeply about these issues. Our relationships are important to us because they are important to our heavenly Father who has called us here. I sincerely hope that the requirement for us to adhere to these new guidelines is short-lived and that we can soon go back to our previous way of interacting with others. We will continue to monitor the situation and will inform you when it is again prudent for us to remove these restrictions from you. Let me be clear though: all of us will be functioning within the limitations of these guidelines until further notice."

Not everyone was happy with the new directives, of course. There was some grumbling and some of our teammates even withdrew membership from our team shortly afterward. They joined another team on the other side of our city—a team with less restrictive policies. For me, though, my trust for Heinrich grew even more that day. He had skillfully demonstrated one of the most critical qualities for leading others through risk: shepherding.

Shepherding is not only important during times of risk, of course. God desires leaders to shepherd his people in the manner that he has modeled for us. We are to be under-shepherds of the Great Shepherd. The role of an under-shepherd is radically different than most conventional leadership roles. It implies service and sacrifice. Leaders who function well in normal environments, who have good leadership skills, will fail in a high-risk environment if they do not embrace under-shepherd traits and qualities.

Being an under-shepherd and having concern for sheep out in the field is a grave responsibility. Scripture is replete with how God feels about shepherds who do not take care of their flocks (Isaiah 58; Jeremiah 23; Ezekiel 34; 37; Micah 7). The message is clear that this responsibility is not just given by God, but that the shepherd is expected to carry it out with care and dedication. The well-being of the flock is clearly linked to the action (or inaction) of the under-shepherd. God strongly denounces those leaders who thoughtlessly mishandle the ones who have been entrusted into their care.

There are two distinct roles of leading those who serve in situations of risk: leaders on the field and leaders who are responsible for sending and overseeing them from home. The perspectives and immediate responsibilities of each are different and the suggestions below may be helpful to consider for either leader when responsible for staff in these kinds of situations.

Essentials for Risk Leadership

Modify Your Leadership Style

Risk leadership requires a noticeably different approach than leading in low-risk environments. Shepherding staff through risk will likely mean an uncomfortable departure from a leader's customary way of doing things. Effective risk leadership will require energy, fresh insights, and dynamic shifts in outlook.

Most personnel who have responded to God's calling to the extent that they have moved across cultural lines are both exceedingly motivated and competent. What highly motivated and competent staff need from their leaders under most conditions is encouragement, appropriate resources, and a delegating leadership style.[236] Skillfully adopting this style of leadership in normal conditions will build an important trust deposit that a leader will be required to draw upon as danger increases.

As a team moves more deeply into risk environments, a leader must transition his style from delegating to directive. This is on a continuum that is proportional to the degree of risk faced. On the extreme end of the continuum is an actual crisis situation. In those cases, a leader will behave almost solely in a directive manner. Imagine a team evacuating a burning building. A good leader will clearly communicate directions with a command required for the danger faced.

The leaders are significant contributors to the normalizing response field-based workers may need to make in risk analysis, and to point out the need for evacuation and/or rest. It is crucial for leaders to be purposeful in helping field workers establish and accept their own risk analysis criteria and response plans.[237]

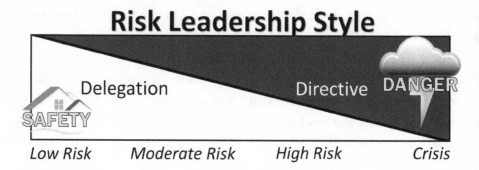

Prior to experiencing a crisis, as risk increases leaders should increase their directive decision-making and communication while decreasing the amount of decision-making authority extended to individual team members. However, this by no means should be understood as a suggestion that leaders begin to embrace a top-down leadership style. As challenging as it seems, it is important for leaders to communicate empathy, awareness, and willingness to hear input (even input that cannot be integrated).

A Well-Developed Personal Conviction Regarding Risk

If you are a leader like my husband, Neal, you probably picked up this book, glanced through the table of contents, and immediately flipped ahead to this chapter on leadership. That's okay—I get it. When God guides his selected followers toward shepherding roles, he also implants in them a spirit-driven passion for developing those gifts. Please do not think that this chapter is the sole leadership piece though. The entire book is intended to help the reader though a process that integrates their faith into dealing with risk. My hope is that after reading this chapter, you'll return to Chapter 1 and use this book and other resources to inform the maturation of your own beliefs regarding serving God through risk.

It is essential that leaders have a well-developed personal conviction about fulfilling God's call while facing danger. This belief must go beyond a cerebral, analytically settled theology of risk; it must incorporate one's own emotional, internal, and spiritual belief about suffering in the context of a faith calling. Preferably, a leader's risk convictions have been grown through his or her own in-the-trenches experiences.

For those in leadership at the sending office who have never had to live through a risky situation, it is wise to consider in some depth the issue of living with risk and through dangerous situations. While the exercise is a bit removed when done outside the situation, it can be a helpful first step in gaining insight to your field staff. Developing a personal statement on risk as if you were going to live in the situation of what your staff are living in will be helpful. Review the guide on how to write a personal statement of risk, found in Appendix E.

Crucial Leadership Skills in Crisis

There are crucial skills to get and resources to develop. For example, a leader would practice running through scenarios to consider who would do what in crisis, and whom they call in the event of a kidnapping. What are the protocols regarding publicity and media? Who communicates with families? There are excellent training organizations who specialize in this. As senders and field leaders, thinking ahead in areas of debriefing, insurance, media, medivac, and on-the-spot pastoral care would really mitigate the consequences of trauma.

Develop Awareness at the Home Office

It is not uncommon for sending leaders at the home office to be removed from field work by many years or they may not have served outside their own country. Many staff in oversight positions, for example, have never experienced living in hostile environments, or the risks they faced may have been considerably different. These leaders are still able to effectively care for field staff but need to acknowledge the need to learn and grow in their understanding. No effective leader assumes they know all they need to, but they will ensure there is a continual learning and growing of their home office and field staff.

Humility is especially important here. Develop awareness of how people act under extreme stress as well as the mental effects resulting from experiencing life-and-death experiences and the "dripping faucet stress" of twenty-first-century field work.

Reserve Judgment of Staff

While the evaluation of field staff's well-being is ongoing, it is wise to hold off on drawing any conclusions during the early weeks after their arrival home. The stress on the field in high-risk situations is often incomprehensible to those back in the home office. If the team and the individual field personnel have been under great duress for a long time, suspend making conclusions of how they really are until they've had a substantial (at least three-month) rest. Ask questions of the staff; don't make judgments before sitting down for several hours and listening with your heart.

It took Neal and me awhile to recover from the effects of living under extreme stress in the high-risk situation. After four years of leading a large team in a high-risk environment, it took our bodies three months to recover from the physical symptoms of prolonged elevated stress, and a full year until we both felt emotionally "normal" again and spiritually energized.

Trust Your Gut Feeling

Leading in risk is like leading through a quagmire in the thickest of fog; there are many uncertainties with the people we need to lead and steward. A gut feeling is also called "intuition." It is "judgment (1) that appears quickly in consciousness, (2) whose underlying reasons we are not fully aware of, yet (3) is strong enough to act upon."[238] Intuition, or gut feeling, is something that is unexplainable; it is different from the leading of the Holy Spirit. To ask someone why they feel a certain way when it is a "gut feeling" will not result in a satisfactory answer. "It is a form of intelligence that a person cannot express in language. Don't ask for reasons if someone with a good track record has a bad gut feeling."[239]

There is no rational set of metrics that may support this gut feeling. It may go against the prevailing wisdom. But this gut feeling in the majority of cases is right and should not be dismissed just because there is not a logical or spiritual reason. This is one "tool" that must be factored in to decision-making in risk.

Practice Wise Risk Communication

It is the leader's job to communicate vision with the rest of the staff. This is even more important in ongoing risk situations. Restating the vision often helps to focus and unify the team. And it keeps partners back home engaged and remembering to pray.

Risk communication is proven to be most effective when it addresses the probability of frequency of risk events and the absolute risk (as opposed to the relative risk). It also must include the degree of belief about the event, the likelihood of occurrence, as well as the potential negative and positive outcomes should that event occur.[240] It should include information about facts, values, options,[241] and Spirit-infused opinions. The goal when communicating in risk is that those most affected by risk taking are enabled to make the best possible decisions.

The types of words used will make your communication more or less clear and effective. Words such as these will more clearly communicate analytical assessments:[242]

- "we judge"
- "we assess"
- "we estimate"
- "probably"
- "likely"
- "very likely"
- "unlikely"
- "remote"
- "may"
- "might"
- "we cannot dismiss"
- "we cannot rule out"
- "we cannot discount"

Additionally, spiritual and rational risk assessments can be supported by using terms such as "high confidence, moderate confidence, low confidence" in both the reliability of the risk analysis and the people engaging in the risk event.[243]

How does effective risk communication increase the resiliency of your staff? Having worked through an identifiable method of risk assessment, weighing a range of potential outcomes, the trust your staff will have in your leadership will increase. Additionally, having methodologically analyzed information, there is increased personal control over behavior because one is prepared. The staff person is better equipped to view the risk event from a spiritual and pragmatic perspective. You will know you have done your job to effectively communicate what is necessary when additional information will not affect the choices you or your staff will make.[244]

Read Up on the Psychology of Risk

There are over a thousand studies on the psychology of risk. "The cognitive approach to risk-taking has dominated the field of risk discussion. But analysis of risk perception and decision-making that fails to consider the affect [emotions, whether positive or negative] attached to a hazard or the emotional state of the individual is inevitably flawed."[245]

Studies on the psychology of risk demonstrate that the decades of emphasis on the cognitive aspects of risk—what people are thinking, how to rationally assess things difficult to predict—have long neglected the emotional side of risk, as well as predictable human behavior. People are predictable in risk. Although the secular studies do not factor in what people of faith will do under the power of the Holy Spirit, they can still equip leaders with useful tools. (Appendix A suggests several good books on the psychology of risk.)

Realize that people are not their normal selves when experiencing extreme stress, or when experiencing stress every day for days, months, and years on end. Reading more on the psychology of stress will give a better understanding of how people normally behave so that "abnormal" reactions are more easily spotted.

Affirm Those Who Have Risked

We see this especially in the Romans 16:4 and Philippians 2:26 verses. Even when you as the leader don't agree with something someone in risk did, you don't like them, or you hear criticism about them, they still deserve to be commended. Those who have risked, who have done their best in the circumstances considering their limitations, deserve the same commendation that Paul gave Epaphroditus in front of the Philippian church. Affirm those who have risked their lives for the sake of the gospel and for caring for the flock who are in their care in a high-risk environment.

The Greek *parabaleusamenos* used in Philippians 2:30 is translated with the same Greek idiom as *paradidomi*, and indeed it is a synonym.[246] But it has a slightly different nuance to it in the way Paul used it. As mentioned earlier, Paul intentionally used this word because it is used only here and is not found anywhere else in the New Testament or Septuagint (the first Greek translation of the Old Testament).[247]

In the sense Paul used it, Epaphroditus put aside and disregarded personal safety for the sake of Christ for another human being. There is no passivity in the verb tense—he actively put himself in danger and risked his life. Epaphroditus was no coward. He demonstrated the height of courage by willingly taking enormous personal risks to come to the aid of a person in need. He did not "save" his life, but rather hazarded it to do for Paul and for the cause of Christ what the Philippian Christians did not or could not do. He is a hero of the faith and is held up in the middle of the letter to the Philippians as an example for all of us to follow.[248]

Is it possible that Paul, by his use of *parabaleusamenos,* is issuing a challenge to Christ-followers and rebuking "easy-going Christianity which makes no stern demands, and calls for no limits of self-denying, self-effacing sacrifice?"[249]

Paul also commends Prisca and Aquila in front of the entire Roman church. This "is the only place in the New Testament where the verb 'to thank' has a human object."[250] Thanking people publically, affirming them for their character and faithfulness in risk, is an important part of shepherding those who have risked, but it also helps Christ's body increase in praise and gratitude for God's working through those chosen men, women, and children.

Develop a Risk Understanding Within the Home Office Culture

One of the psycho-social factors that increase resilience for people in stressful situations is to have a home organization that can be characterized by a graceful and caring attitude. Sending staff need to be aware of the stress under which the field-based workers are living. The leaders of the organization play a key role in modeling, demonstrating, inviting, and expressing grace and support to the field workers. This will enhance the sense of relational safety and promote healthy communication.

Alongside of this, it is important for the sending staff to also develop strong risk-management skills. A home office that is informed, professional, and responsive and has developed the policies and actions necessary for crisis response will increase not just a *sense* of relational safety but, crucially, the real physical safety of the team. A sending staff who learn and develop understanding of the issues will be a sending staff who are able to engage in times of crisis with the appropriate language and insight to be truly supportive.

Invest in Your Own Care

Leading through risk demands a lot from leaders. It is unrealistic to think that a leader can simply maintain a normal pace of productivity while also adding the demands of risk leadership, assessment, and mitigation responsibilities. Wise leaders will make their own care a priority.

It is not uncommon as the consequences of potential risk become more severe for field staff to leave. This means there are less people to accomplish the same tasks. It would be a mistake for leaders to think they can take on more roles in risk. Instead, a leader must become focused and prioritize even more strictly what the primary tasks are. The weight of risk on a leader must be taken into account as a factor in work strategy.

These are all parts of investing in your care—you are pacing yourself in risk so that you lead and shepherd your team well.

Unhelpful Responses

There are at least four unhelpful responses from leaders about risk that we will now discuss.

Not Accurately Naming Reality

Being willing to die for Jesus, while arguably a mental decision, is not the same as willingly and knowingly exposing your children, spouse, and, if you are the team leader, your team to the possibility of death, and having to live with that risk day in and day out. Help your staff and yourself honestly assess the reality of what the staff are facing and let them decide how much of the reality that they are facing they can really live with.

When it is clearly too risky for specific staff based on their mental, emotional, and spiritual health, help them to discern God's voice. Give them permission to make the choice to leave and help them see this as a viable, and sometimes wise, option that the Lord gives us in times of risk. They may ask you to assess if they have enough faith or ask you if they have failed. Let the Holy Spirit be the one to interpret the reality of how they have handled what they have been called to do in the risk moment.

Totally Disavowing That Risk Is a Theological Possibility

One experienced veteran said, "I totally do not agree with your idea on risk … for the Christian, risk doesn't exist." This may easily lead to overspiritualization, restating problems with psychologically positive terms such as the peace and joy of following Jesus, while ignoring the real emotions involved in attacking the gates of hell.

Let's say for a minute that you are the leader and you believe risk is not a reality Christians face. But you are leading folks in their twenties and thirties who are concerned about risk and want to discuss it. By closing down the conversation, you may be leaving your staff frustrated with no one with whom to process the difficult challenges. This leads to less respect of you as a leader, lack of team loyalty and buy-in, and it lowers individual and team resiliency.

Minimizing or Overspiritualizing the Risk

"There really isn't risk in the end, is there?" is what one national influential leader related. What he meant was that since all followers of Jesus go to heaven anyway, it really is not that big of a deal to risk, suffer, and die for the sake of the gospel. This is not a helpful statement to increase emotional resilience of staff on the field. It prohibits personnel from processing the tangible negative impact experienced while facing immediate risk and prospective losses. Pointing to future restoration at some point will likely be a significant encouragement, but it is usually unsupportive when wrestling with potential loss.

Not Using a Holistic Approach

Risk affects all aspects of an individual. Unprocessed emotions resulting from being in a high-risk event or long-term risk situation can lead to physical manifestations of stress, psychological disorders (depression, panic attacks, effects of trauma, PTSD, etc.), loss of faith in God, relational strain (marital, parental, team, etc.), and more. Under-shepherds who do not take into account all facets of an individual and instead suggest that they shouldn't feel that way or they only need to take those thoughts captive are disavowing the real and physical effects of risk, even if nothing "bad" actually happened. Overspiritualization is dangerous and does harm to the internal growth and resilience of cross-cultural workers by keeping them from naming the reality of what they have gone through and grieving the losses experienced.

Lifting Weights: Developing (Faith) Muscle

The term "faith muscle" was coined by Michael Frost and Alan Hirsch. In their book *The Faith of Leap: Embracing a Theology of Risk, Adventure and Courage*, they discuss the organizational death resulting from a team or organization finding equilibrium. When there is equilibrium, the ability to adapt to change is lost. The right amount and pacing of change and variety need to be cultivated and embraced. Of course as under-shepherds, awareness of the stages of team life and the changing field situation are factors that also must be accounted for. It's an understatement that life on the field is full of transitions, losses, and changes. People living cross-culturally can only handle a certain amount of change in a short period of time.

As under-shepherds, understanding all these dynamics, and being able to articulate the vision and guide people through change is a required skill for leading people through high-risk situations. Knowing how to create organizational environments where certain (positive or healthy) risk-taking behaviors are stimulated, being open to unfolding challenges, and allowing people the ability to face issues and come up with their own inputs to solutions to problems will increase the faith muscle of individuals, teams, and organizations, creating a culture able to quickly adapt and capitalize on opportunities for spiritual transformation.

What Are Some Right Expectations Leaders in Risk Situations Should Have?

Expect to Be Criticized

Psychology of risk studies reveal that people think in hindsight that they could have judged the risk better than the other person. Thus, it is natural to criticize. Leaders in risk situations have many hard decisions to make, and the personality and leadership style will impact how those decisions are made. Expect criticism. In humility, consider what you would change next time or how you will handle things differently in the future based on the person you are becoming because of the risks you've handled as a leader. It may be easy to discount those who criticize and have most likely not walked in your shoes. But it is wise to remember that even poorly given feedback is still useful.

Expect to Develop a Highly Focused Empathetic Mind-set[251]

If you didn't have the experience and skill to make quick decisions, you'll learn pretty quickly in risk situations. This type of mentality involves applying four ways of thinking effectively under pressure. First, all decisions are personal in nature. Second, leaders know that the decisions they make will leave their own mark on their character. "The way you are perceived, and the way you perceive those whom your decisions will affect will increase the pressure you face in the decision-making process."[252]

Third, leadership under pressure requires empathy, which is a critical ingredient in the decision-making process. Empathizing with the people you are stewarding will enable increased discernment of how people are doing in the risk situation. Fourth, as discussed previously, careful, rational calculations must be done, especially in high-risk situations. Sound judgment is the ability to incorporate numerous variables, including uncertainty and intangible elements of risk and stewardship, and to make a high-quality decision.

Expect That Being a Leader in Risk Will Cost You

It may affect your physical, emotional, and your spiritual health. Your hair may turn gray or white while leading in risk. Neal's did. It will affect your spouse and your children. It may cost you some relationships. Those who criticize may no longer be your friends after your time leading in risk is over. You will never be the same as before, but hopefully you will become a richer person with increased awe and experience of God.

Expect to Care for Your People

This includes caring for the safety of their physical being, but also their mental, emotional, and spiritual well-being. These elements of a whole person still need to be stewarded and included in the risk assessment and management strategies. Steward your staff well through the Lord's leading.

Expect to Experience Bearing Pain for Your Staff

Sometimes leaders can't fix the problem, and they know their team is hurting. Mark Thibodeaux describes leadership as "the capacity to hold the pain without the ability to fix it, to let go of mental quick fixes, and the courage to look deeply at the reality and respond with love and compassion."[253] It is not easy to minister compassion and tears to hurting sheep, but sometimes this is the type of leadership needed in certain situations with specific staff.

When leading a team, it's hard to know how people would respond in high-risk and dangerous situations. A study of disasters and how people responded revealed five key lessons that may be applicable for cross-cultural high-risk situations. Here are the five main lessons derived from research on examining people's responses to situations that would normally evoke terror and panic:

1. Disaster plans in place prior to a risk event rarely work in practice.

2. Rigid, top-down planning often failed because communications systems were dysfunctional and the plans were targeted at the wrong things or failed to encompass the potential for change in an external context.

3. Flexibility in planning is vital.

4. Victims responded with collective resourcefulness, responding effectively and creatively.

5. Panic was rare among those affected by the disaster. There was an absence of complaints and irrational behavior.[254]

The "X" Factor

A significant factor in people's responses in high-risk situations and events is the role of the Holy Spirit. The Holy Spirit's strengthening power enabling leaders, individuals, and teams to respond in risk with courage and clarity is difficult to account for but can be unhesitatingly relied upon. A friend drew me out for hours, listening to the hardships Neal and I went through, and she asked at the end, "How did you ever make it through all that?" Some combination of mental fortitude, holding tightly to the spiritual reality of God sitting on his throne in calmness, helped me steady my breath and choose to keep persevering another day.

What was fascinating to Neal and me was the people who had all the training and preparation surprisingly didn't do as well as some of those who had no formal training and preparation for the risk situation we were in. As leaders, we do our best to prepare people and create a climate for people to flourish in risk—spiritually, mentally, emotionally, and relationally. It really is possible.

Application

1. What steps are the Holy Spirit whispering to you to do more of?

2. What unhelpful leadership response are you most likely to do?

3. What attitudes or behaviors is God asking you to repent of?

4. What other expectations have you had of leading in risk that you are becoming aware you have?

Chapter 13 Summary

1. Essentials for risk leadership:

- Modify your leadership style. Risk leadership requires a noticeably different approach than leading in low-risk environments.

- Develop a personal conviction regarding risk. It is essential that leaders have a well-developed personal conviction about fulfilling God's call while facing danger.

- Develop an awareness at the home office. It is not uncommon for sending leaders at the home office to be removed from field work by many years or they may not have served outside their own country.

- Reserve judgement of staff. While the evaluation of field staff's well-being is ongoing, it is wise to hold off on drawing any conclusions during the early weeks after their arrival home.

- Trust your gut feeling. Leading in risk is like leading through a quagmire in the thickest of fog; there are many uncertainties with the people we need to lead and steward.

- Practice wise risk communication. Restating the vision often helps to focus and unify the team, and it keeps partners back home engaged and remembering to pray.

- Read up on the psychology of risk. Studies on the psychology of risk demonstrate that the decades of emphasis on the cognitive aspects of risk have long neglected the emotional side of risk, as well as predictable human behavior.

- Affirm those who have risked. Those who have risked, who have done their best in the circumstances considering their limitations, deserve the same commendation that Paul gave Epaphroditus in front of the Philippian church.

- Develop risk understanding within the home office culture. Sending staff need to be aware of the stress under which the field-based workers are living.

- Invest in your own care. Wise leaders will make their own care a priority.

2. Unhelpful responses: There are at least four unhelpful responses from leaders about risk that we will now discuss.

   - Not accurately naming reality. Being willing to die for Jesus is not the same as willingly and knowingly exposing your children, spouse, and, if you are the team leader, your team to the possibility of death, and having to live with that risk day in and day out.

   - Totally disavowing that risk is even a possibility. This may easily lead to overspiritualization, restating problems with psychologically positive terms such as the peace and joy of following Jesus, while ignoring the real emotions involved in attacking the gates of hell.

   - Minimizing or overspiritualizing the risk. Pointing to future restoration at some point will likely be a significant encouragement, but it is usually unsupportive when wrestling with potential loss.

   - Not using a holistic approach. Unprocessed emotions resulting from being in a high-risk event or long-term risk situation can lead to physical manifestations of stress, psychological disorders, loss of faith in God, and relational strain.

3. Lifting weights: developing (faith) muscles. As under-shepherds, understanding all these dynamics, and being able to articulate the vision and guide people through change is a required skill for leading people through high-risk situations.

4. What are some right expectations leaders should have?

   - Expect to be criticized no matter what you do and how well you do it.

   - Expect to develop a highly focused empathetic mind-set.

   - Expect that leading in risk will be costly—it may affect your physical, emotional, and your spiritual health.

   - Expect to care for your people, including caring for the safety of their physical being, but also their mental, emotional, and spiritual well-being.

- Expect to experience pain-bearing for your staff: Sometimes leaders can't fix the problem, and they know their team is hurting.

5. The "X" factor. A significant factor in people's responses in high-risk situations and events is the role of the Holy Spirit. The Holy Spirit's strengthening power enabling leaders, individuals, and teams to respond in risk with courage and clarity is difficult to account for but can be unhesitatingly relied upon.

chapter 14

Thoughts from an Under-Shepherd

The risk event is an honor to experience and a privilege to steward with all that it does in and through us for God's glory and for the increase of his kingdom. In the risk moment we have the opportunity to experience our heavenly Father unlike any other time and place.

There are two key scriptures that sustained me during our years in Afghanistan. Meditating on the ancient words of Daniel and King Nebuchadnezzar especially ministered to my heart, increased my wonder and awe of God, and provided a much-needed perspective on the days I just wanted to pack up the children and go home.

King Nebuchadnezzar and the Throne of Heaven

In Chapter 3 we discussed the battle between the Israelites and the Amalekites. At the end, we saw the permanence of God's hand on his throne in heaven. Later on in the book of Daniel, we read a prayer of praise by Daniel and a blessing on God from King Nebuchadnezzar that point us to the throne room of God. After God revealed to Daniel the king's dream, his prayerful response gives perspective for living through evil times:

> Blessed be the name of God forever and ever,
>   to whom belong wisdom and might.
> He changes times and seasons;
>   he removes kings and sets up kings;
> he gives wisdom to the wise
>   and knowledge to those who have understanding;
> he reveals deep and hidden things;
>   he knows what is in the darkness,

and the light dwells with him.
To you, O God of my fathers,
    I give thanks and praise,
for you have given me wisdom and might,
    and have now made known to me what we asked of you,
        for you have made known to us the king's matter
        (Daniel 2:20–23 ESV).

The Lord set up the king, prime minister, president, or dictator in the host country in which you are living. As in Daniel's time, so in ours—nothing has taken God by surprise. He is the same God for us as he was for Daniel. Each ruler will eventually end, and one day God's complete justice will reign supreme in all the earth. Reading the Scriptures and seeing every mention of the nations reminds us that there is a time coming when all will be made right. We must not despair or give up hope, even when we cannot see justice and righteousness in the dusty village or city in which we are walking.

After King Nebuchadnezzar's sanity returned to him, he looked up to heaven and did four things—he blessed, he praised, he honored God, and then he proclaimed:

For his dominion is an everlasting dominion,
    and his kingdom endures from generation to generation;
all the inhabitants of the earth are accounted as nothing,
    and he does according to his will among the host of heaven
        and among the inhabitants of the earth;
and none can stay his hand
    or say to him, "What have you done?"
    (Daniel 4:34–35 ESV).

King Nebuchadnezzar lived the rest of his life humbly praising, extolling, and honoring the King of heaven. We will get to meet him one day in heaven. He encourages us to remember that the Lord does his will in heaven and on earth, and no one can stop him from doing what he pleases.

The perspective of the Lord sitting at rest on his throne in heaven is life-saving to remember. One day, toward the end of our time there, I was walking on the dusty streets of Kabul. We had just finished about eight months of an almost total lockdown and had been given freedom of movement just in the few blocks close to our home. I was on my way to visit with a colleague to get some security sensitive information I knew she couldn't communicate via cell phone.

As I looked down, I saw clouds of dust swirling around my feet and rolling up my *chapan.*[255] The swirling powdery brownness of dust and dirt moving up the blackness of my robe touched my soul. I immediately starting sinking into depression and cried out, "Lord, no one is remembering us, no one is praying for us!" In a millisecond I sensed a heavy, dark spirit of depression descending upon the back of my neck and latching on. At the same time, I heard the Lord ask me, "What do you have in your purse?"

The cards in my purse popped into my mind. We had been trained how to survive kidnappings, and in the purse clutched tightly around my shoulder was a small travel Bible, my money and ChapStick, and a small laminated collection of cards. The women from one of our partnering churches had written verses and personalized them with my name as their prayers for me.

Then the Lord asked me, "How many e-mail addresses are receiving your monthly newsletter and have committed to pray for you?"

"Two hundred twenty," I responded.

"Good, now don't look down at the dust," I felt him say. "Keep your eyes up, and focus your mind on the holiness surrounding my throne."

"Okay, Lord. I don't know what that means, but I'll try." As I determinedly focused the eyes of my mind on his throne in heaven, the spirit of depression let go of the back of my neck and receded. I lifted up my eyes to see the people around me, and I began to reengage in my usual prayer walking.

Why the focus on God's throne? By focusing on the throne located in eternity, I was reminding myself of where I had come from, whose I was, and what my purpose was. Likewise, as we engage with God and focus on God's eternal throne, then we remind ourselves where we have come from, whose we are, and what our purpose is.

Exclusivity and Fullness

The throne of God is by far the most exclusive place in existence: "The LORD has established his throne in the heavens, and his kingdom rules over all" (Psalm 103:19 ESV). It is exclusively God's. It's been occupied since before time: "Your throne, O God, is forever and ever" (Psalm 45:6). It has never been vacant and it never will be vacant. In fact, when we experience the presence of the Lord, his throne is never far away. It is much more than a seat to sit in; rather, it represents authority, power, rule, and dominion. We welcome its presence.

A Seat of Authority

A throne is the emblem of authority. From the throne official kingdom business is ratified, decrees are made, and judgments pronounced. The psalmist declared, "Righteousness and justice are the foundation of Your throne ..." (Psalm 89:14).

Spending time each day before the throne is called "throne moments," which can be experienced anywhere. I regularly have these at my kitchen sink! Throne moments ensure the grounding of our lives upon righteousness and justice. They bring a right perspective and straightness to our beings that empowers us in the midst of risk. Throne moments activate kingdom principles. Before the throne of God, our actions, thoughts, and motives are scrutinized for complying with God's precepts. Such moments have an amazing effect on the believer. They bring kingdom balance in an otherwise unbalanced and broken world.

Remember the description of God's throne in Revelation? One of the characteristics is that there is a sea like glass emanating from his throne. It's not chaotic waters like Genesis 1:2. Rather, the water is calm and peaceful. The peace surrounding his throne touches our souls as we meditate on him in the depths of our hearts.

The Throne Is Occupied and Mobile

God reigns from his throne, even when it doesn't seem like it or we cannot feel him. The psalmist said, "God reigns over the nations; God sits on His holy throne" (Psalm 47:8). We need to be reminded that the throne of God will never be vacant. It cannot be stolen. He cannot be out-muscled or overpowered. The throne is secure and established forever: "Son of man, this is the place of My throne and the place of the soles of My feet, where I will dwell in the midst of the people of Israel forever" (Ezekiel 43:7).

God's throne is mobile, which means that it appears wherever God manifests his presence. It is carried by the cherubim—it is not standing on the ground (Ezekiel 1:25–26). In Hebrews 4:16, we are encouraged to draw near to the throne of grace with boldness that we may receive mercy and find the timeliness of his grace that helps us in every need.

How do we draw near to this throne? One great way is to pursue the presence of God in worship. Through our praise, God comes seated on the throne, carried by the angels, into our circumstances and lives. What a tremendous thought! He is our help for every need.

A Rainbow around His Throne

"It shall come about, when I bring a cloud over the earth, that the bow will be seen in the cloud" (Genesis 9:14). The bow only comes after darkness and storms. In heaven, the rainbow is *always* over his throne. There are no storms or darkness in heaven. Not only is it over God's throne, but it encircles his throne, signifying completeness and wholeness (Ezekiel 1:28; Revelation 4:3). By focusing our minds and hearts on the serenity, power, righteousness, and justice, which are characteristics of God's throne and throne room, the storm that may be raging in our hearts is stilled, and we are strengthened to face with courage the risk moment he has called us to steward.

A Final Exhortation: Act Like a Mentsh

Stay alert, stand firm in the faith, behave like a *mentsh,* grow strong
(1 Corinthians 16:13 CJB).

Finally, the phrase used in 1 Corinthians 16:13—"stand firm"—means that we are to act with wisdom and courage like a full-grown adult in Christ, not as a babe or a child. The word *mentsh* means a good, reliable person; a real human being, energetic, moral, and compassionate.[256] The command to "behave" applies to all followers of Christ—male and female, adult or child. Act like one who is eating food, not still nursing at the breast (Hebrews 5:12). This command really is, "You all act like those who are mature in the faith."

What does this look like in risk? We see a description of it in Hebrews 10:32–39 (ESV):

> But recall the former days when, after you were enlightened, you endured a hard struggle with sufferings, sometimes being publicly exposed to reproach and affliction, and sometimes being partners with those so treated. For you had compassion on those in prison, and you joyfully accepted the plundering of your property, since you knew that you yourselves had a better possession and an abiding one. Therefore do not throw away your confidence, which has a great reward. For you have need of endurance, so that when you have done the will of God you may receive what is promised. For,
>
> > "Yet a little while,
> >   and the coming one will come and will not delay;
> > but my righteous one shall live by faith,
> >   and if he shrinks back,
> > my soul has no pleasure in him."
>
> But we are not of those who shrink back and are destroyed, but of those who have faith and preserve their souls.

In the margin of my Bible, I have written, "I must have resolve, strength of will, determination, backbone, high morale, courage, devotion, persistence, tenacity, and an unrelenting mind-set. I will not shrink back but press on for my King." Beloved, our cause is a worthy and noble one, for we serve the King of kings and the Lord of lords. We are called to go out and fight Amalek, which is a call to ongoing spiritual warfare.

We cannot sit by and passively accept evil; nor can we ignore it or pretend that it doesn't exist.

We cannot sit by and passively accept evil; nor can we ignore it or pretend that it doesn't exist. We must call evil by its name and exercise spiritual authority over it. The weapons of our warfare have divine power to destroy enemy strongholds.

We are protected by the armor of God and the weapons of light. It is steady faith in God's power that will give us victory over the powers of darkness.

Yahweh says this to us, "Do not be afraid and do not be dismayed at this great horde, for the battle is not yours but God's" (2 Chronicles 20:15 ESV). In this day, this place, and this generation, we engage in battle and fight and destroy the gates of hell in our neighborhoods. We serve a God of peace who will crush Satan under our feet (Romans 16:20). So we take up the sword of the Spirit, which is the Word of God, and war with Christ's love and forgiveness on behalf of the righteousness won for us at the cross.

Remember, there is no armor for our backside, so we will not shrink back or turn away, but be sober and vigilant. We will endure so we are characterized as a generation with courageous combat faith, with a wartime mentality, men and women who will do the right thing even when we are afraid—men and women, and boys and girls with the heart of our King.

Risk Reading List

Against the Gods: The Remarkable Story of Risk by Peter L. Bernstein

A Certain Risk: Living Your Faith at the Edge by Paul Richardson

A Practical Guide to Risk Management by Thomas S. Coleman

God Is a Warrior: Studies in Old Testament Theology by Tremper Longman and Daniel G. Reid

God's Missionary by Amy Carmichael

How to Measure Anything: Finding the Values of Intangibles in Business (and workbook) by Douglas W. Hubbard

Risk: A Very Short Introduction by Baruch Fischhoff

Risk Savvy: How to Make Good Decisions by Gerd Gingerenzer

Strategic Risk Taking: A Framework for Risk Management by Aswath Damodaran

Take the Risk: Learning to Identify, Choose, and Live with Acceptable Risk by Ben Carson

The Faith of Leap: Embracing a Theology of Risk, Adventure and Courage by Michael Frost and Alan Hirsch

The Prophets by Abraham J. Heschel

The Psychology of Risk by Glynis Breakwell

The Psychology of Risk-Taking Behavior by R. M. Trimpop

Catalogue of Questions on Cross-Cultural Risk

Expectations and Risk[257]

- Convictions about God. My "God-box broke." What is it I believe when faced with famine, great loss, injustice, disaster, and tragedy? God is not behaving the way I thought he would. He is unpredictable. What will sustain me when I have no answers?

- Convictions about the way life works. Life should be fair. People should be trustworthy. God should answer prayer quickly. Goodness will be rewarded. Evil will be punished. When these things are not so, then what?

- Convictions about myself. Which "me" am I? I am a good, patient, kind, and reasonable person. I am really pretty brave and resilient. I can handle hardship, most suffering, and considerable deprivation. How then do I explain when I am angry, resentful, self-pitying, demanding, fearful, and suspicious?

- Convictions about people. My good friends won't let me down. They will stand up for me when I am slandered or misrepresented. People can generally be trusted. They will keep their word if they possibly can. And when I am let down by others, what do I do? Do I stop trusting anyone? What should I do? What are my deep-seated convictions about being part of a body? Do I consider trust, love, cooperation, and community to be a nourishing part of life?

- Convictions I hold about growth and maturity, and the value of suffering and pain.

- I believe we are basically good and all want to grow to be like Jesus, and the way to do that is through the normal events of life. Surely the stress and pressure of the workplace is enough to develop Christlikeness! How then will I interpret injustice, the feeling that God is absent or unjust, or the sudden loss of a loved one?

Faith and Risk

- In what or in whom are we placing our trust? Is there integrity (alignment) between our actions and what we say we believe? Would an observer deduce from our lives that we are trusting in God?[258]

- Is God in it? This is the difference between faith versus presumption. Godly decision-making cannot always be reduced to simple behavioral choices (Numbers 13-14; Judges 11; Acts 5).[259]

- Is the activity proposed something that God is pleased with and with us?[260]

- Does Christ call us to die for him physically at all costs or be ready to die for him at all costs?[261]

- What is the line where the risk is too high to remain?[262]

- What core values guide the decision-making and how do these values depict God's character?[263]

- What did specific people of God do when they faced risk, and how did God respond to what they chose to do?[264]

- Is the risk taken motivated out of a personal love for Christ and his purposes?[265]

- Is there balance in how we are viewing our adversary, enemies of God yet enemies to be loved?[266]

- Is there balance between trust in God for the outcome but not presuming on him for a miracle?[267]

- What is motivating you?[268]

- What is it I strongly believe about God, his character, his relevance, and his care?[269]

- What is it I strongly believe about God and prayer, his power and ability, his willingness to intervene on my behalf, and his promises to deliver, provide, and protect?[270]

- What is it I strongly believe about living in a fallen world as a believer engaged in ministry, a ministry that challenges the kingdom and powers of darkness?[271]

- What is it that I strongly believe about the importance and value of being part of a community with close relationships? How do I account for the frailty and weakness of people, as well as my own?[272]

- What is it I believe about myself, my vulnerability or invulnerability to pain and suffering, my readiness to endure, my resilience, and my commitment for the long haul? What is it I believe about the value of hardship and pain and suffering in my life?[273]

Qualifying Risk[274]

- Is there a qualitative difference between risk-related choices made by Christians versus non-Christians in furthering their cause (not our works, but our relationships)?

- What meaning is attached to the possible death?

- What is the correct balance for this situation of our effort and God's work (Colossians 3; Luke 9–10; Nehemiah 4:20–21)?

- Can we identify and classify in biblical terms the actual risk that is proposed?

Culture and Risk[275]

- What do we deem as absolutes but are really culturally influenced expectations of how things should be?

- What is the minimum expectation of acceptable risks that accompany mature Christian discipleship?

- Do I approach decision-making from a more individualistic versus a more community-based worldview? How does my cultural background influence my approach to decision-making? Whether the culture is honor/shame, or righteousness/guilt, or power/fear-based society may also influence how people make decisions and the emotional and cognitive aspects in their approach to and acceptance of danger and risk.

- Are there cultural differences to risk tolerance that need to be addressed in order to arrive at meaningful understanding?

Organizations and Risk

- When considering a ministry risk issue, what kind of situation would characterize a "failure" in God's eyes?[276]

- Where is what is good for the organization in conflict with what is good for the individual?[277]

- How should organizations working in the same community resolve differences in the threshold of acceptable versus unacceptable risk?[278]

- Are there hidden and possibly ungodly motivations or agendas by the individual or organization that need to be surfaced and addressed?[279]

- Are there areas in which the risk and benefits to individual and organization are not aligned where there may be conflicting "interests" influencing decision-making?[280]

Resources and Risk

- Is there careful deliberation in the decision-making process to avoid making an unwise, rash, and regrettable decision or promise?[281]

- What (or whom) are we seeking to protect? Is it something Jesus calls us to die to? (Jesus calls us to die to "good things"—our families, farms, and even our own lives.)[282]

- Is the risk worth taking if the outcome is certain temporal failure or death?[283]

- Is there proper due diligence done on our part as individuals and organizations to prepare for worst-case scenarios?[284]

- What action would produce the clearest message to the world that we value

Jesus above everything else?[285]

- Are we approaching the situation from a perspective of scarcity or abundance?[286]

Myself and Risk[287]

- Are you placing a higher value on risk analysis than on God's wisdom?

- Do you believe that if you make the right decisions it will turn out okay?

- Are you expecting that how well you perform in the moment of risk according to worldly success standards will be an indicator of achievement? In other words, what does "successful risk" look like for you in this situation? Do you need to change your picture?

- Are you listening more to reason than to your heart and the Holy Spirit? Where's the balance?

- Are you being shaped more by your outward circumstances than by inner reflection?

- Are you looking for outward approval by people, your main sending office, or governing boards instead of by inner recognition by God? (Criticism will come, from someone, no matter what you do.)

- Are you struggling to find your destiny or are you striving to bring about God's purposes? Where is devotion versus service in your priorities?

A List of Dangers and Potential Traumas

- Fierce nationalism
- Xenophobia
- Fear of ancestral spirits
- Fundamental Islam
- Ethnic rivalries between churches
- Ethnic rivalries in villages or cities
- Slander by government officials
- Visa denials
- Detention by government officials
- Search of person, home, or personal property by government officials
- Robbery
- Rape of women, boys, girls
- Kidnapping
- Torture
- Overt satanic attack
- Demonic harassment and attack of children
- Murder: beheading, crucifixion, gunshot, or burned alive
- Suspicion of being spies
- Foreign children accused of bad behavior
- Sexual harassment of mothers, daughters, and sons
- Sickness
- Constant bouts with diarrhea and the ruining of the immune system
- Exposure to environmental toxins that lead to cancer or other maladies

appendix d

B's Robbery Recovery Recipe

This is for one dough recipe to make pizza, Stromboli, donuts, or cinnamon rolls. My friend B used this recipe for twenty years in Indonesia raising her own family, then gave it to me in Kabul, Afghanistan, a couple days after we were held at gunpoint by ten Afghan men and our house ransacked and robbed.

The significance of this recipe was that our friend came over to the house and made this dough and then made all four items—pizza, Stromboli, donuts, and cinnamon rolls—so that our home was filled with smells to replace the memories of the robbers. I've used B's recipe for my own family for about fifteen years so far in three different countries.

You'll need:

- 2 tablespoons of yeast

- 2 cups of water

- ½ cup of sugar

- 2 teaspoons of salt

- ½ cup of oil

- 6 cups of flour

Proof the yeast in ½ cup of warm water with 2 tablespoons of sugar. Once activated, pour the water and yeast mixture into a bowl with 1 ½ cups of water and the rest of the sugar. Mix in ½ cup of oil and 2 teaspoons of salt. Then add 1 cup of flour at a time, mixing well between each addition.

Knead the dough five to seven minutes until it becomes elastic. Place in an oiled bowl and cover. If rushed, try to let rise at least forty-five minutes before shaping into desired product. It is best if it can rise until double. Then punch down and shape.

Donuts

If used for donuts, roll out to desired thickness and cut into donuts. Let rise at least ½ hour before frying. The trick to good donuts is having the oil at the right temperature. Make sure the oil stays between 350° and 380°F.

Cinnamon Rolls

For cinnamon rolls, roll out all the dough into a rectangle ¼ inch thick. Spread softened or melted butter (2–6 tablespoons) across the dough with your hands or a spoon. Sprinkle cinnamon roll mixture over the dough. Roll tightly and pinch together the seams. Using a scissors, cut the dough into desired thickness of rolls and place in greased pan. Bake at 350°F for twenty-five to thirty minutes until golden brown.

Cinnamon roll mixture:
- 1 cup of brown sugar, or 1 cup white sugar and 1 tablespoon of molasses
- 2 teaspoons of cinnamon
- ¼ teaspoon of cloves (optional)
- a pinch of salt

Glaze:
- 1 ½ cups of powdered sugar, or pour 2 cups of sugar into a blender and blend until powder. Measure out 1 ½ cups.
- 3 tablespoons of cream cheese or sour cream, softened
- 3 tablespoons of buttermilk or milk
- ½ teaspoon of vanilla extract

Drizzle over the baked cinnamon rolls and serve.

Pizza

After dough has risen, separate dough into fist-sized balls. Let rise a second time on a floured pan. After the dough has doubled in size, roll out into a circle on a floured pan and make your thin crust pizza. If a thicker crust is desired, simply press several dough balls into a greased and floured pan and make the pizza. Bake at the hottest temperature your oven can get (ideally 500°F) on the lowest rack (closest to the heat).

Stromboli

After the dough has doubled in size, roll the dough into a large rectangle ¼ inch thick. Spread pizza sauce and desired pizza toppings across the dough, then roll as in cinnamon rolls. Pinch seems together and carefully place the Stromboli on a baking sheet. Do not cut the Stromboli before baking. Bake at 350°F until golden brown for approximately thirty minutes at two thousand feet elevation.

Note: Customize B's recipe for savory recipes by adding Italian spices to the flour when making pizza or Stromboli dough.

appendix e

Risk Action Plan

If we are aiming for a plan to outwit the schemes of the enemy, then we also want to be clear about our objective. Our objective with this book and the RAM workshop is to provide a holistic risk response strategy to strengthen field-based workers in the middle of risk situations. The strategy will look different for each person and each risk event or situation.

Putting all the elements described in this book and workshop into a plan of action, it is important to identify which of those elements organized into the following steps the Lord is leading you to work on as you prepare for risk or as you navigate through risk. Note that some of the steps you may not be able to put to use until you are in the risk situation. The guide is intended to be used before and during risk, and it can be a helpful tool in analysis and debriefing after a risk experience as you seek to understand more deeply what God has led you through.

What practical steps are needed to reduce fear and anxiety, increase calmness and confidence, and launch you through the risk opportunity to fulfill what God has called you to do? The steps you may need to implement may change for each risk event and your stage of life (singleness, early parenthood, etc.). Here they are.

Step One: *Thinking Shift*

Step Two: *Develop Discernment in Risk*

Step Three: *Identify the Holy Spirit's Voice*

Step Four: *Three Practical Stewardship Lists*

Step Five: *Emergency Planning/Evacuation Plan*

Step Six: *Improve Security Profile*

Step Seven: *Write a Personal Statement of Conviction on Cross-Cultural Risk*

Step Eight: *Danger Evaluation Assessment*

Step Nine: *Endurance Methods*

Step One: Thinking Shift

1. What shift in your thinking needs to occur when you consider stewardship and risk (Chapter 4)?

2. What resources do you need to carefully account for, preserve, and increase in your service to the Master (Chapters 4 and 11)?

3. Alternatively, what are you being called to pour out in this event (Chapter 4)?

4. Risk myths: Choose one risk myth which impacted you (Chapter 9), and write down the myth and correction, and thoughts you have about it.

Step Two: Develop Discernment in Risk (Chapter 5)

Evaluate the past twenty-four hours of your internal thought and emotional life through this grid:

1. Am I more loving, faith-filled, and hopeful?

2. Am I currently moving toward God or away from him in my thoughts, feelings, and actions?

3. Which of the questions are most helpful to you right now and how would you answer them?

   - What is the most loving thing to do?

   - What is the most hopeful thing to do?

   - What is the most faith-filled thing to do?

   - Are my decisions in risk moving me toward God or away from God?

   - Am I relying on false gods of my own making?

   - What is the most strategic thing to do at this moment for the kingdom of God?

Step Three: Identify the Holy Spirit's Voice (Chapter 5)

1. How do you hear the Holy Spirit speaking uniquely to you?

2. In what combination of the six ways discussed is the Holy Spirit leading you in this risk event? What other ways do you discern his leading in risk that were not listed?

    *   Security consultants
    *   Community
    *   Family
    *   Bible
    *   The Holy Spirit's voice
    *   Leadership and authorities, both expatriate and local leaders
    *   Dreams and visions

3. Where do you sense God's presence and God at work?

4. Where is receptivity to the gospel occurring? What changes are necessary to engage those opportunities?

5. What does wisdom, prudence, and discernment look like in this risk situation?

Step Four: Three Practical Stewardship Lists (Chapter 11)

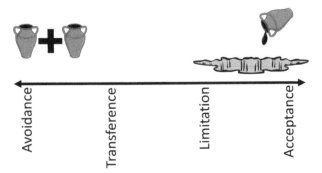

Avoidance · Transference · Limitation · Acceptance

1. Make a list of all the resources you are responsible to steward and what would impact you if you lost them. These include irreplaceable items, but also items with special meaning and those which are expensive or challenging to replace.

2. Pray and ask the Lord to bring to mind those items that would impact you with the feeling of "loss."

3. Pray about what the Lord is asking you to do: mitigate the loss of them as best you can or pour them out for his glory?

   A. Physical: home, office, and people. Make a list of who you are responsible for stewarding in risk (i.e., family, staff, nationals, others).

   B. Nonphysical: fruit (of ministry, of eternal lives), opportunities, digital security, and others.

   C. Self: relationship with God, relationships with others, emotions, and physical body:

      • Relationship with God:

         o Core questions: What aspects of God's character are you having the hardest time trusting right now? What core question are you really asking?

         o Location of your spiritual journey (Chapter 5): How would you describe where you are on your spiritual journey with God? Using Nouwen's five categories of movement, describe your spiritual awareness of where you are at in your relationship with God:

            a. From opaqueness to transparency

            b. From illusion to prayer

            c. From sorrow to joy

            d. From resentment to gratitude

            e. From fear to love

- o Foundations of faith: Which one or two foundations of faith from Abraham Heschel is the Holy Spirit asking you to cultivate regularly for the next season to increase your faith (Chapter 5)?

    a. Wonder

    b. Awe

    c. Indebtedness

    d. Praise

    e. Remembrance

    f. Doing righteousness

- Relationships with others: How are you handling the impact of risk in your relationships with your family, your teammates, your national colleagues, your authorities and leaders, and the culture around you?

- Emotions: Describe your awareness of accepting the reality that decisions you think you are making logically are in fact influenced considerably by your emotions. Identify, acknowledge, and normalize your emotions.

    o How are you feeling about the perceived risk and outcome?

    o How may God be leading you through your emotions?

    o Find constructive ways to handle strong emotions. What is the most helpful way to you personally to process your strong emotions? (Talk to a trusted friend, journal, etc.)

    o Understand how your emotions affect your decision-making in risk, and incorporate this into the risk analysis accordingly. Specifically, how are you handling your fear? Are your fears making you more pessimistic, or are you experiencing a great deal of anger that is causing you to "feel" more in control and therefore more optimistic?

- Physical: What practical strategies can you implement to care for your physical needs in the risk environment?

  o Energy: What would be helpful for stewarding your mental and emotional energy so that you have "margin" for the emergencies and crises that arise in the risk situation?

  o Health: What do you need to do for sleep management? What food planning do you need to implement to receive adequate calories to help you endure through risk?

Step Five: Emergency Planning/Evacuation Plan

Keep a list of items to take and things to do in a safe place where it can be quickly and easily found in an emergency. Prioritize the list, and work through it systematically when the emergency arises.

1. Five-Minute List: Make a list of what you will grab if you only have five minutes to evacuate. Keep the items to only two kilos (4.4 pounds).

2. Two-Hour List: Make a list of action steps if you have two hours to pack.

3. Twenty-Four to Thirty-Six-Hour List: Make a list based on having two days to pack.

4. Clean the House: Go through your home and office with the mind-set of someone looking to find "evidence" against you. What books and papers should you shred or burn before leaving the house? Keep a list of what you need to get rid of so you don't forget items that can be used against your national colleagues in your absence.

5. Evacuation Criteria: What evacuation criteria do you have for when you personally feel like it is too dangerous to stay? Write these down, and if the situation reaches that point, then pray to discern if the Lord is calling you to stay anyway.

Step Six: Improve Security Profile

1. What additional relationships do you need to develop to enhance your own security profile and risk assessment ability?

2. What other ways can you improve your own personal security in the risk situation?

3. What do you need to learn for the risks you are facing? (Learn how to avoid surveillance, learn how to see if someone is following you, organize a planned and randomized schedule of daily activities, develop a Crisis Response Team, etc.)

Step Seven: Write a Personal Statement of Conviction on Cross-Cultural Risk

Take time to write your own statement of cross-cultural risk. This is a short explanation of what you will grasp tightly in risk. Break this down into the following steps:

1. Identify a verse or section in the Bible that ministers to your heart, that causes that "didn't our hearts burn within us?" feeling. Summarize that verse or section in your own words, using verbs and adjectives that resonate with your passion and heart for your calling.

2. Make sure that part of your personal statement includes a conviction of how you will act when hardships come. We see this principle clearly demonstrated in Psalm 46. The psalmist declared how he will respond before anything happens. This is an essential aspect to a theology-of-risk statement.

3. Put it all together, refine it, and then request feedback from a few trusted people who understand what you are trying to do.

4. Teach it to your children as young as possible, print and frame it, and then place it in a place where you will be reminded of it every day. Review it regularly so it becomes part of you. Here is one sample: "Our purpose

is to live by simple trust and confidence in God, unflinching, unawed, and undismayed by the troubles we may face, holding staunchly to our calling and enduring steadfastly with our gaze fixed on Christ (Hebrews 11:24–27)."

Step Eight: Danger Evaluation Assessment Worksheet

The generalized steps for cross-cultural danger (risk) assessment are:

1. Organize an Excel spreadsheet or some other format for analyzing the various potential danger threats and traumas you are exposed to.

2. Organize the list on an increasing scale of negative impact. Which of these are you most concerned about? Think about reorganizing the list based on their impact on you.

3. Use the Risk Bow Tie Sheet to analyze each risk on its own. List all possible causes and all predictable outcomes to that risk event.

4. Make a plan for getting regular streams of information and how you will regularly keep up on the information and analysis.

5. Use the following worksheet to calculate the probabilities of those risk events and likelihood of outcome.

Engage in due diligence analysis. List the primary (most impacting) risks first, and then list the secondary risks. Analyze each one on the risk grid, incorporating as much independent data as possible (embassy information, local informants, Friday mosque preaching, security reports focused on the area, internal security reports from within the NGO community, and analysis from outside experts, etc.).

A Tool for Measuring and Comparing Risk

Objective: To blend the subjective evaluation of risk levels with an objective tool that can be used to measure and compare risk levels in applicable categories.

Step One: Determine Applicable Categories

Just as a finance manager would create a customized chart of accounts that would apply to her company's situation, a team leader creates risk categories that apply to the risks associated with the team's operating environment. Take care to choose categories general enough to measure risks but detailed enough to provide thorough information. An example of a list of risk categories might be:

- Assault (includes physical assault, robberies, and bombings).

- Kidnapping (includes abductions and hostage taking).

- Political unrest (includes riots, coups, and election instability).

- Health (includes outbreaks and a lack of medical care).

Step Two: Create a Graph to Evaluate and Measure Four Factors Associated with Events within the Risk Categories

Each axis of the graph will be used to plot one of the four factors. These factors are:

- severity (the weight of the impact on individuals and team),

- frequency (the rate at which the events occur),

- geographic proximity (the closeness of events), and

- demographic proximity (a measurement of similarities the team shares with the targets of the events).

The assessment graph will look something like the graph on the following page.

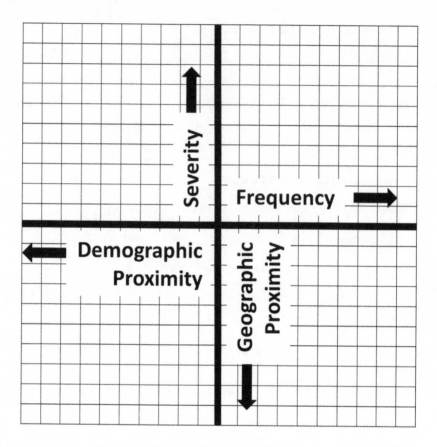

Step Three: Define the Suitable Scale for Measuring Risks

For this example, a 0–10 scale is used to plot the evaluated levels of factors in each risk category. Providing corresponding descriptive words is helpful for adding continuity when multiple people will be assessing the risk. For example:

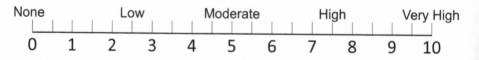

Step Four: Create a Table to Record the Assessed Levels

	Severity	Frequency	Geographic Proximity	Demographic Proximity
Assault	2	8	9	1
Kidnapping	7	4	9	8
Political Unrest	2	6	10	1
Health	8	4	9	3

Step Five: Plot the Results

Plot the results of the table on the graph and connect the four points to create a visual image of the risk level for each category. Using the previous example, the visual aid for the assessed risk in the category of assault would look like this:

The visual image shows a low risk of assault in the areas of severity and demographic proximity, but a high risk of assault in frequency and geographic proximity. Plotting all of the results would look like this:

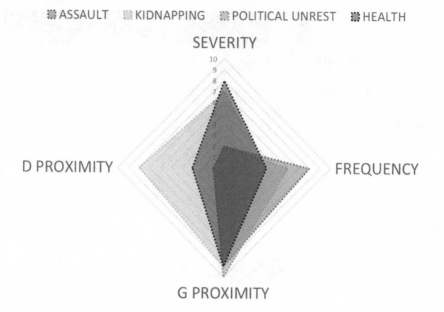

This shows all categories of danger and helps in developing a risk reduction strategy so the risks can be assessed and mitigated in order of perceived priority.

Now that you have looked at all the risks, including the low severity but ongoing frequent risks, pray about what the Holy Spirit is calling you to do. Is he asking you to avoid risk, accept risk, or be somewhere in the middle by either transferring or limiting risk? Of all of these, limiting risk is perhaps the hardest. Ask the Lord to show you a story from the Bible that is an example of what he may want you to do.

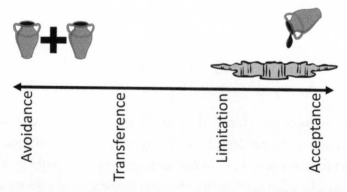

A free digital PDF of this Risk Action Guide is available at http://better-than-gold-faith.blogspot.com/

Step Nine: Endurance Methods (Chapter 11)

What tools, methods, and resources do I need to develop and have on hand in order to run well, rest well, and finish well in risk?

1. Physical tools: taking care of myself, eating, sleeping, etc.

2. Mental-emotional tools: keeping emotional margin for my family and teammates.

   - How I can "off-load" the cares of the day to have margin for others?

   - What brings me energy?

3. Spiritual tools: keeping a vital relationship with God thriving.

   - Worship videos, YouTube videos, books, personal retreats. What tools do I need to develop to spend time with God?

4. Social-relational tools: plan who to have over for dinner and develop friendships.

   - What relaxation is available to me to create in this environment? (Be creative!)

5. Culture-security stress tools: acknowledge when you've had a "bad culture day" and celebrate "good culture days."

6. Mental-spiritual perspective: actively cultivate eternal perspective.

   - One way to do this is by strategically inviting folks from frontline activities and asking them to share their stories of where they see God at work. Ask them questions like: Where do you see God at work? What is keeping you energized right now?

   - Another way is to think of a faith hero you have from any time period, someone who joyfully went through more difficulties (from your perspective) than what you are going through, and use them as a tool of encouragement. Use this not to feel guilty but to be able to keep running your race in a positive way. It's the mentality that if they could do it, then so can I.

notes

1. Verses like Matthew 10; 12; 16:24–26; John 15:20; Acts 14:22; 2 Timothy 3:12; 1 Peter 1:6–7; and 4:12–14 all make this clear.

2. John Piper, *Risk Is Right: Better to Lose Your Life Than to Waste It* (Wheaton, IL: Crossway, 2013), Kindle Location 132.

3. John Bunyan, L. Edward Hazelbaker, *Pilgrim's Progress in Modern English* (Hatfield, S. Africa: Van Schaik, 2000), Kindle Location 1519.

4. I am indebted to Abraham J. Heschel and Psalm 139:7–18 for this language.

5. This is from Neal's and my private monthly newsletter to donors in 2009. This number approximated through analysis of protected, unpublished documents of the missionary history of Afghanistan in our possession.

6. Her name was changed to protect my friend.

7. Paul Borthwick, *Western Christianity in Global Missions: What's the Role of the North American Church?* (Downers Grove: IVP, 2012), 25.

8. Todd Johnson, "World Christian Trends." (Lecture in Lausanne Bi-Annual International Leadership Meeting, Budapest, Hungary, June 18–22, 2007); in Borthwick, *Western Christianity,* 48.

9. Quote of Miriam Adeney in Borthwick, *Western Christianity,* 48.

10. Deseree Whittle, "Missionary Attrition: Its Relationship to the Spiritual Dynamics of the Late Twentieth Century," *Caribbean Journal of Evangelical Theology, June* (1999), accessed June 21, 2016, www.biblicalstudies.org.uk/pdf/cjet/03_68.pdf.

11. William Taylor, *Too Valuable to Lose: Exploring the Causes and Cures of Missionary Attrition* (Pasadena: William Carey Library, 1997). See also http://www.

missionfrontiers.org/issue/article/mission-frontiers-missionary-attrition-series-part-1 for more information.

12. Unnamed sources in private conversations with me in 2011–2014.

13. Dr. Laura Mae Gardner, in private correspondence with me, August 1, 2011.

14. Center for the Study of Global Christianity, *Christianity in Its Global Context: 1970–2020* (South Hamilton, 2013), 7.

15. Ibid.

16. Dr. Stephen Sweatman, president of Mission Training International, at PTM 2011 Conference, Plenary Speech.

17. These statements are based on the research found at "Marriage and Divorce Statistics," https://www.barna.org/family-kids-articles/42-new-marriage-and-divorce-statistics-released; "WHO Study: 1 in 3 Women Sexually or Physically Abused," Design & Trend, www.designtrend.com/articles/5060/20130620/who-study-1-3-women-sexu-ally-abused.htm; and "1 in 6 Male Sexually Abused By Age 18," United Press International, www.upi.com/Health_News/2010/05/25/One-in-six-males-sexually-abused-by-age-18/UPI-40381274765260/, all accessed June 21, 2016.

18. I was unable to locate who coined this term, but wanted to note that it is not original to me.

19. Abraham Heschel, *Who Is Man?* (Stanford, CA: Stanford University Press, 1965), 2.

20. Ibid., 2.

21. Ibid., 13, paraphrase of Heschel.

22. Kelly and Michele O'Donnell, Newsletter, Resiliency Toolkit: Member Care Update, November 2015.

23. This approach of playing a theological "game" is taken from Rabbi David Fohrman.

24. My hermeneutical methodology was to use a Jewish rabbinical approach. I consulted the very helpful guide, "Six Questions to Ask of the New Testament" found in G. K. Beale and D. A. Carson, *Commentary on the New Testament Use of the Old Testament* (Grand Rapids, MI: Baker Academic, 2007), xxiv–vi. However, I primarily used a Jewish rabbinical methodology along with an exegetical inquiry to establish connections between the Old and New Testaments. I employed Rabbi Hillel's principles of biblical interpretation, outlined by Brad Young's in *Meet the Rabbis: Rabbinic Thought and the Teaching of Jesus* (Grand Rapids, MI: Baker Academic, 2007), 169. I also incorporated Rabbi Gorelik's explanation of the four methods of interpretation based on Bachya ben Asher's work of the thirteenth century called Pardesh: Peshat, Remez, Derash, and Sod in his lectures *The Essentials: The Importance of Hebrew Time and Space* (Tustin: Eshav Books, 2006), 16.

Gorelik states:

At the very end of the thirteenth century (1291 C.E.), the Bible scholar Bachya ben Asher of Saragossa noted that there are four way of interpreting Scripture. These came to be known by the acronym pardes, spelled pay resh dalet samech—prds. The pay of pardes stands for peshat, meaning literal explanation of the text." The commentator seeks to explain the plain meaning of the text and no more. The resh of pardes stands for remez, meaning "allusion, allegory, symbolism." The commentator compares words and phrases in one part of the Bible to similar words and phrases in other parts of the Bible and draws inferences from them. The dalet of pardes stands for derash, a form of the word midrash, meaning "interpretation." Here the commentator probes beneath the literal meaning or a word or phrase in order to uncover an ethical or moral lesson that is thought to be implicit in the text. The samech of pardes stands for sod, meaning "mystery, secret." These methods of interpretation are used in varying degrees and combinations by biblical commentators. ... (They do so in order to) resolve obscurities and contradictions in the biblical text and to extract moral lesson from it. 13 a. Shabbat 63a (cf. Yevamot [Levirates] 11b, 24a) A verse cannot depart from its plain meaning (i.e, its peshat).

Additionally, the exegetical methodologies of Nechama Leibowitz described in *To Study and to Teach* by Shmuel Peerless gave additional guidance on the comparative textual analysis between the three New Testament pericopes and the Exodus 17 chapter. Her book, *Nehama Leibowitz: New Studies in the Weekly Parasha* (seven volume set) by Lambda Publishers gave additional guidance on Exodus.

Greek and Hebrew word studies and analysis of the idiomatic language used by Jesus, Luke, and Paul are summarized here. While Paul used *pardesh* in the New Testament to refer to Exodus 17 and Deuteronomy 7 and 20, I didn't incorporate that discussion from my doctoral dissertation here. As Dr. Skip Moen writes in Today's Word (10/27/15), "There is a very old rule in Jewish exegesis: the meaning derived from the text must never contravene or undermine the plain meaning of the text. That is to say, *derash, remez* or *sod* cannot invalidate *peshat*." The study of this book is consistent with this rule but is applied to both the New Testament and Old Testament. The testaments are consistent in their interpretation of risk but find their full expression based on the foundation of Christ's work on the cross done before the foundation of the world was laid (Revelation 13.8).

To paraphrase Aviya Kushner (*The Grammar of God*), this is a book written to people currently in a situation like I found myself in Afghanistan, and in that sense, a personal outworking of what I wished to have had as a mom in a high-risk situation. It is not an attempt to write a systematic theology. This is a suggested spiritual and practical understanding of biblical risk practically and holistically applied to contrast the current material available on a theology of risk. Any errors in understanding and applying a Christocentric Hebraic philosophical worldview integrated with the rabbinic methodology and words of the rabbis of the Talmud and the thoughts of the theologians cited are my own.

25. David Bivin, "Cataloging the New Testament's Hebraisms," *Jerusalem Perspective*, accessed June 21, 2016, http://www.jewishstudies.eteacherbiblical.com/cataloging-the-new-testaments-hebraisms-parts-1-5/.

26. Thorleif Boman, *Hebrew Thought Compared with Greek* (New York: Norton, 1960). Here Boman amply describes the differences between the Greek and Hebrew worldviews, and this sheds light on how idioms explain the concept of risk. Also, Robert Gorelik, *A Collection of Hebrew Idioms: Understanding the Language of Heaven* (Tustin, CA: Eshav Books, 2007), 1. By analyzing the Greco-Roman view scholars have brought into exegesis since the second century AD, we can better compare Hebraic thought with biblical thought. Skip Moen writes, "Exegesis cannot begin with the words of the Bible. It must begin with the *thought forms* we bring to the words of the Bible and to recognize those prior thought forms we will need someone or something to confront and challenge our usual way of thinking. 'Outside the box' must become a part of every exegesis" (Today's Word, 10/27/15).

27. Wilhelm Gesenius, Samuel Prideaux Tregelles, *Gesenius' Hebrew and Chaldee Lexicon to the Old Testament Scriptures* (Bellingham, WA: Logos Bible Software, 2003), רָהַב, 111 Column B.

28. *The Complete Jewish Bible with Rashi Commentary,* www.chabad.org, accessed December 17, 2015, http://www.chabad.org/library/bible_cdo/aid/9878#showrashi=true. (Mechilta d'Rabbi Shimon ben Yochai, Pirkei d'Rabbi Eliezer ch44, Yalkut Shimoni, Jonathan.)

29. Timothy Friberg, Barbara Friberg, and Neva F. Miller, *Analytical Lexicon of the Greek New Testament, Baker's Greek New Testament Library* (Grand Rapids, MI: Baker Books, 2000), 52, ἀνασκευάζοντες.

30. Johannes P. Louw and Eugene Albert Nida, *Greek-English Lexicon of the New Testament: Based on Semantic Domains* (New York: United Bible Studies, 1996), 21.7, 238.

31. The Greek word used is *paradidomi* and this is the only place in the New Testament where it is translated as "risk." Gerhard Kittel, Geoffrey W. Bromiley, and Gerhard Friedrich, eds, *Theological Dictionary of the New Testament* (Grand Rapids, MI: Eerdmans, 1964), 170.

32. The Hebrew term for the priestly blessing is Birkat Kohanim, also known as Nesi'at Kapayim, the "lifting of the hands," because of the priests' uplifted hands through which the divine blessings flow (see Numbers 6:23), accessed June 21, 2016, http://www.chabad.org/library/article_cdo/aid/894569/jewish/The-Priestly-Blessing.htm.

33. Tim Hegg, *The Letter Writer: Paul's Background and Torah Perspective* (Israel: First Fruits of Zion, 2002), 190.

34. Spicq, Ceslas, and James D. Ernest, *Theological Lexicon of the New Testament* (Peabody, MA: Hendrickson Publishers, 1994), Vol 3, 22.

35. Dr. Lee Allison, private correspondence with me on October 20, 2015.

36. The first place "Lord Jesus Christ" is used is in Acts 11:17. See Hegg, *The Letter Writer*, 188. Hegg states, "the addition of Lord in the combined terms may emphasize Yeshua's eternal sovereignty and His unity with the Almighty."

37. *Paradidomi* used in the context of suffering and persecution: Matthew 10:17, 19, 21; 17:22; 20:18–19; 24:9; 26:2, 15; 27:2, 18, 26; Mark 9:31; 10:33; 13:9, 11, 12; 15:1, 10, 15; Luke 9:44; 18:32; 20:20; 21:12, 16; 23:25; 24:7, 20; John 18:30, 35–36; 19:11, 16; Acts 3:13; 12:4; 21:11; 22:4; 27:1; 28:17; Romans 4:25; 1 Corinthians 5:5; 13:3; 2 Corinthians 4:11.

38. *Paradidomi* in the context of stewardship: Matthew 25:20, 22.

39. *Paradidomi* in the context of the Word of God being delivered to others by Jesus and Paul: Luke 1:2; 4:5; Acts 6:14; 16:4; 1 Corinthians 11:2, 23; 15:3; 2 Peter 2:2, 21.

40. *Paradidomi* in the context of battle: 1 Corinthians 15:24; Jude 3.

41. The Hebrew *natan* is used at least 116 times with the object "into the hand." This phrase is used 115 of the 116 times in warfare. The usage of *paradidomi* and similar use in the Old Testament demonstrate the warfare connection.

42. Spiros Zodhiates, *The Complete Word Study Dictionary: New Testament* (Chattanooga, TN: AMG Publishers, 2000), 4961.

43. Louw-Nida, 21.8.

44. William Arndt, Frederick W. Danker, and Walter Bauer, *A Greek-English Lexicon of the New Testament and Other Early Christian Literature* (Chicago: University of Chicago Press, 2000), 1042.

45. James Swanson, *Dictionary of Biblical Languages with Semantic Domains: Greek* (New Testament) (Oak Harbor: Logos Research Systems, Inc., 1997), 5719.

46. See also Genesis 49:24; 1 Samuel 7:12; Psalm 118:22; Isaiah 28:16; Daniel 2:34, 45; Zechariah 3:9; Matthew 21:42; Mark 12:10; Luke 20:17; Acts 4:11; Romans 9:33; 1 Corinthians 10; 1 Peter 2:6–8.

47. Nairy Ohanian, "Member Care Needs for Missionaries Serving in High-Risk Locales, DMin Dissertation," (Columbia Seminary and School of Missions, 2011), 19.

48. Nahum M. Sarna, *Exodus,* The JPS Torah Commentary (Philadelphia: Jewish Publication Society, 1991), 95.

49. Jeffrey H. Tigay, *Deuteronomy,* The JPS Torah Commentary (Philadelphia: Jewish Publication Society, 1996), 236.

50. They were not to forget what the Amalekites did to Israel (Exodus 17:14), to remember what Amalek did (Deuteronomy 25:17), to destroy them utterly (Deuteronomy 25:19), to punish Amalek (1 Samuel 15:2, 3, 18), and to execute the Lord's fierce wrath against Amalek (1 Samuel 28:18). Later wars with Amalek occurred in the stories of Joshua, Saul, David, Gideon, and Esther (Haman was an Amalekite, which is why he hated the Jews).

51. John J. Parsons, "Amalek and Spiritual Warfare: Further Thoughts about Shabbat Zachor," accessed December 16, 2014, http://www.hebrew4christians.com/Scripture/Parashah/Summaries/Tetzaveh/Amalek/amalek.html.

52. Ibid.

53. William G. Braude and Israel J. Kapstein, *Pĕsikta Dĕ-Rab Kahăna: R. Kahana's*

Compilation of Discourses for Sabbaths and Festal Days (Philadelphia, PA: Jewish Publication Society, 2002), 51.

54. Rabbi Nosson Scherman and Rabbi Meir Zlotowitz, eds, *The Stone Edition Chumash* (New York: Menorah Publications, 2013).

55. Jack B. Scott, "116 אָמַן" Edited by R. Laird Harris, Gleason L. Archer Jr., and Bruce K. Waltke, *Theological Wordbook of the Old Testament* (Chicago: Moody Press, 1999).

56. Rabbi Gorelik expounds on the meaning of God's hands in his book *A Collection of Hebrew Idioms: Understanding the Language of Heaven* (Tustin: Eshav Books, 2007), 31. Some verses citing God's hands as an expression of the Holy Spirit include 1 Kings 18:45–19:9; 2 Kings 3:15–16; Ezra 7:27–28; Ezekiel 1:3; 37:1; Nehemiah 2:1–8; Luke 1:66; Mark 10:16; Acts 6:3–6.

57. Most Western scholars just explain the geographic location of Rephidim. Rabbinical commentary, however, states that it means much more than that. For the whole explanation see Braude and Kapstein, Pěsikta Dě-Rab Kahăna, Piska 12, Section 321, 768.

58. Sarna, *Exodus,* 94.

59. The NIV says in Exodus 17:16, "Because hands were lifted up against the throne of the LORD." This is contrary to the majority of two thousand years of rabbinical commentary on the meaning of this verse and contrary to many other translations of this verse. Synthesizing the rabbinical view of the Hebrew meaning with textual analysis, I think the progression of the use of hands is more likely. Israel's slothful hands, Moses's steady hands, and God's permanent sovereign hands.

60. Frank Seekins, *Hebrew Word Pictures: How Does the Hebrew Alphabet Reveal Prophetic Truths?* (Hebrew Heart Media, 2012).

61. Quoting Rashi in *The Complete Jewish Bible with Rashi Commentary,* www.chabad.org, accessed June 21, 2016, http://www.chabad.org/library/bible_cd/aid/9878#showrashi=true.

62. Ibid.

63. Joel F. Drinkard, "Religious Practices Reflected in the Book of Hosea," *Review and Expositor* 90, No 2 (1993, Spring): 209.

64. Sarna, *Exodus,* 96.

65. *The Compete Jewish Bible with Rashi Commentary,* www.chabad.org, accessed June 21, 2016, http://www.chabad.org/library/bible_cdo/aid/9878#showrashi=true; quoted from Midrash Tanchuma, end of Ki Theitzei. Rabbis also use Amos 1:11 and Zechariah 14:9 as a Midrash on Exodus 17:6.

66. Avivah Gottlieb Zornberg, *The Particulars of Rapture: Reflections on Exodus* (New York, NY: Schocken Books, 2001), Kindle Location 5590.

67. Parsons, "Amalek and Spiritual Warfare," http://www.hebrew4christians.com/Scripture/Parashah/Summaries/Tetzaveh/Amalek/amalek.html.

68. Tremper Longman and Daniel G. Reid, *God Is a Warrior: Studies in Old Testament Theology* (Grand Rapids, MI: Zondervan, 1995).

69. Ibid, Kindle Location 1676.

70. I was unable to locate the source for this summary.

71. Longman and Reid, *God Is a Warrior,* 336.

72. Ibid, 378.

73. Jerry L. Schmalenberger, "Stewardship and War's Collateral Damage," *Currents in Theology and Mission* 29:4 (August 2002): 456–458.

74. William L. Hendricks, "Stewardship in the New Testament" *Southwestern Journal of Theology* 13 No 2 (1971): 25–33.

75. Jesus demonstrates in this a Hebraic mind-set—holding two opposing truths in tension. A Greco-Roman (Western) viewpoint is that there is only one right answer.

The Holy Spirit is a creative, powerful Spirit who clearly leads at times what seems to be wasteful in the human economy and at other times he leads in ways that carefully measure and account for what has been entrusted. Both are correct when based on the Spirit's leading.

76. Brad Young, *Parables: The Jewish Tradition and Christian Interpretation* (Grand Rapids, MI: Baker Academic, 1998), Kindle Location 1533.

77. Ibid., Kindle Location 1542.

78. Gerald F. Hawthorne, *Philippians,* Vol 43, Word Biblical Commentary (Dallas: Word Inc, 2004), 167.

79. My call to steward the safety of my family may look different from others.

80. Name changed to protect my friend.

81. Frederick Buechner, *"Stewardship of Pain,"* Program 3416, first air date January 27, 1991, accessed June 21, 2016, http://www.30goodminutes.org/index.php/archives/23-member-archives/229-frederick-buechner-program-3416cago.

82. Thank you, G and P.

83. Warren W. Wiersbe, *Be Comforted: Feeling Secure in the Arms of God* (Wheaton: Victor Books, 1992), 26.

84. Jill Briscoe, *Faith Enough to Finish* (Grand Rapids, MI: Monarch Books: 2007); Stuart Briscoe, *Hearing God's Voice Above the Noise* (Wheaton: Victor Books 1991), and *Dry Bones* (Wheaton: Victor Books, 1989); and Abraham J. Heschel, *The Prophets* (New York: Harper Collins, 1962).

85. Paul writes about this in Romans 13:1–7; Ephesians 6:1–3; 1 Timothy 2:1–3; 6:1–21; and Titus 3:1. And Peter writes in 1 Peter 2:13–14; 5:5.

86. A reading of the writings of the saints going back to the second century AD and continuing up through both Eastern and Roman and Protestant church writings, the saints are remarkably consistent on this one issue.

87. Heschel, *The Prophets,* ix.

88. Henri Nouwen, *Discernment: Reading the Signs of Daily Life* (New York: Harper-Collins, 2015).

89. Rose Mary Dougherty, *Group Spiritual Direction: Community for Discernment* (Mahwah, NJ: Paulist Press, 1995).

90. Nouwen, *Discernment,* 114.

91. Ibid.

92. Mark Thibodeaux, SJ, *God's Voice Within: The Ignatian Way to Discovering God's Will* (Chicago: Loyola Press, 2010).

93. This material is taken from Ministry of Reconciliation, Voices of Deception Illustration, http://mor-mn.com/.

94. This spirit is named in at least two *Time* magazine articles. One example is a quote of Saddam Hussein on March 24, 2003: "O heroic mujahedeen, hit your enemy hard!" Saddam said. "O noble Iraqis, with your strength and spirit of jihad ..." accessed June 21, 2016, http://content.time.com/time/world/article/0,8599,436056,00.html. Also, the practice of receiving spirits' in Islam is well attested. In the Wakhan, a description of the use of shrines is described: "At each shrine, one notices a specific place where oil or clarified butter is applied. If there is a depression in the rock, a wick may be placed in the oil/ butter and the shrine illuminated, or open oil lamps may be placed at the spot. As Iloliev notes, 'Shrines were constructed by believers to have a more direct contact with supernatural powers at the places where the saints were buried or were believed to have performed some miracle. . . . And to receive spiritual blessing (barakat) from them' (Iloliev 2008a, 46). Such places where the relationship with the sacred could be mediated were likely part of the indigenous belief system before the coming of Islam. Shrine sites are the locus for integration and assimilation of indigenous beliefs into Islamic discourse and for reaffirming and mobilizing a shared sense of the sacred in the landscape." John Mock, "Shrine Traditions of Wakhan, Afghanistan," *Journal of Persianate Studies* 4 (2011): 117–145.

95. A complete list of amulets and the jinn is found in Dudley Woodberry's course "Folk Islam" found on the World of Islam 2.0 cd. This may be purchase from Global Mapping.

96. Nouwen, *Discernment*, 114.

97. Ibid.

98. Dougherty, *Group Spiritual Direction*, Kindle Location 385.

99. We may not understand, but we still trust, and the Lord doesn't seem to mind a good argument!

100. Skip Moen, *Today's Word*, July 29, 2014.

101. William G. Braude, and Israel J. Kapstein, *Pĕsikta Dĕ-Rab Kahăna: R. Kahana's Compilation of Discourses for Sabbaths and Festal Days* (Philadelphia, PA: Jewish Publication Society, 2002), 367.

102. The five opposing sets of stages are taken from Henri Nouwen's book *Discernment: Reading the Signs of Daily Life* (New York: HaperCollins, 2015). Tom Ashbrook has more of a checklist approach in his book *Mansions of the Heart.*

103. Abraham J. Heschel, *Essential Writings Selected with an Introduction by Susannah Heschel* (Maryknoll: Orbis Books, 2011), 35.

104. Author unknown.

105. Watchmen Nee, *Spiritual Discernment* (New York: Christian Fellowship Publishers, 2014), Kindle Location 207.

106. Ibid.

107. John C. Merkle, *The Genesis of Faith* (New York: Macmillan Publishing, 1985), 51.

108. Abraham J. Heschel, *The Insecurity of Freedom* (New York: Farrar, Straus and Giroux, 1966), 115. In Chapter 8, Heschel explains in detail this term he coined "depth theology."

109. Merkle, *The Genesis of Faith*, 50.

110. Ibid, 163.

111. Ibid.

112. John Warwick Montgomery, *The Suicide of Christian Theology* (Newburgh: Trinity Press, 1996), 217.

113. Ibid., 218.

114. This is taken from Merckle's summary of Heschel's discussion on awe.

115. Merkle, *The Genesis of Faith*, 170.

116. Abraham J. Heschel, *God in Search of Man* (New York: Farrar, Straus and Giroux, 1955), 74.

117. Merkle, *The Genesis of Faith*, 161, and Heschel, *God in Search of Man*, 45.

118. The miracle of the burning bush was that Moses took time to observe the bush burning, and he realized it was not burning up. How long did he have to look at it? Some minutes of time. In an age where the human attention span is reduced to seven seconds or less, we have to work at cultivating the skill of observation. Moses was able to observe the effect of the raising and lowering of his arms, accept the mystery of it, and enter into a moment of God's supernatural work through the very mundane and sweaty efforts of men fighting.

119. Merkle, *The Genesis of Faith*, 175.

120. Abraham J. Heschel, *Who Is Man?* (Stanford: Stanford University Press, 1965), 106.

121. Ibid., 181.

122. Merkle, *The Genesis of Faith*, 185.

123. Heschel, *God in Search of Man*, 138.

124. Abraham J. Heschel, *Man Is Not Alone: A Philosophy of Religion* (New York: Farrar, Straus, and Giroux, 1951), 163.

125. Heschel, *God in Search of Man,* 287.

126. Robert Gorelik, *A Collection of Hebrew Idioms: Understanding the Language of Heaven* (Tustin: Eshav Books, 2009) 43.

127. Entrust 4, *Developing a Discerning Heart* (Colorado Springs: Entrust 4, 1899), 64.

128. Jeff Iorg, *The Character of Leadership: Nine Qualities That Define Great Leaders* (Nashville: B & H Books, 2007).

129. Heschel demonstrated in *The Prophets* quite conclusively that the emotions of God are consistent with a sovereign and omnipotent God. The issue of free will is not the same issue for the Jews as it is for Christians. Heschel also answers this in his writings: We see in Jesus Christ the entire range of emotions demonstrated in a sinless life. Jesus Christ, the representative of the Father, shows us that God has emotions and is deeply moved by human beings. The philosophical view of the self-sufficiency of God automatically means He is not in need nor moved by humans. I do not agree with this view, as it does not provide a consistent philosophical and hermeneutical approach to theology.

130. Abraham J. Heschel, *The Prophets, Vol 1 and 2* (New York: Harper and Row, 1962), Vol 2, 2.

131. Skip Moen, *God, Time, and the Limits of Omniscience: A Critical Study of Doctrinal Development* (Oxford: Oxford University, 1979). Moen's summary answers some of the modern debate of God's impassibility by concluding that this theological issue arose with the total Hellenization of Christianity and complete break from Judaism between AD 200–250.

132. Heschel, *The Prophets,* 162.

133. John C. Merkle, *Abraham Joshua Heschel: Exploring His Life and Thought* (New York: Macmillan, 1985), 73.

134. Theomorphically.

135. Merkle, *Abraham Joshua Heschel*, 81.

136. Heschel, *The Prophets*, Vol. 2, 212.

137. Earl and Elspeth Williams, *Spiritually Aware Pastoral Care: An Introduction and Training Program* (New York: Paulist Press, 1992), 18.

138. Ibid., 17–18.

139. *The God Who Risks* is John Sander's theology of risk, focusing on God's changing emotions. I responded to this in another publication, as have others.

140. Whichever view a cross-cultural worker chooses to take on God's foreknowledge and sovereign control does not impact one being able to engage responsibly in risk analysis and management.

141. Frost and Hirsch, in their book *The Faith of Leap*, do a great service for the church, encouraging the church to risk for the cause of Christ and not just "maintain the status quo." However, *Facing Danger* is about the cross-cultural risk for the sake of Christ. While I appreciate the premise of their book for an anemic Western church that needs to be challenged to risk for the cause of Christ, for the sake of the narrow focus of this book I prefer Heschel's phrase "the leap of action." He uses this phrase to refocus attention on the act of believing, rather than the content of believing. In the same way, I advocate for a focus on the act of risking and all it entails to refocus attention less on dogma and more on action. It thus accounts for the nephesh, that is the whole person as understood by the Old Testament writers.

142. Baruch Fischoff, John Kadvary, *Risk: A Very Short Introduction* (Oxford: Oxford University Press, 2011), Kindle Location 345.

143. Ibid., Kindle Location 835.

144. R. M. Trimpop, *The Psychology of Risk-Taking Behavior* (Amsterdam: North-Holland, 1994), 4.

145. Ibid.

146. Kenneth Bailey, *Paul Through Mediterranean Eyes: Cultural Studies in 1 Corinthians* (Downers Grove: IVP Academic), Kindle Location 188.

147. Jakob J. Petuchowski. "Faith as the Leap of Action: The Theology of Abraham Joshua Heschel," *Commentary Magazine Online,* July/Aug 2014, accessed June 21, 2016, www.commentarymagazine.com/article/faith-as-the-leap-of-action-the-theology-of-Abraham-Joshua-Heschel/htm.

148. Abraham J. Heschel, *God in Search of Man: A Philosophy of Judaism* (New York: Garrar, Straus, and Giroux), 5.

149. Private correspondence with me. My sixth grade teacher, Mr. N's name is withheld for security reasons.

150. Gerd Gingerenzer, *Risk Savvy: How to Make Good Decisions* (New York: Penguin Group, 2014), 11.

151. Ibid., 15.

152. Ibid.

153. Ibid.

154. Ibid., 23.

155. Ibid.

156. See Appendix A: Risk Reading List.

157. Marvin Rausand, *Risk Assessment: Theory, Methods, and Application* (Hoboken: Wiley, 2011), Chapter 1.

158. Mobile Member Care Team, www.mmct.org, has Member Care while Managing Crisis, also renamed as Crisis Response Training. This is one of the few trainings available in helping leaders and pastoral-care staff learn how to care for their people through crisis

and how to put together Crisis Response Teams. Fort Sherman and CCI also have excellent trainings focusing more on the practical side of Crisis Response Teams.

159. Rausand, *Risk Assessment*, 76.

160. Hubbard, *How to Measure Anything: Finding the Values in the Intangibles*, 136.

161. Aswath Damodaran, *Strategic Risk Taking: A Framework for Risk Management* (Upper Saddle River: Pearson Education, 2008), Kindle Location 526.

162. Glynis Breakwell, *The Psychology of Risk* (Cambridge: Cambridge Univerity Press, 2014).

163. Ibid., 102.

164. Hubbard, *How to Measure Anything*, 7.

165. Ibid., 7.

166. Abraham J. Heschel, *God in Search of Man* (New York: Farrar, Straus and Giroux, 1976), 136. See also Genesis 3:9 and 2 Chronicles 16:9.

167. Abraham Link, "Risk, Crisis Management and the Missional Heart of God," (Egypt meetings on Crisis, Cairo, September 1, 2006). Penname used to protect the security of author and organization.

168. Glenn Penner, "Is the Blood of the Martyrs Really the Seed of the Church?" www. persecution.net, 26 July 2008, 1, accessed June 22, 2016, vomcanada.com/download/ seed.pdf

169. Ibid.

170. Marvin Wilson, *Exploring our Hebraic Heritage*, Kindle Location 3504.

171. *Epilanthánomai* and *eklanthánomai* are two Greek words which mean "to forget."

172. Joseph Ton, *Suffering, Martyrdom, and Rewards in Heaven* (University Press of America, 1997), 301–314.

173. G. K. Beale, *The Book of Revelation: A Commentary on the Greek Text,* New International Greek Testament Commentary (Grand Rapids, MI: Eerdmans, 1999).

174. R. M. French, trans., *Way of the Pilgrim* (Quality Paperback Book Club, NY, 1998), 34.

175. Peter Bernstein, *Against the Gods: The Remarkable Story of Risk* (New York: John Wiley & Sons, 1996), Kindle Location 5898.

176. This is taken from the Jewish Virtual Library, accessed June 22, 2016, https://www.jewishvirtuallibrary.org/jsource/Judaism/pikuach_nefesh.html.

177. See http://blog.eteacherhebrew.com/jewish-religion/pikuach-nefesh-the-value-of-life/ for more information regarding this.

178. *Sanhedrin* 74a–b.

179. Glynis Breakwell, *The Psychology of Risk* (Cambridge: Cambridge University Press, 2014), 29.

180. This is taken from https://www.google.com.tr/?gws_rd=cr&ei=HNbuVcD8OMihsAHbi7mICg#safe=strict&q=define+endurance.

181. N. Ohanian, "Member Care Needs for Those Serving in High Risk Locales," DMin Dissertation, 2011.

182. Breakwell, *The Psychology of Risk,* Kindle Location 7346.

183. This is from Skip Moen, accessed June 22, 2016, http://skipmoen.com/2013/06/06/is-this-faith/, quoting Brad Young in *The Parables: Jewish Tradition and Christian Interpretation* (Grand Rapids, MI: Baker Academic, 1998), 50.

184. Glynis Breakwell, *The Psychology of Risk* (Cambridge: Cambridge University Press, 2014), Kindle Location 3160.

185. Ibid., Kindle Location 3159.

186. Ibid., Kindle Location 3196.

187. Ibid., Kindle Location 3649.

188. Curt Thompson, *Anatomy of the Soul: Surprising Connections Between Neuroscience and Spiritual Practices that can Transform Your Life and Relationship*s (Carrollton: Nunn Communications, 2010), 7.

189. Breakwell, *The Psychology of Risk,* Kindle Location 3376.

190. Curt Thompson, June 25, 2014 talk to Barnabas International Staff.

191. Mark Thibodeoux, SJ, *Hearing God's Voice: The Ignation Way to Discovering God's Will.* (Chicago: Loyola Press, 2010), Kindle Location 648.

192. Peter Scazzero, *Emotionally Healthy Spirituality* (Nashville: Thomas Nelson, 2006), 69.

193. Travis Bradberry, *Emotional Intelligence 2.0* (San Diego: TalentSmart, 2009).

194. Paul Richardson, *A Certain Risk: Living Your Faith on the Edge* (Grand Rapids, MI: Zondervan, 2010), Kindle Location 389.

195. Breakwell, *The Psychology of Risk,* Kindle Location 3649.

196. Charles Schaefer, PhD, in personal correspondence with me in 2015.

197. Breakwell, *The Psychology of Risk,* Kindle Location 338.

198. Ibid., Kindle Location 3357.

199. Ibid., Kindle Location 3658, citing Slovic and Peters, 2006a, 2006b.

200. Hans-Rüdiger Pfister, and Gisela Böhm, "The multiplicity of emotions: A framework of emotional functions in decision making." *Judgment and Decision Making,* vol. 3, No 1, January 2008: 5–17, accessed June 23, 2016, http://www.journal.sjdm.org/bb1/bb1.html.

201. Breakwell, *The Psychology of Risk,* Kindle Location 3159.

202. Ibid., Kindle Location 3376.

203. Ibid., Kindle Location 3376.

204. Marcus Jastrow, *A Dictionary of the Targumim, the Talmud Babli and Yerushalmi, and the Midrashic Literature and II* (London; New York: Luzac & Co.; G. P. Putnam's Sons, 1903), 1656.

205. Thibodeoux, Kindle Location 1137.

206. Breakwell, *The Psychology of Risk,* Kindle Location 3548.

207. Ibid., Kindle Location 3548.

208. Charlie Schaefer, PhD, in personal correspondence with me in 2015.

209. Breakwell, *The Psychology of Risk,* Kindle Location 3557.

210. Ibid., Kindle Location 3567.

211. Thibodeoux, Kindle Location 1077.

212. Breakwell, Kindle Location 3562.

213. There is an 80 percent chance of not being raped. This data is from a secure-sensitive source.

214. Breakwell, Kindle Location 3275.

215. Ibid., Kindle Location 3167.

216. Gerd Gingerenzer, *Risk Savvy: How to Make Good Decisions* (New York: Penguin Group, 2014), 11.

217. Ibid., 10–13.

218. There are many discussions on the theory proposed by Martin Seligman's *Theory of Learned Helplessness.* Here I referenced from https://www.mentalhelp.net/articles/cognitive-theories-of-major-depression-seligman/. This type of depression is a

normalized experience and is alleviated with stress-reducing activities, and recognition that it is situational.

219. "An Overview of Expatriate Adjustment Measurement and Reanalysis of the CernySmith Assessment of Cross-Cultural Adjustment" to be published in *Journal of Psychology and Theology, Missions Edition,* 2016. The attached article was recently submitted to the *Journal of Psychology and Theology* for peer review and hopefully acceptance for publication in a special mission's edition of the journal.

220. Dan Allender and Tremper Longman III, *The Cry of the Soul: How Our Emotions Reveal Our Deepest Questions About God* (Colorado Springs: NavPress, 1994), Kindle Location 171.

221. Quote from teaching by Mimi Wilson at a Women of the Harvest Retreat in the Middle East in 2006.

222. Breakwell, *The Psychology of Risk,* Kindle Location 3548.

223. Ibid., Kindle Location 3557.

224. Ibid., Kindle Location 3567.

225. James Dietz, "Christianity for the Technically Inclined: Risk Assessment, Probability, and Prophecy," *Global Journal of Classical Theology* 4, No 2 (2004, June 1): 1.

226. J. Oswald Sanders, *Spiritual Leadership: A Commitment to Excellence* (Chicago: Moody Press, 1994), 127.

227. Peter L. Bernstein, *Against the Gods: The Remarkable Story of Risk* (New York: John Wiley & Sons, 1996), Kindle Location 5851.

228. Paul Richardson, *A Certain Risk: Living Your Faith at the Edge* (Grand Rapids, MI: Zondervan, 2010), Kindle Location 1576.

229. This information is drawn from Skip Moen, accessed June 23, 2016, http://skipmoen.com/2015/10/16/the-last-24/?mc_cid=8b4a92dff6&mc_eid=b7d46581e2.

230. These were the evacuation plans Neal and I used throughout our time in Afghanistan. We kept our lists and pictures up-to-date, and rehearsed with each other and our kids as appropriate what we would need to do in an emergency. These evacuation plans were first published in CAME MC Newsletter, December 2014, Vol 2 No 11.

231. John Warwick Montgomery, *The Suicide of Christian Theology* (Newburgh: Trinity Press, 1996), 218–219.

232. J. Oswald Sanders, *Spiritual Leadership: A Commitment to Excellence* (Chicago: Moody Press, 1994), 127.

233. Peter Bernstein, *Against the Gods: The Remarkable Story of Risk* (New York: Wiley & Sons, 1998), Kindle Location 5909.

234. Glynis Breakwell, *Psychology of Risk* (Cambridge: Cambridge University Press, 2014), 220.

235. Neal Hampton, *A Tool for Measuring and Comparing Risk* (Hampton, 2014). Used with permission.

236. Ken Blanchard, *Leading at a Higher Level, Revised and Expanded Edition: Blanchard on Leadership and Creating High Performing Organizations* where he addresses a "Self-Reliant Achievers Need a Delegating Style."

237. Charlie Schaefer, PhD, in personal correspondence with the me in November 2015.

238. Gerd Gingerenzer, *Risk Savvy: How to Make Good Decisions* (New York: Penguin Group, 2014), Kindle Location 1631.

239. Ibid., Kindle Location 1640.

240. Ibid., 26.

241. Baruch Fischoff and John Kadvary, *Risk: A Very Short Introduction* (Oxford: Oxford University Press, 2011), Kindle Location 1999.

242. Ibid., Kindle Location 1970.

243. Ibid., Kindle Location 1980.

244. Ibid., Kindle Location 1816.

245. Glynis Breakwell, *Psychology of Risk* (Cambridge: Cambridge University Press, 2014), Kindle Location 3159.

246. Johannes P. Louw, Eugene Albert Nida, *Greek-English Lexicon of the New Testament: Based on Semantic Domains* (New York: United Bible Studies, 1996), 21.7.

247. The exact same form of this word is only found one other place in the world: In an ancient (second century AD) inscription found at Olbia on the Black Sea, and it means "to daringly expose oneself to danger."

248. Gerald F. Hawthorne, *Philippians*, Vol 43, Word Biblical Commentary (Dallas: Word, 2004), 167. Quoting de Jonge from *Light from the Ancient East*, 84–85, 88; cf. de Jonge, NovT 17 [1975], 297–302.

249. If one assumes unity of the book as one letter by Paul, a highly trained rabbi, then it is possible Paul has ably employed the "prophetical rhetorical template" here as Kenneth Bailey amply demonstrates he did in 1 Corinthians. It may be that this pericope, Philippians 2:19–30, chiastically is the structural center of the letter. If this is the chiastic center, using Timothy and Epaphroditus as examples for the church, then his use of risk merits even more attention. O'Brien, D. F. Watson, and Culpepper all point to the force of Paul's use of these godly examples in the location they are found. Culpepper demonstrates the strong verbal parallels in Philippians showing the unity of the letter throughout with Timothy and Epaphroditus as the pinnacle example of Paul's main force of argument. "The imitation of the servanthood of Christ and of men like these is the strongest spiritual antidote to the dangers of legalism, perfectionism, and dissension created by rivalry for power among church leaders. He suggests that while the main focus is 2:5–11, the middle section (2:19–30) is what brings the integrity, origin, and message of Philippians" together. It contrasts the issues of a false Christology (of glory instead of suffering); a misguided soteriology (of perfection rather than a working out of salvation); and of distorted eschatology (deliverance from evil now rather than the future). See Peter Thomas O'Brien and D. F.

Watson in New International Greek Text Commentary, *The Epistle to the Philippians: A Commentary on the Greek Text*, (Grand Rapids, MI: Eerdmans, 1991), 315. Also see R. Alan Culpepper, "Co-workers in Suffering Phil 2:19–30," *Review and Expositor,* 77 no 3 (1980, Summer): 357.

250. Leon Morris, *The Epistle to the Romans*, The Pillar New Testament Commentary (Grand Rapids, MI: Eerdmans, 1988), 532.

251. David Amerland, "The Sniper Mentality: 4 Ways to Think Better Under Pressure," *Forbes,* April 2014, 2, accessed August 22, 2014, www.forbes.com/sites/netapp/2014/05/14/sniper-mentality-leader/.

252. Ibid.

253. Mark Thibodeoux, SJ, *Hearing God's Voice: The Ignation Way to Discovering God's Will* (Chicago: Loyola Press, 2010).

254. Glynis Breakwell, *The Psychology of Risk* (Cambridge: Cambridge University Press, 2014), Kindle Location 3603.

255. A *chapan* is a long Iranian robe.

256. David H. Stern, *Complete Jewish Bible: An English Version of the Tanakh (Old Testament) and B'rit Hadashah (New Testament)* (Clarksville, MD: Jewish New Testament Publications, 1998).

257. Organization A.

258. Organization B.

259. Organization C.

260. Organization C.

261. Organization D.

262. Organization D.

263. Organization D.

264. Organization D.

265. Organization C.

266. Organization C.

267. Organization C.

268. Organization A.

269. Organization A.

270. Organization A.

271. Organization A.

272. Organization A.

273. Organization A.

274. Organization C.

275. Organization C.

276. Organization B.

277. Organization C.

278. Organization C.

279. Organization C.

280. Organization C.

281. Organization C.

282. Organization B.

283. Organization C.

284. Organization C.

285. Organization B.

286. Organization B.

287. Skip Moen, Skip Moen's Word Study, *Todays Word*, www.todaysword.com.

bibliography

Allender, Dan and Tremper Longman III. *The Cry of the Soul: How Our Emotions Reveal Our Deepest Questions About God.* Colorado Springs: NavPress, 1994.

Amerland, David. "The Sniper Mentality: 4 Ways to Think Better Under Pressure," *Forbes,* April 2014, www.forbes.com/sites/netapp/2014/05/14/sniper-mentality-leader/.

Arndt, William, Frederick W. Danker, and Walter Bauer, *A Greek-English Lexicon of the New Testament and Other Early Christian Literature.* Chicago: University of Chicago Press, 2000.

Bailey, Kenneth. *Paul Through Mediterranean Eyes: Cultural Studies in 1 Corinthians.* Downers Grove: IVP Academic.

Beale, G. K. and D. A. Carson. *Commentary on the New Testament Use of the Old Testament.* Grand Rapids, MI: Baker Academic, 2007.

Beale, G. K. *The Book of Revelation: A Commentary on the Greek Text.* New International Greek Testament Commentary. Grand Rapids, MI: Eerdmans, 1999.

Bernstein, Peter. *Against the Gods: The Remarkable Story of Risk.* New York: John Wiley & Sons, 1996.

Bivin, David. *Cataloging the New Testament's Hebraisms,* Jerusalem Perspective, http://www.jewishstudies.eteacherbiblical.com/cataloging-the-new-testaments-hebraisms-parts-1-5/.

Boman, Thorleif. *Hebrew Thought Compared with Greek.* New York: Norton, 1960.

Borthwick, Paul. *Western Christianity in Global Missions: What's the Role of the North American Church.* Downers Grove: IVP, 2012.

Bradberry, Travis. *Emotional Intelligence 2.0.* San Diego: TalentSmart, 2009.

Braude, William G. and Israel J. Kapstein, *Pĕsikta Dĕ-Rab Kahăna: R. Kahana's Compilation of Discourses for Sabbaths and Festal Days.* Philadelphia: Jewish Publication Society, 2002.

Breakwell, Glynis. *The Psychology of Risk*. Cambridge: Cambridge University Press, 2014.

Briscoe, Jill. *Faith Enough to Finish*. Grand Rapids, MI: Monarch Books, 2007.

Briscoe, Stuart. *Hearing God's Voice Above the Noise*. Wheaton: Victor Books, 1991.

——. *Dry Bones*. Wheaton: Victor Books, 1989.

Buechner, Frederick. "Stewardship of Pain," Program 3416, First air date January 27, 1991, http://www.30goodminutes.org/index.php/archives/23-member-archives/229-frederick buechner-program-3416cago.

Center for the Study of Global Christianity, *Christianity in Its Global Context: 1970–2020* South Hamilton, 2013.

Chabad.org. *The Complete Jewish Bible with Rashi Commentary*, http://www.chabad.org/library bible_cdo/aid/9878#showrashi=true. (Mechilta d'Rabbi Shimon ben Yochai, Pirke d'Rabbi Eliezer ch44, Yalkut Shimoni, Jonathan.)

CAME MC Newsletter, December 2014, Vol 2, No 11.

Damodaran, Aswath. *Strategic Risk Taking: A Framework for Risk Management*. Upper Saddle River: Pearson Education, 2008.

Dietz, James. "Christianity for the Technically Inclined: Risk Assessment, Probability, and Prophecy." *Global Journal of Classical Theology* 4, No 2 (2004, June 1).

Dougherty, Rose Mary. *Group Spiritual Direction: Community for Discernment*. Mahwah, NJ: Paulist Press, 1995.

Drinkard, Joel F. "Religious Practices Reflected in the Book of Hosea," *Review and Expositor* 90, No 2, 1993, Spring.

Entrust 4. *Developing a Discerning Heart*. Colorado Springs: Entrust 4, 1899.

Fischoff, Baruch and John Kadvary. *Risk: A Very Short Introduction*. Oxford: Oxford University Press, 2011.

French, R. M. (trans). *Way of the Pilgrim*. New York: Quality Paperback Book Club, 1998.

Frost, Michael and Alan Hirsch. *Faith of Leap: Embracing a Theology of Risk, Adventure and Courage*. Grand Rapids, MI: Baker Books, 2011.

Gesenius, Wilhelm, and Samuel Prideaux Tregelles. *Gesenius' Hebrew and Chaldee Lexicon to the Old Testament Scriptures*. Bellingham, WA: Logos Bible Software, 2003.

Gingerenzer, Gerd. *Risk Savvy: How to Make Good Decisions*. New York: Penguin Group, 2014.

Gorelik, Robert. *The Essentials: The Importance of Hebrew Time and Space*. Tustin: Eshav Books, 2006.

——. *A Collection of Hebrew Idioms: Understanding the Language of Heaven*. Tustin: Eshav Books, 2007.

Hawthorne, Gerald F. *Philippians*, Vol 43, Word Biblical Commentary. Dallas: Word, 2004.

Hegg, Tim. *The Letter Writer: Paul's Background and Torah Perspective*. Israel: First Fruits of Zion, 2002.

Hendricks, William L. "Stewardship in the New Testament." *Southwestern Journal of Theology* 13, No 2 (1971).

Heschel, Abraham J. *God in Search of Man: A Philosophy of Judaism*. New York: Farrar, Straus and Giroux, 1955.

——. *Man is Not Alone: A Philosophy of Religion*. New York: Farrar, Straus and Giroux, 1951.

——. *Moral Grandeur and Spiritual Audacity*. New York: Farrar, Straus and Giroux, 1996.

——. *The Prophets*. New York: Harper Collins, 1962.

——. *Who Is Man?* Stanford: Stanford University Press, 1965.

Hechel, Susannah. *Abraham Joshua Heschel: Essential Writings Selected with an Introduction*. Maryknol: Orbis Books, 2011.

Hubbard, Douglas. *How to Measure Anything: Finding the Values in the Intangibles*. Hoboken, NJ: John Wiley & Sons, 2007.

Iorg, Jeff. *The Character of Leadership: Nine Qualities That Define Great Leaders*. Nashville: B & H Books, 2007.

Kellemen, Robert W. and Susan M. Ellis. *Sacred Friendships: Celebrating the Legacy of Women Heroes of the Faith*. Winona Lake: BMH Customs Books, 2009.

Kittel, Gerhard and Geoffrey W. Bromiley, and Gerhard Friedrich, eds, *Theological Dictionary of the New Testament*. Grand Rapids, MI: Eerdmans, 1964.

Link, Abraham. "Risk, Crisis Management and the Missional Heart of God." (Egypt meetings on Crisis, Cairo, September 1, 2006.)

Longman III, Tremper. and Daniel G. Reid. *God Is a Warrior: Studies in Old Testament Theology.* Grand Rapids, MI: Zondervan, 1995.

Louw, Johannes P. and Eugene Albert Nida, *Greek-English Lexicon of the New Testament: Based on Semantic Domains.* New York: United Bible Studies, 1996.

Merkle, John C. *The Genesis of Faith.* New York: Macmillan Publishing, 1985.

——. *Abraham Joshua Heschel: Exploring His Life and Thought.* New York: Macmillan, 1985.

Ministry of Reconciliation. Voices of Deception Illustration.

Moen, Skip. *God, Time, and the Limits of Omniscience: A Critical Study of Doctrinal Development.* Oxford: Oxford University, 1979.

Montgomery, John Warwick. *The Suicide of Christian Theology.* Newburgh: Trinity Press, 1996.

Morris, Leon. *The Epistle to the Romans,* The Pillar New Testament Commentary. Grand Rapids, MI: Eerdmans, 1988.

Nee, Watchmen. *Spiritual Discernment.* New York: Christian Fellowship Publishers, 2014.

Nouwen, Henri. *Discernment: Reading the Signs of Daily Life.* New York: HarperCollins, 2015.

O'Donnell, Kelly and Michelle. Newsletter, Resiliency Toolkit, Member Care Update, November 2015.

Ohanian, Nairy A. "Member Care Needs for Missionaries Serving in High-Risk Locales." DMin Dissertation. Columbia Seminary and School of Missions, 2011.

Parsons, John J. "Amalek and Spiritual Warfare: Further Thoughts about Shabbat Zachor," http://www.hebrew4christians.com/Scripture/Parashah/Summaries/Tetzaveh/Amalek/amalek.html.

——. "Warfare with Amalek: Further Thoughts Shabbat Zachor," www.hebrew4christians.com/Scripture/Parashah/SummariesKi_Teitzei/.

Peerless, Shmuel. *To Study and to Teach: The Methodology of Nechama Leibowitz.* Urim Publications, 2005.

Penner, Glenn. "Is the Blood of the Martyrs Really the Seed of the Church?" www.vomcanada.com, 26 July 2008, 1, http://www.vomcanada.com/download/seed.pdf

Petuchowski, Jakob J. "Faith as the Leap of Action: The Theology of Abraham Joshua Heschel."

Commentary Magazine Online, July/Aug 2014, www.commentarymagazine.com/ article/ faith-as-the-leap-of-action-the-theology-of-Abraham-Joshua-Heschel/htm.

Rausand, Marvin. *Risk Assessment: Theory, Methods, and Application.* Hoboken, NJ: John Wiley & Sons, 2011.

Richardson, Paul. *A Certain Risk: Living Your Faith on the Edge.* Grand Rapids, MI: Zondervan, 2010.

Sanders, John. *The God Who Risks: A Theology of Divine Providence.* Downers Grove: IVP, 1998.

Sanders, J. Oswald. *Spiritual Leadership: A Commitment to Excellence.* Chicago: Moody Press, 1994.

Sarna, Nahum M. *Exodus*, The JPS Torah Commentary. Philadelphia: Jewish Publication Society, 1991.

Scazzero, Peter. *Emotionally Healthy Spirituality.* Nashville: Thomas Nelson, 2006.

Scherman, Rabbi Nosson and Rabbi Meir Zlotowitz, eds. *The Stone Edition Chumash.* New York: Menorah Publications, 2013.

Schmalenberger, Jerry L. "Stewardship and War's Collateral Damage." *Currents in Theology and Mission* 29:4 (August 2002).

Scott, Jack B. "116 אמן." Edited by R. Laird Harris, Gleason L. Archer Jr., and Bruce K. Waltke. *Theological Wordbook of the Old Testament.* Chicago: Moody Press, 1999.

Seekins, Frank. *Hebrew Word Pictures: How Does the Hebrew Alphabet Reveal Prophetic Truths?* Hebrew Heart Media, 2012.

Swanson, James. *Dictionary of Biblical Languages with Semantic Domains: Greek (New Testament).* Oak Harbor: Logos Research Systems, Inc., 1997.

Taylor, William. *Too Valuable to Lose.* New York: IVP, 1997, and 2007 WCL on "Worth Keeping: Global Perspectives on the Best Practice in Missionary Retention."

Thibodeaux, Mark, SJ. *Hearing God's Voice: The Ignation Way to Discovering God's Will.* Chicago: Loyola Press, 2010.

Thompson, Curt. *Anatomy of the Soul: Surprising Connections Between Neuroscience and Spiritual Practices That Can Transform Your Life and Relationships.* Carrollton: Nunn Communications, 2010.

Tigay, Jeffrey H. *Deuteronomy*, The JPS Torah Commentary. Philadelphia: Jewish Publication Society, 1996.

Ton, Joseph. *Suffering, Martyrdom, and Rewards in Heaven*. University Press of America, 1997.

Trimpop, R. M. *The Psychology of Risk-Taking Behavior*. Amsterdam: North-Holland,1994.

Whittle, Deseree. "Missionary Attrition: Its Relationship to The Spiritual Dynamics of the Late Twentieth Century." *Biblical Studies*. (1999, June), www.biblicalstudies.org.uk/pdf/cjet/03_68.pdf.

Wiersbe, Warren W. *Be Comforted: Feeling Secure in the Arms of God*. Wheaton: Victor Books, 1992.

Williams, Earl and Elspeth. *Spiritually Aware Pastoral Care: An Introduction and Training Program*. New York: Paulist Press, 1992.

Wilson, Marvin. *Exploring our Hebraic Heritage: A Christian Theology of Roots and Renewal*. Grand Rapids, MI: Eerdmans, 2014.

Woodberry, Dudley. "Folk Islam" World of Islam 2.0 CD.

Young, Brad. *Meet the Rabbis: Rabbinic Thought and the Teaching of Jesus*. Grand Rapids, MI: Baker Academic, 2007.

——. *Parables: The Jewish Tradition and Christian Interpretation*. Grand Rapids, MI: Baker Academic, 1998.

Zodhiates, Spiros. *The Complete Word Study Dictionary: New Testament*. Chattanooga, TN: AMG Publishers, 2000.

Zornberg, Avivah Gottlieb. *The Particulars of Rapture: Reflections on Exodus*. New York: Schocken Books, 2001.

RAM Training
(Risk Assessment and Management)

This is a two-day training utilizing the adult-facilitated methodology. It is geared to all cross-cultural workers, from candidates to veterans. Come prepared to dig in and work together as a group to understand a theology of risk. The topics include:

The Basics:
- Bible background
- How to write a statement of conviction on risk

Assessing Risk:
- Stewarding resources
- Danger risk assessment
- Discernment of Holy Spirit
- The twelve risk myths
- Developing a risk action plan

Managing Risk:
- Leading your team well
- Communication and risk
- Children and risk
- Endurance strategies
- Risk and loss mitigation
- Emotions and risk

About the RAM Trainers

Anna Hampton shares God's Word woven with personal experiences from living and working for almost a decade in war-torn Afghanistan and over twenty-five years of ministry experiences traveling in almost sixty countries of the world. She holds four degrees, including a Doctor of Religious Studies. Her passion is for Christ and encouraging others to develop daring, better-than-gold faith. She is a Bible teacher and conference speaker at international women's events in Central Asia, the Middle East, and in the US. Visit her at her blog at http://better-than-gold-faith.blogspot.com/.

Anna's husband, Neal Hampton, is a life-long student, practitioner, and trainer in the area of shepherd leadership and life development. He has worked with hundreds of field leaders across multiple sectors in the for-profit, nonprofit, parachurch, and educational worlds. He has over twenty years of experience serving in the Central Asia and Middle Eastern regions as a humanitarian aid worker, and later as the country director of a large multinational team during a difficult period in Afghanistan. Among the wide variety of topics that he addresses, are shepherd leadership, leader development, developing interpersonal skills, leadership in high-risk environments, stress assessment and resiliency, and critical incident debriefing.

To schedule the full two-day training, then contact us at
nealhampton@pobox.com.

CPSIA information can be obtained
at www.ICGtesting.com
Printed in the USA
BVHW071305050819
555095BV00004B/343/P